Teaching ESL/EFL Listening and Speaking

This guide for teachers and teacher trainees provides a wealth of suggestions for helping learners at all levels of proficiency develop their listening and speaking skills and fluency, using a framework based on principles of teaching and learning. By following these suggestions, which are organised around four strands—meaning-focused input, meaning-focused output, language-focused learning, and fluency development—teachers will be able to design and present a balanced programme for their students.

Updated with cutting-edge research and theory, the second edition of *Teaching ESL/EFL Listening and Speaking* retains its hands-on focus and engaging format, and features new activities and information on emerging topics, including:

- Two new chapters on Extensive Listening and Teaching Using a Course Book
- Expanded coverage of key topics, including assessment, pronunciation, and using the internet to develop listening and speaking skills
- Easy-to-implement tasks and suggestions for further reading in every chapter
- More tools for preservice teachers and teacher trainers, such as a sample unit, a "survival syllabus", and topic prompts

The second edition of this bestselling book is an essential text for all Certificate, Diploma, Masters, and Doctoral courses for teachers of English as a second or foreign language.

Jonathan M. Newton is Associate Professor and Director of the MA TESOL programme at Victoria University of Wellington, New Zealand.

I.S.P. Nation is Professor Emeritus in Applied Linguistics at Victoria University of Wellington, New Zealand.

ESL & Applied Linguistics Professional Series
Eli Hinkel, Series Editor

Language Curriculum Design
2nd Edition
John Macalister and I.S.P. Nation

Teaching Academic L2 Writing
Practical Techniques in Vocabulary and Grammar
Eli Hinkel

What English Language Teachers Need to Know Volume II
Facilitating Learning, 2nd Edition
Denise E. Murray and MaryAnn Christison

English Morphology for the Language Teaching Profession
Laurie Bauer with I.S.P. Nation

Conversation Analysis and Second Language Pedagogy
A Guide for ESL/EFL Teachers, 2nd Edition
Jean Wong, Hansun Zhang Waring

English L2 Reading
Getting to the Bottom, 4th Edition
Barbara M. Birch and Sean Fulop

Teaching ESL/EFL Reading and Writing, 2nd Edition
I.S.P. Nation and John Macalister

Reconciling Translingualism and Second Language Writing
Tony Silva and Zhaozhe Wang

Teaching ESL/EFL Listening and Speaking, 2nd Edition
Jonathan M. Newton and I.S.P. Nation

For more information about this series, please visit: www.routledge.com/ESL-Applied-Linguistics-Professional-Series/book-series/LEAESLALP

Teaching ESL/EFL Listening and Speaking

Second edition

Jonathan M. Newton and I.S.P. Nation

Second edition published 2021
by Routledge
52 Vanderbilt Avenue, New York, NY 10017

and by Routledge
2 Park Square, Milton Park, Abingdon, Oxon, OX14 4RN

Routledge is an imprint of the Taylor & Francis Group, an informa business

© 2021 Taylor & Francis

The right of Jonathan M. Newton and I.S.P. Nation to be identified as authors of this work has been asserted by them in accordance with sections 77 and 78 of the Copyright, Designs and Patents Act 1988.

All rights reserved. No part of this book may be reprinted or reproduced or utilised in any form or by any electronic, mechanical, or other means, now known or hereafter invented, including photocopying and recording, or in any information storage or retrieval system, without permission in writing from the publishers.

Trademark notice: Product or corporate names may be trademarks or registered trademarks, and are used only for identification and explanation without intent to infringe.

First edition published by Routledge 2008

Library of Congress Cataloging-in-Publication Data
Names: Newton, Jonathan M., author. | Nation, I. S. P., author.
Title: Teaching ESL/EFL listening and speaking / Jonathan M. Newton, I.S.P. Nation.
Identifiers: LCCN 2020020304 (print) | LCCN 2020020305 (ebook) | ISBN 9780367195519 (hardback) | ISBN 9780367195533 (paperback) | ISBN 9780429203114 (ebook)
Subjects: LCSH: English language–Study and teaching–Foreign speakers. | English language–Spoken English–Study and teaching. | Listening–Study and teaching. | English teachers–Training of.
Classification: LCC PE1128.A2 N496 2021 (print) | LCC PE1128.A2 (ebook) | DDC 428.0071–dc23
LC record available at https://lccn.loc.gov/2020020304
LC ebook record available at https://lccn.loc.gov/2020020305

ISBN: 978-0-367-19551-9 (hbk)
ISBN: 978-0-367-19553-3 (pbk)
ISBN: 978-0-429-20311-4 (ebk)

Typeset in Sabon
by River Editorial Ltd, Devon, UK

Contents

Preface	vii
1 Parts and Goals of a Listening and Speaking Course	1
2 Beginning to Listen and Speak in Another Language	17
3 Listening	37
4 Extensive Listening	60
5 Language-focused Learning through Dictation and Related Activities	74
6 Pronunciation	92
7 Learning through Task-based Interaction	120
8 Learning through Pushed Output	139
9 Teaching Using a Course Book	164
10 Language-focused Learning: Deliberate Teaching	183
11 Developing Fluency	206
12 Assessing Progress	223
Conclusion	244
Appendix A The Survival Syllabus	246

Appendix B	Topic Types	250
Appendix C	Topics for Listening and Speaking	252
Appendix D	Sample Unit from Riddiford and Newton (2010)	255
References		259
Index		281

Preface

This book is intended for teachers of English as a second or foreign language. It can be used both for experienced teachers and for teachers in training. In its earlier forms, this book has been used on graduate diploma and Masters level courses, and with teachers in training.

The second edition of this book contains numerous changes and updates and two new chapters, Chapter 4, Extensive Listening, and Chapter 9, Teaching Using a Course Book, making a total of twelve chapters. The chapter on extensive listening partly reflects the increasing interest in extensive reading and the continuing awareness of the importance of comprehensible input through listening and reading for learning. The chapter on using a course book addresses a common reality that many teachers, through choice or command, use a course book. A course book cannot cover all that is needed in a course and does not provide enough repetition for learning to occur.

In this second edition, each chapter is now followed by three tasks and suggestions for further reading that could be used with teachers-in-training. The tasks focus on understanding and applying some of the ideas covered in the chapter.

Several of the techniques described in this book can be found at https://tinyurl.com/Language-Teaching-Techniques. The videos are short and very practical and are a useful supplement to the descriptions in this book.

The book has three major features. First, it has a strong practical emphasis—around a hundred teaching techniques are described in the book. Second, it tries to provide a balanced programme for developing the skills of listening and speaking. It does this by using a framework called the four strands. These are called strands because they run through the whole course. They are the strands of meaning-focused input, meaning-focused output, language-focused learning, and fluency development. In a well-balanced language programme covering the four skills of listening, speaking, reading, and writing, each of the four strands should have roughly equal amounts of time and, ideally, should cover the same content. The organization of the book largely reflects these four strands. Third, wherever possible, the ideas in this book are research-based. This is reflected in the principles that are described at the end of Chapter 1 and that are referred to throughout the book. The idea that lies behind these principles is that it is not a wise idea to closely follow a particular method of language teaching, such as communicative language teaching or the direct method. It is much more sensible to draw, where possible, on research-based principles that can be adapted or discarded as new research evidence becomes available.

We have attempted to write the book using clear and simple language. Wherever possible, technical terms have been avoided. However, in a few cases, with terms such as *negotiation, pushed output*, and *extensive listening*, technical terms have been used and explained in the text. This book, thus, does not require any previous knowledge of second language acquisition theory or language teaching methodology.

Chapter 1 gives an overview of the four strands. This overview is also very relevant for the companion book to this one, called *Teaching ESL/EFL Reading and Writing* (also available in a second edition). Chapters 2–4 deal largely with listening (a form of meaning-focused input). Chapters 5, 6, and 10 deal with language-focused learning, paying particular attention to dictation and its related activities, to pronunciation, and to the learning of vocabulary, grammar, and discourse. Chapters 7 and 8 focus on speaking (meaning-focused output). These chapters look at how speaking activities can be designed to encourage language learning. Chapter 9 focuses on using and supplementing a course book, and particularly on making sure that the course is well balanced, with plenty of opportunities for repetition to occur. Chapter 11 deals with fluency development, which is the fourth of the four strands. Where English is taught as a foreign language, fluency development is often neglected. Fluency development is important at all levels of proficiency, and even beginners need to become fluent with the few items of language that they know. Chapter 12 deals with monitoring and testing.

As a result of working through this book, teachers should be able to design a well-balanced listening and speaking course that provides a good range of opportunities for learning. They should also be able to use a course book well, supplementing it with extensive listening and reading, and fluency development. The teacher's most important job is to plan so that the learners are learning useful things, so that the best conditions for learning occur, and so that they are getting a balance of learning opportunities. This book should help teachers do this.

The reviewers of the book before it was published provided many helpful and frank comments that led us to see the book through others' eyes. We are very grateful for this.

Both this book and its companion volume, *Teaching ESL/EFL Reading and Writing*, were largely written and used in our own teacher training courses before they were offered for publication. There was, thus, a lot of input from the teachers who were studying on these courses.

We would feel that the book's purpose has been achieved if, as a result of reading it, teachers learn some new techniques and activities, understand why these activities are used, and see how they fit into the larger, well-balanced programme.

Teaching English and training teachers of English are challenging but very rewarding professions. We have both been involved in them for a very long time, and they have given us a great deal of enjoyment. We hope that this enjoyment is apparent in the book and that it will help readers gain similar enjoyment.

1 Parts and Goals of a Listening and Speaking Course

This book uses research and theory on second language acquisition in classrooms as the basis for planning a listening and speaking programme for learners of English as a second or foreign language. As we shall see, the principles underlying the listening and speaking parts of a course are not essentially different from those underlying the reading and writing parts.

The Four Strands

The basic argument of the book is that a well-balanced language course should consist of four roughly equal strands:

1. Learning through meaning-focused input; that is, learning through listening and reading where the learner's attention is on the ideas and messages conveyed by the language.
2. Learning through meaning-focused output; that is, learning through speaking and writing where the learner's attention is on conveying ideas and messages to another person.
3. Learning through deliberate attention to language items and language features; that is, learning through direct vocabulary study, through grammar exercises and explanation, through attention to the sounds and spelling of the language, through attention to discourse features, and through the deliberate learning and practice of language learning strategies and language use strategies.
4. Developing fluent use of known language items and features over the four skills of listening, speaking, reading, and writing; that is, becoming fluent with what is already known.

These four strands are called meaning-focused input, meaning-focused output, language-focused learning, and fluency development. A well-planned language course has an appropriate balance of these four strands. It is through these four strands that learners achieve the learning goals of a language course, namely fluent control of the sounds, spelling, vocabulary, grammar, and discourse features of the language, so that they can be used to communicate effectively. The opportunities for learning language are called strands because they can be seen as long, continuous sets of learning conditions that run through the whole language course. Every activity in a language course fits into one of these strands.

This chapter does not limit itself to listening and speaking, but, because it aims at describing what a well-balanced course is like, it also includes the skills of reading and writing. *Teaching ESL/EFL Reading and Writing* is a companion text to this text on listening and speaking.

There is a tendency for language courses not to balance the four strands and, indeed, to pay almost no attention to some of them. Courses that have a very strong communicative focus often actively discourage formal language-focused learning. There is no justification for this, as second language acquisition research shows that appropriately focused attention to language items can make a very positive contribution to learning (Elgort, 2011; Nassaji, 2017). At the other extreme, there are courses that seem to do little else but focus on formal features of the language, with little or no opportunity to use what has been learned to receive and produce real messages. Perhaps even more commonly, there are courses that provide opportunities to receive and produce messages and pay useful attention to language features, but do not provide opportunities for the learners to become truly fluent in using what they know.

A common-sense justification of the four strands is the time-on-task principle. How can you learn to do something if you don't do that during learning? How can you learn to speak if you don't do speaking? How can you learn to write without writing? The time-on-task principle simply says that, the more time you spend doing something, the better you are likely to be at doing it. This is a very robust principle, and there is no shortage of evidence, for example, that those who read a lot are better readers (Cunningham & Stanovich, 1991), and that those who write a lot usually become better writers. However, it is a simplistic principle and it can be rightfully criticised for ignoring the quality of the activity in favour of the quantity of the activity, and for not taking account of the ways in which language learning differs from other kinds of learning. Nevertheless, as one of a set of principles that do take account of these factors, the time-on-task principle is an important and essential one. Another idea underlying a common-sense approach is that there is something about each of the language skills of listening, speaking, reading, and writing that makes it different from the others. It is, thus, necessary to pay attention to each skill to make sure that these unique features are learned. It is also not difficult to argue that each of these four skills can be broken down even further—for example, that a formal spoken monologue has features that differ from those of friendly conversation, and so on (Biber, 1989). It is also possible to distinguish accuracy from fluency and so see the necessity for providing fluency practice for each of the skills. There are, thus, common-sense justifications for including the four strands in a language course.

The evidence for the strands draws on a large and growing body of research into the roles of input, output, and form-focused instruction in second language learning, and in the development of speaking and reading fluency. In this chapter, we will look at each of the four strands, the research evidence for them, their justification, and how they can be put into practice. The chapter concludes with a set of pedagogical principles based on the strands that can be used to guide the teaching of a language course.

Meaning-focused Input: Learning through Listening and Reading

The meaning-focused input strand involves learning through listening and reading—using language receptively. It is called "meaning-focused" because, in all the work done in this strand, the learners' main focus and interest should be on understanding and gaining knowledge or enjoyment, or both, from what they listen to and read. Typical activities in this strand include extensive listening, extensive reading, shared reading, listening to stories, watching TV or films, and being a listener in a conversation (see Newton (2016) for a chapter-length survey of the four skills, and Newton et al. (2018) for a detailed guide to teaching the four skills in academic contexts).

This strand only exists if certain conditions are present:

1. Most of what the learners are listening to or reading is already familiar to them.
2. The learners are interested in the input and want to understand it.
3. Only a small proportion of the language features are unknown to the learners. In terms of vocabulary, 95–98 per cent of the running words should be within the learners' previous knowledge, and so only five, or preferably only one or two, words per hundred should be unknown to them (Hu & Nation, 2000).
4. The learners can gain some knowledge of the unknown language items through context clues and background knowledge.
5. There are large quantities of input.

If these conditions are not present, then the meaning-focused input strand does not exist in that course. Learning from meaning-focused input is fragile, because there are usually only small gains from each meeting with a word, and because learning is dependent on the quality of reading and listening skills and is affected by background knowledge. Because of this, large quantities of input are needed for this strand to work well. An extensive listening programme is one way of providing this quantity.

Although many researchers criticise Krashen's (1985) input theory, none would disagree with the idea that meaningful, comprehensible input is an important source of language learning. Dupuy (1999) investigated "narrow listening", an approach based on Krashen's ideas. This involved learners listening as many times as they wished to a range of 1–2-minute aural texts on a range of familiar and interesting topics of their choice. The learners in the study reported improvements in their listening comprehension, fluency, and vocabulary, as well as increased confidence in French (the target language). Webb, Newton, and Chang (2013) found that meeting unfamiliar collocations (e.g., buy time, lose touch) during extensive listening to graded readers while reading along led to incidental learning. It was necessary for the young adult Taiwanese EFL learners in the study to meet a collocation more than five times for effective incidental learning, and, as the number of encounters increased, so did their knowledge of the collocations. Among the best-controlled studies of second language extensive reading is Waring and Takaki's (2003) study of vocabulary learning from a graded reader. This study showed that small amounts of vocabulary learning of various strengths occurred incidentally as a result of meaning-focused reading. Elley and Mangubhai's (1981) classic study of the book flood (a programme that encouraged wide reading for pleasure) showed a range of language learning benefits compared with a programme that was largely dominated by language-focused learning (or perhaps more accurately, language-focused teaching).

Compared with well-planned deliberate learning, incidental learning through input is fragile and is dependent on large quantities of input to gain sufficient repetition. Nation and Wang (1999) calculated that second language learners needed to read at least one graded reader every week in order to get enough repetitions to establish substantial vocabulary growth through incidental learning. The gains from meaning-focused input, however, become substantial gains if there are large quantities of input.

Meaning-focused Output: Learning through Speaking and Writing

The meaning-focused output strand involves learning through speaking and writing—using language productively. Typical activities in this strand include talking in conversations, giving a speech or lecture, writing a letter, writing a note to someone, keeping a diary, telling a story, and telling someone how to do something.

The same kinds of condition apply to meaning-focused output as apply to meaning-focused input:

1. The learners write and talk about things that are largely familiar to them.
2. The learners' main goal is to convey their message to someone else.
3. Only a small proportion of the language they need to use is not familiar to them.

4. The learners can use communication strategies, dictionaries, or previous input to make up for gaps in their productive knowledge.
5. There are plenty of opportunities to produce.

Many spoken activities will include a mixture of meaning-focused input and meaning-focused output. One person's output can be another person's input.

Swain's (1985) output hypothesis has been influential in clarifying the role of speaking and writing in second language learning. The output hypothesis was initially formulated to highlight limitations in Krashen's (1985) input hypothesis. Put simply, it claims that, "the act of producing language (speaking and writing) constitutes, under certain circumstances, part of the process of second language learning" (Swain, 2005: 471). The opportunities that output provides for learning are not the same as those provided by input. Swain (1995) suggests three functions for output: (1) the noticing/triggering function, (2) the hypothesis-testing function, and (3) the metalinguistic (reflective) function.

The noticing/triggering function occurs when learners become consciously aware of a gap in their knowledge as they attempt to construct a message in the second language—that is, they do not know how to say what they want to say. Izumi's (2002) research indicates that the effect on acquisition of noticing a gap through output was significantly greater than the effect of noticing through input. This effect can be explained in two ways. First, productive learning involves having to search for and produce a grammatical structure or a word form (including pronouncing a word accurately), whereas receptive learning involves having to find a meaning for a structure or word form. Productive learning typically results in more, stronger knowledge than receptive learning (Griffin & Harley, 1996). Second, varied use involves meeting or using previously met language items in ways that they have not been used or met before and produces deeper learning than the simple retrieval of previously met items (Joe, 1998). Izumi (2002) suggests that the grammatical encoding that is required by output forces learners to integrate the new items into a more cohesive structure. Decoding items from input does not require this same kind of integration. That is, output sets up learning conditions that are qualitatively different from those of input. This is not to say that input is inferior, simply that it is different and, thus, an important part of a balanced set of opportunities for learning.

The full effect of the noticing/triggering function is not complete until a learner has had the chance to make up for the gap that he/she has noticed. This can occur in several ways. First, having noticed a gap during output, the learner is likely to be more alert to language items in input that match the gap. For example, if the learner has difficulty expressing a particular meaning when writing, they later "read like a writer", paying attention to how others say what they wanted to say. This is referred to as moving from semantic to syntactic processing. It is similar to an amateur guitar player not just enjoying a performance by a top-class guitarist of a tune he or she has struggled to play, but also noticing the techniques and chord voicings the performer uses to play it. Second, having noticed a gap during output, learners may successfully fill that gap through a lucky guess, trial and error, the use of analogy, first language transfer, or problem-solving. Webb (2002) found that learners were able to demonstrate aspects of vocabulary knowledge of previously unknown words even though they had not had the opportunity to learn those aspects of knowledge, because they were able to work them out through analogy and first language parallels. Third, having noticed a gap during output, learners may deliberately seek to find the item by reference to outside sources such as teachers, peers, or dictionaries.

Swain's second function of output is the hypothesis-testing function. This involves the learner "having a go" at constructing a message using language they are not sure about. For example, when asked to make a prediction about the future, a learner said, "In the future will be robot working in house" (Newton, personal classroom data). This learner's partial understanding of the will + main verb structure allowed him to express his meaning but also revealed a gap in his knowledge. If he then hears other learners using the correct structure, he may become aware of his gap. Or the teacher may give corrective feedback to prompt him to notice and fix the error. Corrective feedback during communicative classroom interaction has been shown to aid language development (Leeman, 2007; Lyster, Saito, & Sato, 2013). However, there are many ways of giving feedback, and not all are equally effective, a point we discuss in a later chapter.

The third function of output is the metalinguistic (reflective) function. This involves learners working collaboratively to talk about and solve language problems during classroom interaction. Common classroom applications of this idea include activities such as the strip story (Gibson, 1975), dictogloss (Wajnryb, 1988, 1989), where learners work together to reconstruct a text they have listened to, and what Fotos (2002) refers to as structure-based interactive activities in which learners are given grammar problems to solve interactively. In these tasks, grammar structures are the topic of communication. All these activities involve a lot of talk about language, and this talk can contribute to language learning (Swain, 2000; Swain & Lapkin, 1998). Such activities require a deliberate reflective focus on language, typically within the context of language in use. Other activities encouraging metalinguistic reflection include whiteboard or group composition, where learners cooperate to produce one piece of written work, and "Ask and

Answer" (Simcock, 1993), where learners retell a text in an interview format. These activities combine meaning-focused output and language-focused learning, because output becomes the means for deliberately focusing on language features.

It is possible to add a number of additional functions of output. A fourth function involves strengthening knowledge of language items through the way they are used. The most effective use is called "generative or varied use" (Joe, 1998), where the learners use the language items in ways that they have not met or used before. The more generatively something is used, the better it is retained. Additional functions involve developing discourse skills, such as turn-taking and dealing with communication problems, and developing a personal voice or manner of speaking (Skehan, 1998). These are skills that can only be acquired through active participation in meaning-focused speaking.

Language-focused Learning

Language-focused learning has many names—focus on form, form-focused instruction, deliberate study and deliberate teaching, learning as opposed to acquisition, intentional learning, and so on. It involves the deliberate learning of language features such as pronunciation, spelling, vocabulary, grammar, and discourse. The ultimate aim of language-focused learning is to become a more proficient language user, but its short-term aim is to learn language items. Typical activities in this strand are pronunciation practice, using substitution tables and drills, listening to teacher explanations of language items, learning vocabulary from word cards, intensive reading, translation, memorising dialogues, and getting feedback about writing. The deliberate learning of strategies such as guessing from context or dictionary use are also included in this strand. Most of these language-focused learning activities can have a positive effect on learning and language use, but it is important that they are only a small part of the course and do not become the whole course. In total, the language-focused learning strand should not make up more than one-quarter of the time spent on the whole course.

Just as there are conditions for meaning-focused input and output, there are conditions for language-focused learning:

1. The learners give deliberate attention to language features.
2. The learners should process the language features in deep and thoughtful ways.
3. There should be opportunities to give spaced, repeated attention to the same features.
4. The features that are focused on should be simple and not dependent on developmental knowledge that the learners do not have.
5. Features that are studied in the language-focused learning strand should also occur often in the other three strands of the course.

Language-focused learning can have any of these effects:

- it can add directly to implicit knowledge
- it can raise consciousness of language items to help later learning
- it can focus on systematic aspects of the language
- it can be used to develop strategies.

Some activities in the language-focused learning strand, such as dictation, go in and out of fashion, but there is plenty of evidence, certainly in vocabulary learning, that deliberate learning can make a very useful contribution to a learner's language proficiency.

There has long been substantial evidence that deliberately learning vocabulary can result in large amounts of well-retained usable knowledge (Nation, 2013a: 437–478). Evidence also shows that very large amounts of learning can occur in limited amounts of learning time, particularly if learning sessions are increasingly spaced. There is evidence that deliberate learning is effective for the learning of multi-word units (Boers, Eyckmans, Kappel, Stengers, & Demecheleer, 2006) and grammatical features (Williams, 2005), but there is debate over whether this has to be within the context of an overall focus on meaning and communication or whether it can be fully decontextualised (Ellis, 2006; Long, 2015; Williams, 2005). Elgort (2011) has shown that the deliberate learning of vocabulary establishes both implicit knowledge and explicit knowledge at the same time (see Nassaji (2017) for a clear and useful discussion of explicit and implicit knowledge and learning). The deliberate decontextualised learning of vocabulary thus results in the kind of knowledge needed for normal language use.

Becoming Fluent in Listening, Speaking, Reading, and Writing

The fluency development strand should involve all the four skills of listening, speaking, reading, and writing. In this strand, the learners are helped to make the best use of what they already know. Like meaning-focused input and output, the fluency development strand is also meaning-focused. That is, the learners' aim is to receive and convey messages. Typical activities include speed reading, repeated listening, the 4/3/2 technique, the poster carousel/gallery walk activity, 10-minute writing, and listening to easy stories.

The fluency strand only exists if certain conditions are present.

1. All of what the learners are listening to, reading, speaking, or writing is largely familiar to them. That is, there are no unfamiliar language features or largely unfamiliar content or discourse features.
2. There is some pressure or encouragement to perform at a faster than usual speed.
3. There is a large amount of input or output.
4. The learners' focus is on receiving or conveying meaning.

If the activity involves unknown vocabulary, it is not a fluency activity. If the focus is on language features, it is not a fluency activity. If there is no push to go faster or more smoothly, it is not a fluency activity. The fluency strand should make up about one-quarter of the course time. It is time out from learning new items and is a time for getting good at using what is already known.

Studies of fluency development in first language readers have found that fluency practice increases reading fluency, and that assisted fluency activities seem to work better than unassisted activities (Kuhn & Stahl, 2003). Studies of second language readers have also found an increase in fluency as a result of timed practice (Chung & Nation, 2006) and have found transfer of reading speed between the first and second languages when language difficulty is controlled for (Bismoko & Nation, 1974; Cramer, 1975; West, 1941). Studies of the 4/3/2 technique, where the same talk is repeated to different listeners in a decreasing time frame (4 minutes, then 3 minutes, then 2), have shown increases in fluency during the task (Arevart & Nation, 1991; Boers, 2014, 2017; de Jong & Perfetti, 2011; Nation, 1989a; Thai & Boers, 2016). Schmidt (1992) describes a range of theories to explain fluency development. What is common to many of these is that fluency development involves more formulaic use of larger language chunks or sequences (Wood, 2006). Fluency, accuracy, and complexity are most likely interdependent.

There are two major types of second language fluency activity: those that involve repetition of the same material, as in 4/3/2 and repeated listening, and those that do not, as in easy extensive listening or reading.

In the early stages of language learning especially, there is value in becoming fluent with a repertoire of useful sentences and phrases such as those listed in Nation and Crabbe's (1991) survival vocabulary. This fits with Palmer's (1925) fundamental guiding principle for learning to communicate in a second language—*Memorise perfectly the largest number of common and useful word groups!* Palmer explains that "perfectly" means to a high level of fluency. In most language courses, not enough attention is paid to fluency development, possibly because it does not involve the learning of new language items and, thus, is not seen as moving the learners forward in their knowledge of the language.

Balancing the Four Strands

Each strand should have roughly the same amount of time in a well-balanced course that aims to cover both receptive and productive skills. The balancing of time needs to take account of what occurs inside the classroom as well as opportunities for language learning and use outside the classroom. In a longitudinal study of opportunities for 17 Chinese graduate students at a Canadian university to use English, Ranta and Meckelborg (2013) found generally low levels of interactive use of

English compared with higher levels of receptive use, such as listening to lectures, although there was considerable variation among individuals. The authors conclude that the students had "few opportunities to improve their speaking fluency and acquire more idiomatic aspects of English" (p. 24).

A teacher can check whether there is a good balance of the strands by noting the language activities that learners are involved in over a few weeks or a month, classifying each of these into one or more of the four strands and noting how much time each one takes. Ideally each strand should occupy about 25 per cent of the course time.

What justification is there for trying to have an equal amount of time for each strand? Ellis (2005) includes the following principles in his list of principles of instructed language learning:

- Instruction needs to ensure that learners focus predominantly on use.
- Instruction needs to ensure that learners also focus on language features.

The three strands of meaning-focused input, meaning-focused output, and fluency development are meaning-focused strands. They all involve activities where the learners' focus is on communicating and receiving messages. In the meaning-focused input and meaning-focused output strands, this meaning-focused communication pushes the boundaries of learners' knowledge and skill and results in mostly incidental learning of language features. In the fluency development strand, the messages are very easy and familiar ones, but they are still the main focus of the activities. Thus, three of the four strands—and, hence, three-quarters of the time—focus predominately on use, and one strand, the language-focused learning strand, focuses on language features.

There is another justification for this three-to-one balance. Given the same amount of time, deliberate language-focused learning activities result in more learning than the incidental learning from meaning-focused activities. For example, the Waring and Takaki (2003) study showed that, in approximately 56 minutes of meaning-focused reading of a graded reader, four words were learned reasonably well, and another twelve were partially learned. Newton (2013) found that around four new words were learnt for every 30 minutes learners spent doing interactive communication tasks. By comparison, studies of deliberate vocabulary learning when learners study word pairs (2L-1L) result in learning rates of around thirty-five words per hour, which are four or more times higher than the incidental rate (Nation, 2013a: 439; Thorndike, 1908; Webb, 1962). This kind of comparison is not entirely fair, however, because meaning-focused activities have a range of benefits for language learning, such as learning content matter, skill improvement, and enjoyment. Nonetheless, a major justification for language-focused learning is its focused efficiency. This focused efficiency needs to be balanced against the three less efficient, but more widely beneficial, meaning-focused strands.

In spite of these arguments, giving equal time to each strand is an arbitrary decision. It has been suggested that the time given to the strands could change as learners' proficiency develops (Ellis, 2019). There are good arguments, such as those put forward by Ellis, for developing fluency with items such as numbers and useful multi-word phrases right from the beginning of language learning. Then, once basic fluency has been achieved, greater emphasis can be given to language-focused learning, or what Ellis refers to as "explicit accuracy-oriented work" (p. 454). Similarly, learning more about the nature of language, such as its history, etymology, and pragmatic effects, can be a useful support for learning at advanced levels.

Integrating the Four Strands

The four strands are opportunities for certain types of learning. They differ from each other according to the conditions that are needed for the different types of learning. They can fit together in many different ways. For example, in an intensive English programme with many different teachers, there may be different classes for spoken language (listening and speaking), reading, writing, and language study. It would then be important to make sure that the spoken language classes, for example, not only had meaning-focused input and output activities, but also included fluency development activities and only a very small amount of language-focused learning.

In a content-based course that did not have a skill-based division of classes, the four strands could all occur within a unit of work. Language-focused learning could lead into meaning-focused input or output, and this could lead into a fluency activity on the same theme. Alternatively, language-focused learning could occur as it was needed in the context of meaning-focused work. Once again, a good teacher would check to see if, over a week or two, there was a roughly equal amount of time given to each strand.

The four strands work best if the content material of the course, that is the topics covered, are integrated across the four strands. That is, the same topics should be covered in all four strands. This has several positive effects on learning. First, the coverage of the same topics will result in repetition of the language features associated with those topics, and repetition is essential for learning to occur. Second, because the same topics are covered in different strands and across the different skills of listening, speaking, reading, and writing, the repetition that occurs is more likely to be varied repetition, where there are some differences in the repetitions. Such variation increases the quality of the input and results in better retention (Joe, 1998) than verbatim repetition. Third, as learners' familiarity with a topic increases, they move closer to developing fluency with the language features within that topic area.

There are many ways of giving time to the four strands, and these will depend on factors such as the skills and preferences of the teachers, the expectations of learners and the school, the time-tabling constraints, and current beliefs about language teaching and learning. What is important is that, over a period of time, each strand gets about the same amount of time.

Principles and the Four Strands

The following pedagogical principles are aimed at providing guidelines for teachers. They draw on a larger list (Nation & Macalister, 2020a) and can usefully be compared with other lists of principles (e.g., Arnold, Dörnyei, & Pugliese, 2015; Brown, 1993; Ellis, 2005; Long, 2009). The list is organised around the four strands, with the final two principles focusing on what should be covered in a course. Each principle is followed by a brief list of suggestions about how the principle could be put into practice, with an emphasis on suggestions for teaching listening and speaking.

1. *Provide and organise large amounts of comprehensible input through both listening and reading.* This could involve providing an extensive listening programme, reading to the learners, getting learners to give talks for their classmates to listen to, arranging spoken communication activities, and using online platforms for conversational interaction.
2. *Boost learning through comprehensible input by adding a deliberate element.* Note words on the board as they occur in listening, do consciousness-raising activities after communicative tasks, get learners to reflect on new items they meet through listening, and explain problem items that come up in the context of communication activities.
3. *Support and push learners to produce spoken and written output in a variety of appropriate genres.* Use communication activities that involve a range of situations, and use role play.
4. *Provide opportunities for cooperative interaction.* Do group work involving problem-solving and information gap tasks.
5. *Help learners deliberately learn language items and patterns, including sounds, spelling, vocabulary, multi-word units, grammar, and discourse.* Do teacher-led intensive listening, give corrective feedback on speaking, deliberately teach language items, and arrange individual study of language items.
6. *Train learners in strategies that will contribute to autonomous language learning.* Work on guessing from context, train learners in metacognitive listening strategies (Goh, 2000), and model in class

ways to practise listening and speaking that learners can take up out of class.
7. *Provide fluency development activities in each of the four skills of listening, speaking, reading, and writing.* Run a speed reading course, include repeated reading, provide extensive reading and listening programmes, do 4/3/2 activities, and organise a regular 10-minute writing fluency programme.
8. *Provide a roughly equal balance of the four strands of meaning-focused input, meaning-focused output, language-focused learning, and fluency development.* Keep a record of the activities done in the course, the strand they fit into, and the amount of time spent on them.
9. *Plan for repeated coverage of the most useful language items.* Focus on high-frequency items, use controlled and simplified material, and provide plenty of input at the same level.
10. *Use needs analysis, monitoring, and assessment to help address learners' language and communication needs.*

The main aim of this book is to show the wide range of activities that can be used in each of the four strands of a course, to show the research evidence that justifies the existence of the strands, and to show how teachers can monitor and assess the learning that occurs in each of the strands.

A basic assumption that lies behind the book is that it is not wise for a teacher or course designer to ally themselves with a particular method of language teaching. It is much more productive to become aware of the important principles of teaching and learning and to apply these in ways that suit the learners, the teaching conditions, and the skills of the teacher. This may result in courses that use different kinds of teaching and learning activity but that fundamentally draw on the same principles.

Another related assumption behind this book is that teaching and learning activities that have become unfashionable for a variety of reasons may still make a positive contribution to learning if they apply useful principles and if they are focused on worthwhile goals. Thus, in this book, there is considerable discussion of pronunciation practice, structure drills, learning words out of context, dictation activities, and repetition activities. This is because each of these activities, performed in an appropriate way, can contribute to one of the strands of a course. The trick lies in giving them a useful focus and a suitable amount of time.

This book is written for teachers of English as a second or foreign language, and, as a result of working their way through it, they should be able to do the following things:

1. Recognise and describe the range of goals of a language course.
2. Look critically at a language course to see its strengths, weaknesses, and gaps.

14 *Parts of a Listening and Speaking Course*

3. Develop and adapt courses to provide a balance of the four strands in a course.
4. Choose, apply, and monitor a range of activities that will reach useful learning goals.
5. Be able to describe and justify the parts of their language course, drawing on principles derived from research in second language learning and second language teaching.

In each section of this book, there will be discussion of how much time in a course should be given to each of the four strands and the sub-strands within them. Teachers will need to look at opportunities for learning outside class and consider these when planning a course.

Learning Goals

A language learning course is used to reach learning goals. These goals can include the learning of: (1) language items such as sounds, vocabulary, and grammatical constructions; (2) the content or ideas of the subject being studied, such as geography, English literature, mathematics, or cross-cultural understanding; (3) language skills such as listening, writing, fluency in using known items, and strategies for coping with language difficulties; and (4) the organisation of discourse such as rhetorical features and communication strategies. Table 1.1 elaborates these areas. The mnemonic LIST, which contains the first letter of each of the goals (language, ideas, skills, text), is a useful way to remember the goals.

The use of particular language teaching techniques is justified to the extent that they achieve learning goals. This even applies to techniques that are used for fun to give the learners a break, because there are many language teaching techniques that are great fun and achieve very useful learning goals.

The separate listing of specific goals such as pronunciation, vocabulary, and fluency does not mean that there must be a discrete-point approach to teaching. The purpose of such a listing is to make teachers more analytical about their use of techniques and the design of programmes. As we shall see, one technique can achieve several goals, and, at times, it may not be obvious to the learners what the goal is as their interest may be in the message involved in the activity.

Some books describe the skill components and the nature of listening (Rost, 2016) and speaking (Hughes & Reed, 2016). Such descriptions give a teacher more realistic expectations of what may be achieved in a course and what to look for to see if the range of knowledge and skills is being covered. Such descriptions also play a role in sequencing the sub-goals of a course.

The text or discourse goals are clearly related to language goals. Biber's research (1989) has shown that various grammatical aspects of the language tend to form different clusters according to the type of discourse. Biber set up

Table 1.1 Learning Goals

General goals	Specific goals
Language items	pronunciation
	vocabulary
	grammatical constructions
Ideas (content)	curriculum topics
	world knowledge
	cultural themes
Skills	listening, speaking, reading, and writing skills or sub-skills
	accuracy
	fluency
	strategies
Text (discourse)	conversational discourse patterns and rules
	text schemata or topic-type scales

a typology of texts based on the co-occurrence of language features. He found that he was able to group texts according to the language features that frequently occurred or that were typically absent or infrequent. For example, face-to-face interaction is typified by the use of time and place adverbials, first- and second-person pronouns, the present tense, private verbs such as *know* and *think*, and *be* as a main verb. Imaginative narrative is typified by past tense verbs, third-person pronouns, public verbs such as *said*, and present participial clauses.

Biber's findings are important for designing courses, because we can draw the following implications from them:

1. In order to meet the full range of language features, learners need to be exposed to a range of discourse types.
2. Being able to operate well in one kind of discourse—for example, informal conversation—does not mean that a learner has the knowledge to operate well in another kind of discourse—for example, formal speech—because each discourse type makes use of a different cluster of language features.
3. Having to operate in an unfamiliar discourse area is a demanding task for learners and may make them aware of gaps in their command of the language. As Ellis (1990) points out, this awareness is a valuable starting point for language acquisition.

We have looked at the broad features that should make up a well-balanced language course. In the following chapters, we will look in detail at what should make up a well-balanced listening and speaking course.

Tasks

1. Classify these ten activities into the four strands: *extensive reading, feedback on writing, conversation activities, training in metalinguistic listening strategies, easy extensive listening, repeated listening, substitution tables, pronunciation practice, delivering a prepared talk, listening and reading at the same time*. The purpose of this task is help you become familiar with the nature of each of the four strands.
2. The 4/3/2 activity involves giving the same talk on a very familiar topic three times. Each time the speaker gives the talk to a different listener, but each time there is less time (4 minutes, 3 minutes, 2 minutes) to deliver the talk. Working with a partner or in a small group, explain how this activity meets the four criteria for the fluency strand (easy material, pressure to go faster, plenty of practice, a focus on the message). The purpose of this task is to see if you can use learning conditions to justify why a particular activity fits into a particular strand.
3. The principle of the four strands says that a well-balanced course gives equal time to meaning-focused input, meaning-focused output, language-focused learning, and fluency development, and covers much the same content in each of the four strands. How could you check to see if your course applies the principle of the four strands?

Further Reading

Nation (2013b, Chapter 1) has a detailed discussion of the four strands and shows how the principle can be applied to a course. Nation and Yamamoto (2012) apply the four strands to learning a language without a teacher.

The following sources all provide valuable lists of principles to guide language teaching and reflect many of the ideas in this chapter: Arnold, Dörnyei, and Pugliese (2015), Ellis (2005), and Long (2009).

2 Beginning to Listen and Speak in Another Language

The aims of a beginner's course in listening and speaking are: (1) to help the learners to be able to cope with meaning-focused input and meaning-focused output as soon as possible; (2) to motivate them in their language study by getting them to engage in successful listening and speaking; and (3) to make the early learning as relevant as possible to their language use needs.

What Should They Learn?

The content of an English course for beginners will vary greatly according to the age of the learners, their purpose for learning, their educational background and previous experience with English, and whether they are learning in a foreign or second language context. Below is a set of learning priorities for one type of beginners, namely new migrant adult absolute beginners who may have had limited education and who need general everyday English for living in an English-speaking context.

1. *Using a New Alphabet*
    - Recognise and write the letters of the alphabet (including upper- and lower-case letters). This could involve lots of copying tasks
    - Develop phonological awareness that letters in words stand for specific sounds, including vowel–consonant patterns, three-letter words (consonant–vowel–consonant), consonant blends, and so on.

2. *Phrases for Talking about Yourself*
    - My name is ____. I live in ____. I come from ____.
    - I am ____ years old. I am married. I have ____ children.
    - I worked as a ____.
    - I like ____. I don't like ____.

3. *Phrases and Vocabulary for Everyday Life*

- Shopping—food, clothing names, household objects
- Visiting the doctor
- Housing
- Using the internet
- Banking
- Finding a job
- Contacting government agencies

4. *Sight Vocabulary*

- Reading street signs, tickets, labels, and so on

5. *Classroom Expressions*

- Excuse me ...
- Say that again please?
- How do I say this?
- Can you help me?
- How do you spell ____?
- I don't know. I don't understand.
- Please speak more slowly.
- May I go to the toilet?

6. *High-Frequency Words*

- Numbers
- Classroom objects
- Colours
- Time and date words
- Family members
- Parts of the body
- Objects in the home
- Simple question forms.

If the learners are adults who wish to use the language while travelling, then learning the survival vocabulary (Appendix A) is a sensible early goal. This collection of around 120 sentences and phrases has been designed to be immediately useful and to fill the needs of getting to places, finding food and accommodation, being polite, shopping, and getting help. The survival vocabulary is available in many different languages from Paul Nation's resources at www.wgtn.ac.nz/lals/resource.

If the learners are children, then they should learn the high-frequency words of the language, which allow them to listen to simple stories, begin to read graded readers, and do interesting activities. The easiest graded readers use only 75 different words.

Where possible, the course should try to address the learners' language needs and should do this so that the learners can see that this is being done. In small classes, this can involve the use of a negotiated syllabus (Clarke, 1991; Macalister & Nation, 2020: Chapter 10), where the teacher and learners work together to decide what will be dealt with in class.

How Should the Teaching and Learning Be Done?

Five Principles for Teaching Beginners

One way to answer this question is through a set of principles. Here are five principles that are particularly relevant to the teaching of beginners:

1. Meaning — Focus on meaningful and relevant language
2. Interest — Maintain interest through a variety of activities
3. New language — Avoid overloading learners with too much new language
4. Understanding — Provide plenty of comprehensible input
5. Stress-free — Create a friendly, safe, cooperative classroom environment

Notice that the first letter for each of the key words spells out the acronym MINUS. This provides a useful aid for remembering the principles. We now discuss the principles in relation to the teaching of absolute beginners in an ESL context. This is, of course, only one of many contexts for teaching beginners, and so readers will need to consider its relevance to their particular teaching context, and how the examples can be adapted to suit that context.

Principle 1. Focus on Meaningful and Relevant Content

The main focus should be on language that the learners can use quickly for their purposes, rather than on too much grammar explanation or on words that are not directly useful. Here are some simple sentences that can be learned very early in a course so that the learners can use them straight away:

My name is _____.
I come from _____.
I live in _____.
My address is _____.

The teacher could present these sentences orally, one by one, with gestures and lots of repetition and learner involvement. The sentences could then be written on a whiteboard so that the learners can write them down. The written versions then become the basis for pair work. The first aim of this learning is for learners to be able to say these things about themselves without looking at the written version and to understand other learners when they use them. The second aim is for learners to begin to link the written and spoken forms of the words. For learners who are not very familiar with the written form of English, recognising the written form of their name and address is an important early step in building literacy.

One way of checking the usefulness of a phrase or word is to use a computer concordancer to see how many examples of the item can be found in a collection of spoken texts. A useful starting point is www.lextutor.ca/concordancers/

One of the most useful techniques in a listening and speaking programme is the teacher engaging in meaning-focused dialogue with the learners. This dialogue can have many different focuses.

1. *Classroom management.* Perhaps the most realistic kind of dialogue involves the day-to-day running of the classroom. This includes: (1) organising classroom work such as forming groups, using the course book, and calling on learners to perform tasks; (2) managing classroom behaviour; (3) checking attendance; and (4) thanking and praising.
2. *Informal conversation.* The teacher and learners talk about things that happened outside school. Where appropriate, this can be about the learner's family, their hobbies, how they travel to school, favourite food, and so on.
3. *Recalling previous lessons.* The teacher and learners talk about previous class work. This draws on what is hopefully known and familiar and also provides opportunities for revision.
4. *Finding out learners' opinions and ideas.* During an activity, the teacher can ask the learners if they like the particular activity and if they want to do more of it. This dialogue can be the early beginnings of a partly negotiated syllabus.

Principle 2. Maintain Interest through a Variety of Activities

To maintain learners' interest, activities need to be short and varied, and to involve the learners in responding to or using the language. Here are some simple ways to keep learners interested in learning:

- do activities that involve movement
- use real objects and pictures
- plan trips outside the classroom—for example, a trip to a local supermarket linked to a simple food search game

- use songs and simple chants in between other more demanding activities
- introduce and practise new content though games such as bingo.

Principle 3. Avoid Overloading Learners with Too Much New Language

There is usually little need to focus on grammar in the early parts of a course for beginners. Instead, lessons should focus on learning set phrases and words. Teachers often make the mistake of introducing too much new language without giving learners enough opportunities to gain control over this language. A simple rule to keep in mind is "learn a little, use a lot". For example, if the goal is to learn the names for parts of the body, it is better to focus on the most useful words, such as *head, neck, arms, hands, legs, feet,* and so on, and to avoid less-common words such as *elbow* and *ankle*. Note that introducing *elbow* and *ankle* at the same time creates another problem: the similarities between these words (i.e., they sound a bit the same, and their meanings are related) are likely to lead to learners confusing one word for the other.

To apply the principle of "learn a little, use a lot", the body words need to be practised in a variety of ways. These could include picture games, information transfer activities, action games ("Simon says ..."), and bingo. The words can then be used in simple sentence patterns and dialogues such as "How are you? Not so good. My _____ hurts". These activities are described later in this chapter.

Providing the learners with grammatical knowledge about a sentence helps learners get it right in the early stages of learning, but meaningful practice is needed to develop both accuracy in use and fluency in use (Sato & McDonough, 2019).

Principle 4. Provide Plenty of Comprehensible Input

Note that most of these activities mentioned above first involve learners in learning the words through listening and doing before they deepen their learning through using the words in guided speaking. If speaking is pushed too early, learners may be more likely to transfer L1 phonology and to concentrate on mechanical difficulties. Activities such as listen and do, picture ordering, bingo, and information transfer show how listening can be practised in very active ways without requiring much speaking.

Ensuring that input can be understood requires the use of visual aids and contextual support for new language, including pictures, gestures, mime, objects, and experiences out of class. Teachers also need to think carefully about the language they use in class, with the aim of keeping their talk simple but not simplistic or ungrammatical. One way to do this is to always use one form for one meaning. Thus, for example, the teacher needs to decide whether to use "My name is _____" or "I am _____", but not both; "Where are you from?" or "Where do you come from?", but not both.

Early in the course, learners can also learn simple phrases for controlling input such as, "Sorry, I don't understand" or "Please say it again". Displaying these phrases on a large poster makes them readily available throughout a course.

Most of these ideas assume a context in which learners speak a variety of first languages, or the teacher does not speak the learners' first language. Of course, teaching beginners is easier if the learners all speak the same first language and the teacher speaks the first language of the learners. Using translation to convey the meanings of words and phrases is very efficient and is well supported by research as an effective way of communicating meaning. The main disadvantage is that the teacher and learners are tempted to spend a lot of classroom time using the first language instead of the second language. However, as long as the teacher is aware of this danger, then using the first language is a good thing to do and saves a lot of time.

If the learners do not all speak the same first language, and if the teacher does not speak the first languages of the learners, then pictures, gestures, and the use of context need to be used to get meaning across. This is not as difficult as it sounds, and, if the learners also have a well-illustrated course book, the job is easier.

Older learners may make use of bilingual dictionaries that give the meanings of second language words in the learners' first language. These dictionaries differ a lot in quality, but they are extremely useful learning aids. There are now many well-made bilingual dictionary apps. Learners need to have a second language vocabulary of at least 2000 words before they can use monolingual dictionaries where meanings are given in the second language. This is because a vocabulary of around 2000 words is needed to write and understand definitions.

Principle 5. Create a Friendly, Safe, Cooperative Classroom Environment

There is strong evidence that anxiety influences learners' willingness to communicate in a second language (e.g., Yashima, 2002). Therefore, it is particularly important that, in the early stages of learning a second language, learners have successful, low-stress learning experiences. By paying attention to the first four principles, there is a very good chance that these experiences will be plentiful, and that the teacher will already be meeting this fifth principle. Some of the factors that contribute to a positive beginners' classroom are variety, movement, physical comfort, frequent interaction, successful language experiences, and opportunities for learners to experiment and make mistakes without penalties.

Activities and Approaches for Teaching and Learning in a Beginners' Course

Memorising Useful Phrases and Sentences

A quick way of gaining early fluency in a language is to memorise useful phrases. There are several advantages in doing this. First, simple communication can occur at an early stage. For example, learners should be able to say who they are, where they come from, and what they do from the very first language lessons. They should also be able to greet people with phrases such as *good morning* and *good day* and to thank them. Second, memorising phrases and sentences allows learners to make accurate use of the language without having to know the grammar. Third, as we have seen, knowing sentences such as *Please say that again, Please speak more slowly, What does X mean?* allows learners to take control of a conversation and use it for language learning purposes. Fourth, the words and patterns that make up such phrases can make the learning of later phrases and perhaps the learning of later patterns easier. Even at this very early stage of language learning, it is worth showing learners the value of making small flash cards with the second language word or phrase on one side and the first language translation on the other. These cards can be physical or electronic, or both, and are used for recalling the meanings of the words and phrases and, later, recalling the words and phrases. If using physical flash cards, the learner carries a pack of these cards around and goes through them when they have a free moment. For electronic flash cards, there are many apps available for making cards, such as FluentU and Anki, and the British Council website offers practical advice and resources for making and using flash cards. Research has shown that this spaced recall is a very effective way of learning (Nation, 2013a: Chapter 11) and results in the kind of knowledge needed for normal language use.

There are several ways of deciding what sentences and phrases to learn. The following list is ranked in order of importance:

1. The learners think of things they want to be able to say, and the teacher provides the second language phrase to say this.
2. The teacher thinks of the uses the learners need to make of the language and thinks of useful phrases to meet these needs. In some cases, this may involve the teacher talking to the learners about their language needs and observing their daily use of the language.
3. The teacher consults lists of useful and frequent phrases that researchers have developed (Nation & Crabbe, 1991; Nation, 2013b; Shin & Nation, 2008).
4. The teacher follows a course book.

Here is an example of what can happen if not much thought is given to what is taught. Gareth is in his fifth month of learning Japanese in the first year of secondary school. He is speaking to a researcher.

"Tell me something in Japanese, Gareth."
"OK. You ask me questions in English and I'll answer in Japanese."
"Were you born in New Zealand?"
"*We haven't got up to 'yes' yet.*"
"All right. I'll try something else. How old are you?"
"*Do you want me to say the whole sentence because I can only say the number?*"
"That's fine. Just tell me the number."

"…"

"That sounds good. Here's another question. What do you do at school?"
"*No, not that kind of thing.*"
"Sorry. What sort of thing should I be asking you?"
"*Well all the regular things like 'This is a pen' and 'The book is red'. That kind of thing.*"

Practising Sentence Patterns

The next step from memorising phrases and sentences is to learn some productive sentence patterns, that is, sentences where regular substitutions can be made to produce other sentences. These are called **substitution tables**. Here is an example (see www.victoria.ac.nz/lals/resources/george for H.V. George's *101 Substitution Tables*, available for free download).

1	2	3	4	5
I	'll	see	you	tomorrow.
		meet		on Friday.
		call		next week.
				at six o'clock.

The sentence has five parts, but, in the example, substitutions are only made in two of them. When the pattern is first introduced, it is best to have substitution only in one part. The first step is to memorise one sentence, *I'll see you tomorrow*. Then, the teacher gets the learners to take turns around the class making a systematic substitution in one part—for example, *tomorrow, on Friday*, and so on. The teacher should give the learner an oral cue before they make the substitution.

Teacher:	I'll see you tomorrow. On Friday.
Learner 1:	I'll see you on Friday.
Teacher:	next week
Learner 2	I'll see you next week.
Teacher:	at six o'clock
Learner 3:	I'll see you at six o'clock.

When a new pattern or substitution table is introduced, the teacher should start regularly. That is, the teacher should go through the table so that the learners can tell what the next sentence will be, and who will have to say it.

		eating ice-cream
		playing football
	hate	going to the cinema
I	like	studying geography
	love	walking in the evening
		reading comics

For example, when the teacher introduces this substitution table, it can start in a regular way with the teacher saying "I hate eating ice-cream" and then pointing to *playing football*. The first learner in the first row says "I hate playing football". Then the teacher points to *going to the cinema*, and the second learner in the first row says the new sentence, and so on.

T:	I hate eating ice-cream. (points to *playing football*)
L1:	I hate playing football.
T:	(points to *going to the cinema*)
L2:	I hate going to the cinema.

When this is easy for the learners, the teacher can point to phrases in any order. When this is easy for the learners, the teacher points to a phrase and then points to any learner with the other hand. Thus, the learners do not know what phrase will be next and who will be the next person to speak. So, the teacher keeps the exercise interesting by increasing the amount of irregularity in the use of the table (George, 1965).

Another way to keep the exercise interesting is for the teacher to increase the speed of pointing at the table or at the learners. The learners thus have less time to think. The teacher should be careful that the learners do not say the sentences too quickly because of this. This should also be done in a light-hearted and supportive way so as not to increase anxiety.

Another way to keep the exercise interesting is to make the learners use their memory. If the table is written on the board, the teacher can gradually rub out words and phrases. The teacher still points to the whiteboard, but often points to an empty space, and the learners must remember what was there in order to say the sentence. This is called the **disappearing text** technique. To make it easier, when the words are rubbed out, they can be replaced by drawings or words in the first language. Or, after the learners have used a substitution table for a short time, it is rubbed off the whiteboard or the learners close their books. Then, the teacher says parts of phrases, and the learners must say the whole sentence. So, using the above substitution table, the teacher would say, "I hate eating ice-cream. playing." The learners must remember that *playing* was followed by *football* in the table, and so the learner says, "I hate playing football". Then the teacher says "comics", and so on. Doing this applies the principle of retrieval.

There is a danger in the use of substitution tables. The items that are listed in one column—*on Friday, next week, at six o'clock*—tend to be related in meaning and so can interfere with each other. Thus, learners may later incorrectly recall items, such as *on next week, at Friday*. The teacher should plan substitutions with this possibility in mind (for example, don't include *on Friday*) and should look to see if interference is occurring.

So far, we have looked at a range of language-focused activities to use in the beginning stages of a language course, involving memorising phrases and sentences and practising sentence patterns. These are all useful language-focused learning shortcuts to getting started in a language, but do not directly develop the implicit knowledge needed for normal language use. The following activities move closer to meaning-focused input and meaning-focused output, where the focus is on communicating messages. Although many techniques are described below, the teacher should choose a few of these to use regularly. This helps set up known, predictable routines that make classroom management easier and allow the focus to be on the communication rather than on managing the activity. Other activities can be brought in occasionally for variety.

Guiding Listening and Speaking

The prototypical technique for guided listening and speaking is the **What is it?** technique (Nation, 1978). The teacher writes some sentences on the whiteboard. The sentences describe something or someone. Here is an example:

It is thin.
It is black.
It has many teeth.
It is made of plastic.
We can find it near a mirror.
It costs a dollar.
Everybody uses it.
It is used for combing your hair.
What is it?

The teacher shows the learners how to change the sentences to talk about different things. While she does this the teacher follows the plan very closely. For example, *a needle*:

It is thin.
It is silver.
It has a sharp point.
It is made of steel.
We can find it in our house.
It costs ten cents.
You need good eyes to use it.
It is used for sewing things.
What is it?

Then, the teacher gives the learners the name of something—for example, *a pen*—and they must describe it using the plan. She gives a few new words if they are needed in the description. Each learner can be given a different item written on a card to describe. When the learners know how to follow the plan, it can be played as a game. One learner describes something, while the others try to guess what it is. As they improve, the learners can add some sentences that are not in the plan and make other changes. The exercise can be made more controlled by asking the learners to follow the sentence patterns of the plan very carefully. This technique has the following features:

1. Learners can be prepared for the activity by learning and practising a small number of sentence patterns.
2. Communication is important, because the activity has an outcome that depends on successful communication.
3. The learners can do the activity with each other in a form of pair and group work. In this way, the activity provides opportunities for both listening and speaking to occur.
4. Learners can make changes to the activity so that the outcome is not completely predictable.

The following activity has the same features. **Listening grids** (Badger, 1986) involve using listening and often questioning to fill a matrix with information. Table 2.1 gives an example based on what people enjoy watching on television or the internet. Each learner makes a short presentation describing what they like, using the construction "I enjoy watching ...". The rest of the group tick the appropriate places in their grids.

It is only a small step from grids to **surveys**. Each learner has a grid or a list of questions that are then used to gather information from other learners in the class (see Table 2.2). This can be done with each learner moving around the class. Surveys can also move out of the classroom to involve English speakers at home or at work, or learners in another class.

Interview activities provide small-scale question-and-answer interaction. The activities using grids and surveys described above can easily become like small interviews. The person being interviewed needs a source of knowledge—for example, personal experience, a report from a newspaper, part of a science, mathematics, or economics textbook, a picture, or a brief written description. The interviewer needs some guidance on what information to look for and what kinds of question to ask. If, for example, several learners or pairs of learners each have information on different apartments for rent, then they can be interviewed several times by different learners who are using a standard set of questions or the same grid to fill in.

Quizzes are often simply listening activities with an element of competition. The teacher prepares general knowledge questions, incomplete statements, or true/false statements that the learners will hear and try to

Table 2.1 Listening Grids

Person's name	News	Comedy	Game shows	Adventure

Table 2.2 Surveys
(a) *Family*

What's your name?	Have you got any brothers?	Have you got any sisters?	Have you got any children?

(b) Things

What's your name?	Have you got:			
	a car	a bicycle	a cat	a cell phone

answer. There may be two competing teams, with an audience who also write their own answers to the questions. It is not difficult to design quiz questions around a few grammatical constructions.

The airline of Belgium is called _____.
The long thin parts of a comb are called _____.

An element of challenge or competition is also present in **puzzles**. Puzzles may be based on pictures or brief descriptions and give meaning-focused practice in listening.

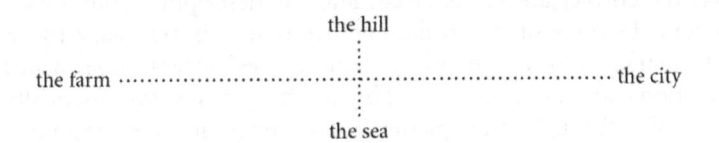

```
                    the hill
                       :
    the farm ..........:............ the city
                       :
                    the sea
```

A boy faces the city.   A girl faces the farm.
What is on his right side?   Where is the hill?
What is behind him?   What is on her left side?

Puzzles based on pictures can involve the use of inference. For example, the learners may have to decide what season it is, what the weather is like on that day in the picture, how old the people are, and so on.

Listen and do activities are used in most classrooms and are the basis of total physical response language teaching (Asher, Kosudo, & De La Torre, 1974). In these activities, the teacher gives commands or makes statements, and the learners do what the teacher says. There are many possible variations on these activities. They can become speaking activities, with the learners saying what to do, and the teacher or another learner doing the action. In **positioning**, some of the learners see a photograph or picture and have to tell other learners how to position themselves to appear like the people in the picture. This can also include the expressions on their faces (Hughes, 1985). Blindfolded learners may be guided through a series of minor obstacles by following the spoken instructions of others.

Bingo is a very adaptable activity that provides learners with lots of listening and vocabulary practice. In "body part bingo" (McKay & Tom, 1999), the teacher first reads simple descriptions of main body parts, and learners guess what is being referred to. Learners then draw a grid with the required number of boxes (3 × 3, 5 × 5, etc.) for the number of body parts. The teacher dictates the names of the body parts, and the learners fill in the grid in any order with these names. The game begins with the teacher reading out descriptions of body parts in random order, and the learners covering the matching words. The first learner to cover a row in any direction calls out "body". He or she then reads back the covered words.

The **listening to pictures** technique (McComish, 1982) is an excellent example of a technique that involves a large quantity of material to listen to and uses a supporting picture to make the language input comprehensible. The learners have a big picture in front of them in which several things are happening. The teacher starts describing the picture, and the learners follow the description while looking at the picture. Occasionally, the teacher includes a true/false statement. If the description is recorded, this can be preceded by a buzz to warn learners that the next statement is a test. The learners write T or F on a sheet of paper, the correct answer is given, and the description continues. Some important features of this technique are that it is very easy to prepare and to mark, and the same picture can be used several times if different descriptions are used with it. The teacher moves systematically and predictably through the picture, describing it. For example, the description may start in the top left corner and move across. This means the learners have little difficulty in following the movement and matching the parts of the picture to the spoken input.

Information transfer activities can be used to help learners produce a description involving several sentences (Palmer, 1982). For example, the information transfer diagram could consist of small pictures and phrases showing the process of cooking a certain food, or making something such as a clay pot. Most of the sentences needed in the description would be in the passive (White, 1978). The learner could repeat the description several times, each time with a different audience and with less opportunity to consult the information transfer diagram.

Techniques for Early Meaning-focused Speaking

The following techniques allow learners to produce spoken language mainly in single sentence turns. The first techniques listed below are directed towards question making. The learners' focus will be largely on the meaning, as there is usually a game-like element of guessing or competition in the activities. As most of the techniques involve learners making the same kinds of sentence around the group, there is the chance for learners to notice what others do and use it to improve their own performance. The design features of modelled repetitive turn-taking, mixed proficiency groups, and productive tasks thus make it possible for learning through comprehending, noticing, comparing, and using to occur.

Descriptions involve the learners making statements based on pictures. The statements may be descriptions, comparisons, predictions, pointing out the differences between two pictures, explanations of what happened before the event shown in the picture, and so on. The learners can take turns producing a sentence each around the group or can call on each other.

Duppenthaler (1988) suggests an interesting variation of "What is it?" called **Hints**. The learners are divided into groups of four or five. Each group thinks of a word in their first language, such as the name of a national dish. The group then prepares one sentence for each learner in the group that describes the word. Then, the learners say the sentences, and points are awarded to the group that guesses it. If, after all the sentences are said, it still cannot be guessed, then the team who made the sentences loses points.

Learners often need practice in forming questions. Gurrey (1955) divides questions into three types—**stages one, two, and three questions.** Stage one questions ask for an answer that can be pointed to, either in a picture or a reading passage—for example, "What is behind the house?", "Who did John meet?" Stage two questions make the learners think. The answer to a stage two question is not directly stated in the passage or cannot be pointed to in a picture. The learners must put certain facts together to find the answer. After a learner answers a stage two question, the teacher can usually ask, "How do you know this?" Here are some stage two questions that are based on a picture: "What season is it?" "What country do these people come from?" To answer these questions, the learners must put certain facts together to find the answers. Stage three questions ask learners to use their imagination—for example, "What are these people thinking about?" "Why does this person like wearing blue clothes?" The questions cannot be answered by looking at a picture or reading a passage. Learners can move through these stages of questions while asking each other questions about an event, a picture, or a story. There is a list that can be used for defining question levels, popularly called "Bloom's taxonomy". Search for this on the internet and look at the five levels and the differences between them.

The learners are divided into tourists and information officers for the **ask and move** activity (Buckeridge, 1988). Each tourist has a different card telling the tourist to find out four or five pieces of information, such as, "Find out the address and opening hours of the museum". The information officers have the answers to these requests, but each information officer does not have all the information. So, it is necessary for each tourist to go to several information officers to find out all the answers. This will involve the information officers answering the same questions several times.

Twenty questions is a well-known activity. The teacher or a learner thinks of an object and writes its name on a piece of paper. The learners ask yes/no questions—for example, "Is it in the room?", "Is it big?" They must guess what it is before they have asked twenty questions. The person who guesses correctly thinks of the next object, and the other learners ask questions.

Questions that are not grammatically correct should not be answered. In another game, a learner can pretend to have a certain job or to be a famous person. The others ask them questions to try to guess their job or who they are. In this game, pronominal questions can be used. Instead of thinking of an object, the teacher can show an unfamiliar object to the class, and, by asking yes/no questions, the learners find out what it is.

In **walk and talk**, the learners form two circles, with a person in the inner circle being paired with a person in the outer circle. The person in the inner circle tells their partner what they did during the weekend. Then they move two persons to the right and tell their new partner. Later, in the whole class, a few learners tell what one of their partners told them.

The learners work in pairs for **the same or different** activity. They each have a sheet of numbered sentences and words. They do not show their sheets to each other. The one with the cross next to number 1 begins speaking. The learner with the sentence says it, and the other learner provides the word. They decide if the sentence and the word refer to the same thing or different things.

Learner A	Learner B
1x It usually has four legs.	1 a chair
2 a boat	2x It flies through the air.
3x It has one eye.	3 a needle
4 a book	4x We can read it.

In another version, the learners decide if the word and the sentence describe the same thing or different things. Instead of words and sentences, only sentences can be used. The learners decide if the two sentences have almost the same meaning or quite different meanings.

Learner A	Learner B
1x A car costs a lot of money.	1 A car is expensive.
2 I agree with you.	2x You and I have the same idea about this.
3x I failed to meet him.	3 We met only once.

The learners are given sets of four words and have to decide which word is the **odd one out**, that is, it does not belong in the set (Burton, 1986). For example, a set can be

grammar-based: *sung, broken, drank, rung;*
vocabulary-based: *hand, heart, leg, ear;*
or content-based: *Delhi, Jakarta, Hanoi, Berlin.*

The learners describe why the word chosen is the odd one out.

All the activities described in this chapter involve group work where the learners interact with each other using very limited English. It is always useful for the teacher to model the activity for the learners before they get involved in their groups.

A Note on Pronunciation

The older the learners, the more important it is to give some direct attention to pronunciation in the beginning stages of language learning. Pronunciation difficulties for most learners are the result of differences between the sound system of their first language and the sound system of the second language. Adults are less likely to pick up the new sounds than young children. (We will look at the reasons for this in Chapter 6.) Giving early attention to difficult sounds such as the beginning of *the* and the beginning of *ship* can be helpful in developing accurate pronunciation. This practice can involve listening to the sounds, distinguishing the sounds, copying the teacher making the sound in easy syllables (consonant plus vowel), looking at the teacher's mouth to see the position of the tongue, teeth, and lips, and getting some simple explanation and feedback from the teacher. This directed attention should only take up a small part of each lesson. Its greatest value is in making the learners aware of the differences between the first and second languages. Pronunciation is looked at in detail in Chapter 6.

Planning a Listening and Speaking Programme for Beginners

There should be regular opportunities for increasing amounts of meaning-focused listening input early in a language course. When planning for this, it is worth making a distinction between just listening to input—**listen and enjoy**—and the various other listening techniques described in this chapter and elsewhere that require some visible response from the learners, such as **listen and draw**, **What is it?**, **listening to pictures**, and **information transfer**.

Listen and enjoy can have its regular daily or weekly time when the learners listen to the continuation of an interesting story, in much the same way as people follow a television serial.

If there is no opportunity or learner motivation for sustained, supported listening outside the classroom (such as through television or the internet), then about a quarter of the listening and speaking class time could be usefully spent on meaning-focused listening, particularly in the early stages of language learning. This will be explored in Chapter 4 on extensive listening.

Care should be taken to see that the listening covers a range of language uses, including fiction and non-fiction, formal and informal, monologue and dialogue, and interactional and transactional. The topics for listening can arise out of the writing programme, the reading programme, or other subjects studied in the school curriculum, such as geography and economic studies.

Here is an example of how meaning-focused listening was made part of a programme for a class of young learners. For these learners, listening was given a high priority.

1. Several days a week, learners listened to an interesting story, chapter by chapter (see Chapter 3 of this book for **listening to stories**).
2. The teacher also read to the learners a complete story taken from a "blown-up" (very large) book. The learners interacted with the teacher during the reading (see *Teaching ESL/EFL: Reading and Writing* (Macalister & Nation, 2020) for more description of this activity). Often, learners heard the same story several times, which helped them develop fluency in listening.
3. The learners did guided-listening activities such as **picture ordering** and **What is it?**
4. The learners did simple group activities where they listened to each other.
5. There was some formal teaching of pronunciation, vocabulary, and grammar.

A well-balanced early listening and speaking lesson or series of lessons could contain the following parts:

- *Meaning-focused input.* The learners engage in dialogue with the teacher, do activities such as listen and do, grids, interview activities, and listening to simple stories.

- *Meaning-focused output.* The learners engage in dialogue with the teacher, do activities such as descriptions, a variety of questioning activities such as asking by numbers and hints, and guided activities such as What is it?, picture stories, and the same or different.
- *Language-focused learning.* The teacher helps the learners with pronunciation, memorising useful phrases and sentences, and substitution tables.
- *Fluency development.* Memorised phrases and sentences are given repeated practice, with an emphasis on reaching a normal speed of production. The learners listen to the same story several times over several days, with the delivery getting faster. The learners do simple, repeated role plays that use the sentences and phrases they memorised and the sentences that they have already practised in substitution tables. They also get very fluent listening to numbers.

An Input-based Task Sequence for Beginner Learners

This sequence starts with a vocabulary focus to teach and consolidate the vocabulary required for understanding classroom instructions.

1. Talk about things in the classroom. Elicit as many words from learners as they know and give the names of unknown items. Learners practise in pairs, moving around the room naming what they see. This gives learners the chance to use any basic vocabulary they already have and to learn a small number of new words.
2. The next step is to build receptive knowledge of the new words without any expectation that learners need to use them in communication. In this step, learners listen to the teacher saying the names of objects and actions and they point to the correct picture in a set of pictures they have been given.
3. The teacher says an instruction, and the learners show or point to the picture of this action. This could be done as a **bingo** activity. This step focuses on short instructions and so emphasizes learning action/verb phrases such as "open your books", "turn to your partner", "get out your book/pen", "read page/book …", "stand up", "sit down". Like Step 2, this is a listen and point task.
4. The teacher says the instruction, and the learners do it. This step removes the visual support of the pictures so that learners have to rely on listening only. They can look around and copy others if unsure. Again, no output is required, as the aim is receptive learning.
5. Do a **Spot the difference** activity using two versions of a list of pictures of common classroom items and actions. Alternatively, do a **split information** activity in which each learner has half the pictures and words for the other half of the pictures, in random

order. The learners take turns reading a word or instruction of describing a picture and their partner has to find the picture or word/action they have heard. This step requires output as learners practise the task in pairs. This is quite a big step from the previous tasks, and so the teacher needs to demonstrate how to do the task to the whole class.

Tasks

1. Choose one of the activities described in this chapter and try it in a small group using your classmates as learners. Take turns in being the teacher. Spend a few minutes commenting on the activity.
2. An information transfer activity can be used for meaning-focused input and meaning-focused output. Look at the activity in the table and be ready to explain how it could be used for listening (receptive use) and speaking (productive use).

Choosing a Scooter

	Ninebot	*Razor E-prime*	*Emicro Falcon*
Cost			
Strength			
Weight			
Time to charge battery			
Size when folded			
Top speed			
Range			

3. Look at a picture or a text and try applying the five levels of Bloom's taxonomy to form questions related to the picture or text.

Further Reading

Use this link to find videos of a range of very useful teaching techniques: https://tinyurl.com/Language-Teaching-Techniques. You may recognise the names of some of the people presenting the techniques.

Although young learners are not necessarily beginners, they often are. For teachers working with young beginners, Pinter (2017) is a guide to useful listening activities.

Look at H.V. George's website (www.victoria.ac.nz/lals/resources/george) for a version of his book *101 Substitution Tables* and his 1985 article about substitution tables.

3 Listening

Why Listening?

> No model of second language acquisition does not avail itself of input in trying to explain how learners create second language grammars.
> (Gass, 1997: 1)

It has been claimed that more than 50 per cent of the time that students spend functioning in a foreign language will be devoted to listening (Nunan, 1998). Despite this, we often take the importance of listening for granted, and it is arguably the least understood and most overlooked of the four skills (listening, speaking, reading, and writing) in the language classroom. As Vandergrift and Goh (2012: 4) point out, "compared with writing and reading, or even speaking, [...] the development of listening has received the least systematic attention from teachers and instructional materials".

Listening is the natural first step to speaking; the early stages of language development in a person's first language (and in naturalistic acquisition of other languages) are dependent on listening. It was long taken for granted that first language speakers needed instruction in how to read and write, but not how to listen and speak, because these skills were automatically acquired by native speakers. But, as Alexander (2020), Brown (1978), and other scholars have shown, both oracy and literacy development benefit from targeted attention in first language education.

Similarly, in second language learning, several writers and researchers in the early 1980s suggested that listening had a very important role (Winitz, 1981). This emphasis on listening was related to a corresponding drop in the importance given to speaking in the early stages of learning, with several writers saying that speaking early in a course should be actively discouraged.

One of the strongest arguments for emphasising listening and delaying speaking is based on a particular view of what it means to learn a language. Some approaches to language teaching, such as the audio-lingual method, have given a lot of importance to speaking. From the very first lesson, these approaches use speaking drills involving repetition and substitution, and so learners do as much or more speaking than listening, because listening is seen as a way to present models that learners immediately copy. The aim of learning a language is to speak, and language is viewed as a type of behaviour.

Approaches that gave more importance to listening are based on different ideas. Nord (1980: 17) expresses this view clearly:

> Some people now believe that learning a language is not just learning to talk, but rather that learning a language is building a map of meaning in the mind. These people believe that talking may indicate that the language was learned, but they do not believe that practice in talking is the best way to build up this "cognitive" map in the mind. To do this, they feel, the best method is to practice meaningful listening.

In this view of language learning, listening is the way of learning the language. It gives the learner information from which to build up the knowledge necessary for using the language. When this knowledge is built up, the learner can begin to speak. The listening-only period is a time of observation and learning that provides the basis for the other language skills.

What conditions are necessary for language learning to occur? Several writers (Krashen, 1981; Newmark, 1981; Taylor, 1982; Terrell, 1982) using different terminology found considerable agreement. Newmark (1981: 39), for example, said:

> A comprehension approach can work ... as long as the material presented for comprehension in fact consists of (1) sufficient (2) language instances (3) whose meaning can be inferred by students (4) who are paying attention.

Terrell (1982) and Krashen (1981) would also add that the learner must not feel anxious or threatened by the situation.

Gary and Gary (1981) described the many benefits of delaying speaking and concentrating on listening. These benefits include the following:

1. The learner is not overloaded by having to focus on two or more skills at the same time—a cognitive benefit.
2. Speed of coverage—receptive knowledge grows faster than productive knowledge. It is possible to experience and learn much more of the language by just concentrating on listening. If learners had to be able to say all the material in the lessons, progress would be very slow.

3. It is easy to move very quickly to realistic communicative listening activities. This will have a strong effect on motivation.
4. Learners will not feel shy or worried about their language classes. Having to speak a foreign language, particularly when you know very little, can be a frightening experience. Listening activities reduce the stress involved in language learning—a psychological benefit.
5. Listening activities are well suited to independent learning through listening to recordings.

The comprehension approach has its critics. Some, such as Gregg (1984), criticised the logic and research evidence that the approach was based on. Others, such as Swain (1985), suggested that it is not sufficient to result in the kind of learning that is needed to produce the language. All these critics, however, agree that language learning courses should contain substantial quantities of receptive activity. They consider that this receptive activity alone, however, is not sufficient for language learning.

Certainly, most of the early research on comprehension approaches to learning was not well done, and both research and theory now consider that there is an important role for early spoken production in a language course. The positive effect of the comprehension approach on language teaching has been to highlight the importance of listening and to direct attention to the development of techniques for providing interesting, successful, and sustained opportunities for listening early in a learner's language learning.

Types of Listening

Listening was traditionally seen as a passive process by which the listener receives information sent by a speaker. More recent models view listening as a much more active and interpretive process in which the message is not fixed but is created in the interactional space between participants. Meanings are shaped by context and constructed by the listener through the act of *interpreting* meaning, rather than receiving it intact (Lynch & Mendelsohn, 2002: 194).

We can distinguish two broad types of listening:

1. One-way listening—typically associated with the transfer of information (transactional listening).
2. Two-way listening—typically associated with maintaining social relations (interactional listening).

Again, we can distinguish traditional, conventional views of listening from more contemporary views. Traditionally, listening was associated with transmission of information—that is with one-way listening. This can be seen in the extensive use of monologues in older listening materials.

Although this is fine, if we are relating primarily to listening in academic contexts, for example, it fails to capture the richness and dynamics of listening as it occurs in our everyday interactions (two-way listening). Most contemporary materials reflect this re-emphasis with a move towards natural-sounding dialogues.

Listening Processes

Listening involves what are referred to as two broad suites of processes—bottom–up and top–down. Bottom–up processes are the processes the listener uses to assemble the message piece by piece from the speech stream, going from the parts to the whole. Bottom–up processing involves perceiving and parsing the speech stream at increasingly larger levels, beginning with auditory-phonetic, phonemic, syllabic, lexical, syntactic, semantic, propositional, pragmatic, and interpretive (Field, 2003: 326).

Top–down processes involve the listener in going from the whole—their prior knowledge and their content and rhetorical schemata—to the parts. In other words, the listener uses what they know of the context of communication to predict what the message will contain and uses parts of the message to confirm, correct, or add to this. The key process here is inferencing.

When we put these two types of processing together, we see listening not as a single skill, but as a variety of sub-skills.

It is possible to make sense of a spoken message by drawing cues from context and picking up a few key words, but without attending to the grammatical form of the message. In other words, comprehension is possible without noticing. This problem with the comprehension approach was identified by Merrill Swain, who investigated language development in French and English language immersion programmes in Canada in the 1970s and 1980s (Swain, 1985). She found that L1 English-speaking students in French immersion classes were performing as well as L1 French students in subject matter, but their writing and speaking were flawed grammatically, despite many hours spent listening to subjects taught in French. Cauldwell (2013: 6) is also critical of the kind of comprehension approach advocated by Krashen (1985) and prevalent in many published textbooks, which Cauldwell describes as an "over-reliance on osmosis". He argues that the assumption in such an approach that, if you listen a lot, your listening skills will improve automatically draws too heavily on research into the role of listening in first language acquisition and so overlooks the importance for L2 learners of deliberate instruction in speech perception processes.

When we have to say or write something, we need to compose the sentence in our head, and this involves more attention to grammar, to the syntactic layer of language. So, although meaning-focused listening is important, learners also need opportunities to pay attention to language details so they can learn those parts of the language system that may not be so important for basic communication but are important for accuracy. Lynch and Mendelsohn (2002) report on a number of recent studies that have shown the importance of bottom–up processing in second language listening.

Tsui and Fullilove (1998) found that more skilled listeners performed better on comprehension questions for which the correct answers did not match obvious content schema for the topic. The implication is that less skilled listeners relied too much on content schemata to assist with guessing. Although this helped with items for which the content schemata matched the correct answer, it did not help when there was no match. A second study by Wu (1998) asked learners to think back on how they derived their answers to multi-choice questions in a listening comprehension test. The responses showed that successful comprehension was closely allied with linguistic (bottom–up processing). So, evidence suggests that learners need to be proficient with these bottom–up processes, and that learners can benefit from being taught how to listen. Lynch and Mendelsohn (2002: 207) suggest the following targets for practice:

- discriminating between similar sounds
- coping with and processing fast speech
- processing stress and intonation differences
- processing the meaning of different discourse markers
- understanding communicative functions and the non-one-to-one equivalence between form and function. (For example, the declarative sentence structure "It's cold in here" in fact functions as an imperative—to request that the window be shut or a heater turned on.)

Field (2003) also argues for more attention to be paid to bottom–up listening skills and presents some detailed proposals for assisting learners with lexical segmentation—parsing the speech stream so as to distinguish word boundaries. According to Field, three speech phenomena make this particularly difficult for language learners:

1. *Reduced Forms (Contractions, Weak Forms, and Chunks)*

    I've lived in Wellington for 10 years.
    Fifty-one high-frequency function words in English contain weak forms. For example, been → bin, his → z, and → ənd, nd, n (Field, 2003: 334). Chunks—*How are you going?*

2. Assimilation and Elision

> For example, [g] or a glottal stop before [k, g]—*good cause* → *goog cause* (ibid.: 331).
> Typically affects the beginnings and ends of words.

3. Resyllabification

> For example, *went in* → *wen tin*
> *made out* → *may dout*
> *(can't) help it* → *hel pit* (ibid.: 332).

These authors support teachers taking more time to raise awareness of speech phenomena and to provide opportunities for learners to develop perceptual control over perceptual processes through activities such as dictations and repeated listening to authentic speech samples.

Experiences with meaning-focused listening provide a fundamental platform for second language development and content learning. These experiences will usually need to be enriched through directed attention to perceptual processing and parsing skills. Teachers need to find an appropriate balance between providing opportunities for listening skill development through meaning-focused listening and through language-focused learning, which focuses on bottom–up listening practice.

Activities for Meaning-focused Listening

In children's classes, the prototypical teacher-fronted listening technique for meaning-focused input is **listening to stories**. The teacher chooses a graded reader that is at the right level for the learners: that is, there are only a few unknown words in the story. The teacher sits next to the whiteboard and slowly reads the story to the learners. Initially, most sentences are read twice and are read slowly. All the time, the teacher is watching to see that the learners understand what they hear. When words come up that the learners might not recognise or that might be unknown to the learners, the teacher quickly writes them on the board and gives a quick explanation, using either a translation, a gesture, pointing, a quick drawing, or a simple second language definition. If the same word or another member of its word family occurs again, the teacher points to it on the board. As the learners become familiar with the story, the teacher reads a little faster and cuts down the repetitions and explanations. The main goal of the activity is for the learners to follow and enjoy the story. After about 10 minutes, the teacher stops at a suitable point, such as the end of a chapter, and the activity ends, to be continued in the next day or so. Listening to the story becomes an eagerly anticipated activity, similar to following a serialised programme on TV.

Listening

This technique has the following features:

1. The learners are interested in what they are listening to.
2. They are able to understand what they are listening to.
3. The material is at the right level for the learners.
4. There are a few unfamiliar or partly unfamiliar items that they can understand through the help of context, or through the teacher's explanation. Some of these items occur several times in the input.
5. There is a little bit of deliberate attention paid to language features, without too much interruption to the flow of the story.
6. There are possibilities for interaction during the listening, as the teacher occasionally asks questions or gets the learners to anticipate what will happen, and as the learners ask the teacher to repeat, slow down, or explain.
7. There is a large quantity of input.
8. Learners do not have to produce much output.

Krashen's (1981) claims for the importance of comprehensible input can be translated into a set of learning conditions—that is, conditions that need to be met for language development through listening. These conditions can be represented by the acronym MINUS and are listed in Table 3.1.

Table 3.1 Conditions for Learning through Input

Conditions	Questions the teacher should ask:
Meaningful	• Is the input a piece of meaningful communication?
Interesting	• Does the input contain useful or interesting information that will attract the learner(s) attention? • What features of the input make it useful or interesting and will engage learners' attention? • How do listening activities engage the learners' interest?
New items	• What learnable language, ideas, skills, or text types (LIST) will learners meet through the listening experience?
Understanding	• Can the learners understand the input? How is the learner assisted with understanding the input (e.g., through the difficulty of the input being controlled or through activities that scaffold learning)? • How are new language items being made comprehensible?
Stress-free	• How are stress and anxiety being controlled?

It is useful to keep these conditions in mind when considering the activities that follow.

In **oral cloze** exercises, the listeners listen to a story, and occasionally (about once in every 50 words) the teacher pauses so that the learners can guess the next word in the story. The word should be easy to guess, and the guessing should not interrupt the story too much. If the learners can produce very little English, a list of possible words can be put on the board for them to choose from, or they can answer in their first language. Immediately after the learners have guessed, the teacher gives the answer.

In **picture ordering** (Flenley, 1982), the learners see a set of pictures that are in the wrong order. They listen to a description of each of the pictures or to a story involving the events in the pictures, and they put the pictures in the right order. Suitable pictures can be found in picture-composition books or on the internet. Instead of using pictures that tell a story, a collection of pictures of faces or cars, for example, can be used. The pictures must be put in the same order as that in which they are described. The same set of pictures can be used again and again with slightly different descriptions and a different order. It is easy to get fluent speakers of English to record descriptions with very little preparation.

The **What is it?** technique (Nation, 1978) has already been described as a way of guiding early listening and speaking. It can also be used to produce large quantities of recorded material for developing the listening skill and is useful as an impromptu technique as well. The teacher describes something, and the learners have to decide what is being described. The description begins with only a little bit of information, and gradually more and more information is revealed. Here is an example:

> I forgot it when I left home this morning. This made me angry because it is useful. I don't like it very much but I need it. Not every person has one, but I think most people do. Some people like to look at it all the time and now many people play with it. Mine is quite heavy.

The rambling description continues with more clues given until the learners guess that a mobile phone is being described. Teachers who are not confident about their own English can follow set patterns when describing.

Same or different exercises can be adapted for listening. Usually in these exercises, learners work in pairs, and one member of the pair has a picture that they describe to their partner. The partner tries to decide whether the two pictures are the same or different. They must not show their pictures to each other. When these exercises are used for listening, all the learners have the same picture, and the teacher has the other picture. This is just like working in pairs, except that the teacher is one member of the pair, and the class is the other member of the pair. There are several types of exercise that can be used in this way. The exercises can consist of several small pictures or just a large picture with several differences (see Chapter 7).

Listen and choose exercises are similar to **picture ordering** and **same or different**. The learners listen to a description and choose the picture that is described from a set of similar but slightly different pictures. It is easy to record such descriptions without much preparation, so that they can be used for self-study listening. The same sets can be used again and again by describing different items in the set or getting different people to record descriptions. The descriptions should not be brief; they should add several bits of irrelevant information, should be repetitive, and should be interesting and lively. Brown (1978) suggests that spoken language is used mainly for social reasons and not for conveying detailed information. Where information is conveyed, it is usually given in short bursts. Long, detailed, informative pieces of spoken English are uncommon. Accordingly, listening exercises should not be too dense—that is, they should not pack too much information into a single utterance.

There are lots of variations on the **listen and draw** exercise. For the following exercises, each learner needs to have a copy of a picture:

1. The learners listen and colour the picture with colours suited to the description.
2. The listeners listen and fill in details on the picture. This can include activities such as having an outline of several heads and having to fill in the details of eyes, nose, moustache, scars, mouth, and hair while listening to a description of several people. Other activities could involve incomplete maps, rooms, outdoor scenes, and cars. A variation of this technique that requires more preparation involves providing small drawings of objects that have to be placed in the right position in a larger picture.
3. The learners listen and label parts of a picture or diagram. The amount of writing required can be reduced by providing a list of the words needed for labelling. I saw this done very well by a teacher talking about her country. The learners had an outline map of the country with some numbered points on it. These points were places. The teacher gave a very interesting description and occasionally indicated when the learners should label the map. This type of activity provides good opportunities for vocabulary learning. For example, the labels can be new words, and the learners discover what objects to label by listening to the description.

Padded questions give a lot of listening practice with a minimal language response. For example, the teacher talks about where she lives and what it is like living there. Pictures on PowerPoint slides can be used to add interest. She then asks the learners, "Where do you live?" Each item consists of a simple question that is preceded by quite a long talk on the same topic. Here is another example:

> I don't come from a small family, but I don't come from a big family either. I have one sister. She's the oldest. She plays the piano very well and can drive anything. My two brothers are older than me. All my brothers and sisters are married and have children. How many people are there in your family?

Padded questions are very easy to make because you can talk about your own experience. They can include questions such as: Where were you born? What is your job? What's your favourite food? What have you read recently? Do you play tennis?

Supporting Listening

We can assist our learners by providing them with support when they do an activity (e.g., around the house—add a list of words or pictures for the learners to see as they listen). This support acts as a temporary bridge that learners use to reach the target. Over time, learners internalise the expertise required to meet the target independently, and the bridge can be removed. We can provide this support in four main ways:

1. By providing prior experience with aspects of the text (i.e., with language, ideas, skills or text-type).
2. By guiding the learners through the text.
3. By setting up cooperative learning arrangements (for example, shared reading approaches).
4. By providing the means by which learners can achieve comprehension by themselves.

Providing Prior Experience

This can be done by rehearsing the text beforehand, using a simple version first, repeating the listening, using language or ideas already within learners' experience while increasing the skill demands of a task, and pre-teaching items. The topic of the text can come from the learners' previous experience and may be based on a first language text. Similarly, working on a theme that continues over several days can provide useful content support for listening activities, because the learners' content knowledge increases as they keep working on the theme.

Providing Guidance during Listening

Learners can be guided through the text by using completion activities, where part of the text is provided, but the learners must fill in the gaps; by using ordering activities, where the main points are provided, and the learners must put them in the correct order; having questions to answer that cover the main points of the input; and having information transfer diagrams to fill in or pictures to label.

Working in Groups to Support Listening

Learners can treat listening as a kind of group work where they are able to negotiate with the person providing the input. This can allow for negotiation to occur during the activity. In note-taking activities, learners can work in pairs to take notes, and, if the lecturer provides time for learners to discuss the input with each other at points during the lecture, this can help those who are getting left behind keep up with what's going on.

Information Transfer

Another group of activities involving a small amount of written language is given the name **information transfer**. In these activities, learners reproduce the message they hear in a new form—for example, when they listen and respond by ordering a set of pictures, completing a map, drawing a picture, or completing a table. A key characteristic of such activities is that they involve a change in the form of the message, but the message remains the same. Listen-and-draw techniques can thus be classified as information transfer techniques. We will now look in detail at information transfer activities.

Most information transfer activities focus the learners' attention on the details of the information used in the activity. There are numerous possibilities. For example, the learners listen to a conversation between a landlady and a new boarder and label a plan of the rooms of the house using the information conveyed in the conversation. Similarly, the teacher talks about her family or an imaginary family, and the learners complete a family tree diagram. Palmer (1982) has an excellent list of other suggestions classified according to the type of diagram used. He uses the categories of maps and plans, grids and tables, diagrams and charts, diaries and calendars, and miscellaneous lists, forms, and coupons. The following suggestions can be added to Palmer's examples:

- The learners listen to a report of a robbery and draw the robbers' route through the house on a diagram of the house.

- The learners listen to descriptions of two languages and note their characteristics on a chart. The chart includes categories such as *script, use of stress, word building processes*, and so on.
- The learners listen to a recorded conversation between a teacher and a parent and put grades and comments on a child's school report.

There are good reasons for using information transfer activities to encourage meaning-focused listening and to support listening. The most obvious learning from information transfer relates to the information in the activity. After doing the activity about the landlady, the boarder, and the plan of the house, the learners would be likely to remember the particular plan of that house. So, in contrast to the use of comprehension questions, the visual structure of a well-designed diagram for information transfer provides a conceptual scaffold to assist comprehension. Put simply, the visual support makes listening easier.

Second, when used with listening, information transfer focuses learners' attention on listening without the extra burden of having to read a list of questions or write long answers. The principle here is that, when the focus is on listening skills, the activity should not require learners to simultaneously read and/or write extensively. Information transfer activities that involve learners tracking a journey on a map or filling in a chart or grid all control the learning burden in this way by requiring a minimal response.

Third, these activities can easily be used to draw attention to important and generalisable text structures and information. For example, good note-taking from a lecture presents the ideas in a diagrammatic way that highlights how the ideas relate to one another. (We discuss note-taking in more detail later in this chapter.) Tree diagrams, maps, and pictures can reveal the conceptual structure of text types as well as the relationships between parts and between ideas in a text. The more generalisable the text structures that an information transfer activity draws attention to, the more generalisable the learning. This approach trains learners to listen strategically for important information. In other words, the conceptual work that learners must do in a well-designed information transfer activity encourages deep understanding and is particularly good for intellectual development in young learners.

Fourth, information transfer encourages deep processing of input. A key question that teachers should ask about an activity is, "What quality of thinking does this activity promote?" Information transfer requires learners to transform the input in some way, and this typically requires more mental effort than copying or responding to comprehension questions. In a sense, then, information transfer activities are **information transforming** activities. It is likely that this deep processing provides good opportunities to learn new vocabulary and grammatical items contained in the spoken or written text, particularly those items that are focused on in the information transfer activity. Research on vocabulary learning indicates that some special attention needs to be given to vocabulary if there is to be substantial learning. This can be done either by putting the vocabulary to be learned in places in the text where most information occurs (Herman, Anderson, Pearson & Nagy, 1987), or by briefly commenting on particular vocabulary during the storytelling (Elley, 1989). To make the most of this learning, the vocabulary would need to be high-frequency or specialised vocabulary that the learners would be sure to need again in their use of English. Nation (1988) discusses a range of goals for information transfer activities.

The above four reasons all focus on the role of information transfer in guiding understanding of input. In addition, information transfer also has a useful role in pushing learners' production. It does this by providing a simplified or diagrammatic representation of the original input that learners can use to "reconstitute" the text in their own words. This can be represented in the following way:

```
LISTEN                                              SPEAK
         ⟶   Information transfer   ⟶
READ                                                WRITE
```

Learners begin by listening or reading and then completing some kind of information transfer diagram. They then take part in a speaking or writing activity in which they retell or rewrite the main ideas in the text using the diagram as a guide. In this way, information transfer provides an intermediary bridge or link between input and output that discourages learners from relying too heavily on direct copying from the original text, but still provides them with a conceptual scaffold for rebuilding the original text in their own words or for another purpose.

Finally, from a practical point of view, information transfer activities can be much easier to produce than sets of comprehension questions. A timeline related to a simple narrative, or a simple radio news item grid such as that in Table 3.2 can easily be sketched onto a whiteboard for learners to copy or created electronically for learners to upload. Alternatively, the diagram can be described to learners who then draw it, thus adding another valuable listening opportunity to the activity. The same diagram can become a template to be used regularly in lessons.

Table 3.2 Radio News Item Grid

News item	Who	What	Where	When
1				
2				
3				
4				

Creating Input for Information Transfer Activities

Although listening materials are readily available, these may not always match the particular needs, interests, and level of a group of learners. Teachers, therefore, can greatly enrich listening opportunities through creating topical, custom-made aural texts. Willis (1996) provides a range of excellent ideas for using recordings of spontaneous speech rather than scripted speech in the classroom. Such recordings have the advantage of containing the features of natural speech that learners will encounter outside the classroom. Here is an example of how such a recording can be made and used with an information transfer activity.

You are teaching a group of international students who have arrived in your city to study in an ESOL summer school. They are interested in exploring accommodation options.

1. Save internet links to various apartments available to rent.
2. Record a conversation between you ("Tom") and a friend ("Ahmed") in which you discuss:

   - information in the various ads and personal preferences regarding this information
   - a ranking of the apartments in terms of preference.

3. Design an information transfer table such as Table 3.3.

Other topics include movies to see, places to visit, job advertisements, ranking topics such as favourite weekend activities, predictions about the future, favourite books, favourite foods, ways to save money and live cheaply—the list is endless.

Table 3.3 Information Transfer Table

Location	Place 1 Aro Valley	Place 2 Kelburn	Place 3 Thorndon	Place 4 Mt Cook	Place 5 City central
Number of bedrooms					
Rent cost					
Distance from campus					
Heating					
Date available					
Features					
Ranking Tom					
Ranking Ahmed					

Most of the activities described above provide some kind of support that makes listening easier. Ways of providing this support that can be used across a range of activities include:

1. *Listening while reading.* While they listen, the learners see the written form of what they are listening to. This can include a written text, a PowerPoint presentation, and captioned movies.
2. *Repeated listening.* There are repeated opportunities to listen to the same text. Repeated reading is a well-established activity for improving reading fluency. Repeated listening using a recorder, DVD, or video, or using input from the teacher should also be of value.
3. *Interactive listening.* In a later chapter, we will look at interactive activities where learners can control the speed, repetitions, and amount of accompanying explanation through interacting with the person providing the input—that is, by asking them to slow down, repeat, clarify, or explain. This broad negotiation can improve comprehension, help learning, and also help develop strategies for dealing with difficult input. Cabrera and Martinez (2001) found that making stories interactional, with comprehension checks, repetition, and gestures, resulted in better comprehension.
4. *Non-linguistic or semi-linguistic support.* Support such as information transfer diagrams, pictures and diagrams, PowerPoint notes, and real objects can all make listening easier if they are directly related to what is being listened to.

Strategies

There is some debate (Field, 2000; Newton, 2017; Ridgway, 2000a, 2000b; Swan & Walter, 2017a, 2017b) about whether strategy training is useful for listening, although Vandergrift and Goh (2018) claim that listening strategies can be taught and do improve comprehension. To a large degree, this debate is about the definition of "strategy", but it does have direct teaching implications. If the here-and-now nature of listening makes strategy use unrealistic, then there is little point in training learners in strategies that cannot be applied. Goh (2000) proposes that the first step in strategy training involves finding out the particular problems that learners face in listening comprehension. Goh identified three categories of listening problems reported by the learners in her study: perceptual processing problems (e.g., not recognising the spoken form of words they know); parsing problems (e.g., unable to form a mental representation from words heard); and utilisation problems (e.g., understand the words but not the gist/intended message).

Learners can benefit from training in listening strategies. Metacognitive strategies involve guiding learners to "think" about their "thinking", so that they can better manage how they learn. As

Vandergrift (2007: 193) notes, skilled L2 listening involves "a skilful orchestration of metacognitive and cognitive strategies". Raising learners' metacognitive awareness of how they listen and teaching them how to effectively manage the listening process are, therefore, important teaching goals (Vandergrift & Goh, 2012). To illustrate the point, a study by Vandergrift and Tafaghodtari (2010) showed that tertiary French as a second language students who were given metacognitive listening strategy training outperformed their peers in subsequent listening comprehension tests. The training guided the learners through four metacognitive processes characteristic of successful L2 listening—predicting, monitoring, evaluating, and problem-solving. The authors conclude that listening performance improves when "listening practice includes opportunities to explain or reflect on the decisions required during the listening task" (p. 488).

Cross (2014) also looked at the effect of metacognitive training, focusing on one learner's listening skill in independent listening to news and current affairs podcasts. The training involved using clues to stimulate background knowledge and develop predictions of content, using the introduction to check and reconsider predictions, noting main ideas, problem identification and resolution through repeated listening, and using a transcript to check the accuracy of the listening. The learner found it useful to use subheadings reflecting the content of the podcast when taking notes and she developed a strategic sequence to follow when doing the listening. As a part of this, she also considered the newsworthiness of each story and developed a critical attitude to the stories. She also considered how the stories were constructed and produced. She reflected on her progress and the skills she developed. What is striking about the Cross case study is how, over time, the learner moved from surface-level comprehension to include more critical, evaluative, and reflective aspects of the listening task. Cowen (2019) suggests using listening logs as a way of getting learners to improve their listening strategies. The log requires the learners to note their pre-, during-, and post-listening strategies and to rate and evaluate their success. The log provides a basis for a discussion of strategies and for reflecting on their use.

Yeldham and Gruba (2014) found that a listening course focusing on bottom–up skills was inadequate and, in their 2016 study, looked at the effect of a range of instructed top–down strategies (predicting, guessing words from context, and inferring content), bottom–up strategies (using stressed words, discourse markers), and general strategies (gaining an overview of strategies, metacognitive control, and developing a text model). The instruction typically involved focusing on a different kind of strategy with each replay of the listening text. Yeldham and Gruba found that learners developed a more balanced range of strategy use, used a wider range of strategies, and combined strategies more effectively. However, there was considerable variation in development across the four learners in the case studies.

Advanced Listening: Note-taking

Note-taking is a meaning-focused listening activity. It is also an essential skill for academic study where learners have to attend lectures in another language, but can be used in various forms at all levels of language proficiency.

Note-taking does two jobs: it stores information for later use, and it provides the opportunity to encode information. These two effects are called the storage effect and the encoding effect.

The storage effect of note-taking is the one that most learners consider to be important. However, as we shall see later, there are reasons why this effect may not be as important as the encoding effect. Learners make use of the storage effect of note-taking when they take notes that they will later use to help recall or revise what occurred in the lecture. Sometimes, note-taking of this type is used to make a record of material that is not well understood so that it can later be studied and understood better. This process is helped if a recording of the lecture is also available for repeated listening.

The encoding effect of note-taking occurs at the time the notes are taken. "Encoding" means changing information from one form to another, as in the information transfer activity described earlier. It can mean changing from a written form to a spoken form, for example. It can also mean changing from one form of organisation of the ideas to another form of organisation. For example, taking notes from a lecture about speed reading may involve a change from a listing form such as:

1. Skilled reading speed = 250–300 wpm
2. Around 90 fixations per 100 words—200 ms per fixation
3. Saccadic jumps

    (a) 1.2 words per jump on average
    (b) 20 ms per jump

to a diagrammatic form such as shown in Figure 3.1.

Evidence of the importance of the encoding effect is that, even with no revision, note-taking helps recall (Barnett, Di Vesta, & Rogoszinski, 1981). That is, the activity of encoding or changing the form of the information helps the note-taker to remember the information that they were encoding. This finding fits in with the depth of processing hypothesis which suggests that the most important factor in remembering is not the amount of effort put into remembering, nor the motivation of the learner, but is the depth or thoughtfulness of the

54 Listening

```
                Skilled reading speed = 25–300 wpm
                   ↙                        ↘
              Fixations                    Jumps
              ↙      ↘                       ↓
     90 per 100 words  200 ms per fixation   20 ms per jump
```

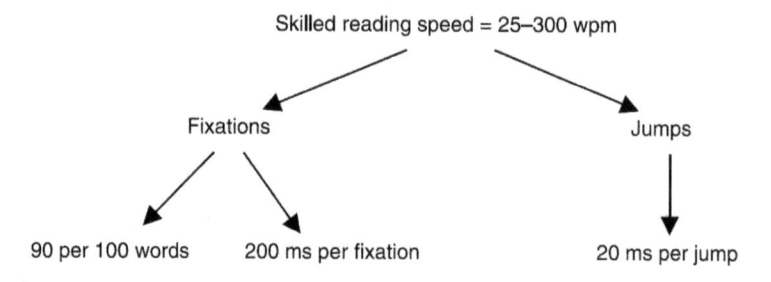

Figure 3.1 Diagrammatic Note-taking

mental processing at the time that learning takes place (Craik & Lockhart, 1972). The more thoughtful the mental activity, the better the learning. For example, repeating an item over and over again to yourself is not as deep as trying to find some mnemonic device that you can attach to the item. This means that note-taking works well when learners know thoughtful ways of encoding.

How to Take Notes

Research on note-taking indicates that the best notes are usually taken in the pauses during a lecture. Good note-taking requires time for thought. If the lecturer's style does not provide enough pauses, then, after the lecture has ended, some time can be used for looking back over notes and reorganising and elaborating them.

The kinds of note that make best use of the encoding effect of note-taking involve changing the information from a linear form to a form that is organised and patterned in a way that makes sense to the note-taker and that reflects the important relationships between the pieces of information in the lecture. There are several ways of doing this. The most creative is to listen to the lecture and find a unique way of representing the ideas. Buzan's (1974) spray or concept diagrams are a way of doing this (see also Hamp-Lyons, 1983: 120). In this kind of note-taking, the topic is placed in a circle at the middle of the page. Then, the various aspects of the topic are attached to the circle and elaborated by lines (see Figure 3.2).

The result is a diagram that changes the linear form of the lecture input into a patterned arrangement that is unique to that lecture. The system is also very flexible as it allows connections to be made between parts that may have been separated in time in the lecture. As Buzan (1974: 87) puts it: "It is the network inside the mind, and not the simple order of word presentation, which is more important to an understanding of the way we relate to words." Mindmeister.com is one of several apps that provide a range of formats for note-taking and mind-mapping

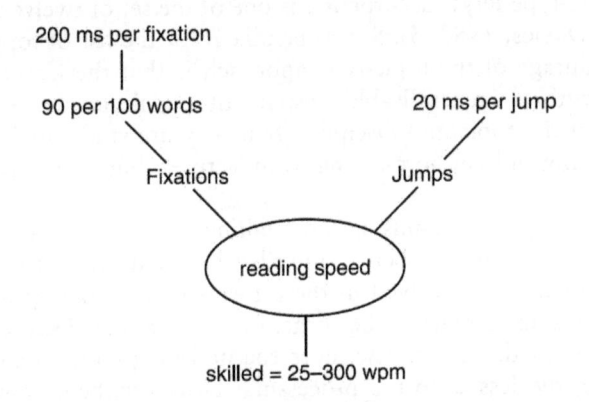

```
                200 ms per fixation
                       |
     90 per 100 words          20 ms per jump
                   \           /
                  Fixations   Jumps
                        \    /
                     ( reading speed )
                           |
                   skilled = 25–300 wpm
```

Figure 3.2 Note-taking about Speed Reading in a Spray or Concept Diagram

Another way of organising note-taking is by relating the information in a lecture to patterns or schema that can be applied to a range of topics. One such set of schemata is Johns and Davies (1983) topic types. There is a chapter on topic types in the companion volume to this book, *Teaching ESL/EFL Reading and Writing*. The topic-type hypothesis states:

> While it is possible to envisage an unlimited range of *topics* which might be identified in ESP texts, there is a strictly limited set of *topic types*. A topic type can be defined by means of its "information constituents"—certain categories of information which consistently co-occur over a wide range of different topics.
>
> For example, the following topics appear on the surface to be quite unrelated: a suspension bridge, a flowering plant, a skeleton, a blast furnace. Nevertheless, in a general sense they are all about the same sort of thing: a *physical structure* of one sort or another. Furthermore, in practice, descriptions of such physical structures consistently provide information which falls into the following categories:
>
> 1. the *parts* of the structure
> 2. the *properties* or *attributes* of the parts
> 3. the *location* of the parts
> 4. the *function* of the parts.
>
> Moreover, texts describing physical structures not only give information which falls into these four categories or slots, but (virtually) no information of any other kind.
>
> (Johns & Davies, 1983: 5; original italics)

The topic-type **Physical Structure** is one of the set of twelve topic types (Johns & Davies, 1983: 5). See Appendix B for the list of topic types.

An advantage of the topic-type approach is that the learners become familiar with a generalisable system that reflects the information structure of the topic and discipline that they are studying. This system is of value not only in note-taking from lectures, but also in reading and writing.

Another way of organising note-taking is to use very structured approaches such as numbered, multilevel lists or tree diagrams. The depth of processing involved in these forms of note-taking depends on the relationship between the organisation of the lecture and the organisation of the notes. The more the notes copy the organisation of the lecture, the less deep the processing. However, being aware of the structure of the lecture helps recall.

For some learners, taking notes may improve the chances of recall of information, at least because it requires attention and, ideally, because it involves thoughtful processing of the information. Not all researchers, however, are convinced of this (Todd, 1996). Generally, short notes are better than long notes, because, in shortening, the note-taker has to make decisions about what is important and what can be left out.

Learning How to Take Notes

First, it is worth discussing note-taking with learners, covering the points described above. Information about deep processing is useful not only for note-taking, but also for other learning.

Second, it is useful for learners to see examples of various ways of taking notes. A useful procedure after learners have learned about spray diagrams, tree diagrams, and ordered lists is to get one learner to take notes during a lecture and, at the beginning of the next lecture, display the notes using a document reader. Both the content and form of the notes are discussed. This has the double effect of providing revision of the previous lecture as well as developing awareness of note-taking skills.

Third, the lecturer can structure lectures to give help with note-taking. This can be done in the following ways:

1. The lecture can be given at a slow rate of delivery, with frequent pauses.
2. Several times during the lecture, there can be breaks for learners to discuss and compare their notes with their neighbours. These small discussion groups during a lecture are sometimes called **buzz groups**.
3. The lecturer can use signals to indicate when information is important and should be noted.
4. The lecturer can provide outline sheets or information transfer tables for the learners to complete while listening to the lecture.

5. The learners can read about the content of a lecture before they listen to it. This allows them to focus on the skills of listening and note-taking because they are familiar with the content.

Learners can be taught how to take notes. Siegel (2016, 2019) trialled a four-step procedure finding that it resulted in the learners taking more information units in their notes. Each step of the procedure was practised for about 30 minutes a week for 2 weeks, over 8 weeks. The first step involved chunking transcripts into information units while listening. The second step also involved transcripts and involved using symbols to mark the transcript for main ideas, supporting ideas, and redundancies. The third step involved listening to short segments of from 30 seconds to 1 minute and noting down key words. The fourth step involved writing notes in simplified form rather than just verbatim. For each step, there was feedback and discussion involving comparison with the teacher's answers. Siegel suggests that including this training is likely to yield better results than just practising note-taking.

Monitoring Note-taking

Because note-taking is such an individual activity, the most useful monitoring is for learners to look critically at their own note-taking. Here is how this could be done:

1. Learners can compare their note-taking with the note-taking of their classmates. One way of doing this is to use the notes-sharing technique described above. The teacher displays a willing learner's set of notes and discusses them. Another way is for the teacher to allow time in lectures for learners to look at their neighbours' notes and to discuss the differences with each other.
2. Learners may be given a checklist to help them evaluate the storage and encoding values of their own notes (see Table 3.4).

Teachers may wish to collect their learners' notes to comment on. This should be for positive comments rather than assessment.

At lower levels of proficiency, note-taking can involve ticking lists of points as they occur, connecting given points by drawing lines between them, having two learners working together to take one set of notes, and completing an incomplete set of notes. Teaching learners how to learn is a very important part of teaching. Many learners use inefficient and ineffective learning strategies (or none at all), and showing them how to learn efficiently and effectively can have a substantial effect on their learning and their attitude to learning and the course. This can be done by making the learners aware of the principles of repetition; retrieval; spacing the repetition and retrieval; and thoughtful, elaborative, and varied processing,

58 *Listening*

Table 3.4 Note-taking Checklist

Why are you taking notes?

- to help remember the lecture content
- to store the lecture content for later study.

To help remember

- Are you putting your own organisation on the notes?
- Are you relating the information to your other knowledge?
- Does the form of your notes help recall the content?

To store the information

- Are your notes clear and well organised?
- Have you chosen the most important information to note down?

Monitoring Meaning-focused Listening

Examining the Teaching Material

It is useful to examine material before it is used for teaching to see if it is likely to reach the learning goals of the lesson. Table 3.1 (p. 43) provides a set of questions that are useful for checking lesson content. The idea behind this kind of analysis is not that we can plan and account for every piece of learning in a lesson, but that teachers should be purposeful and analytical in their design and use of teaching material. They should be able to say why they are using a particular activity and how its design will help learning.

Observing the Activity

Examining the material before it is used is useful to make sure that the learners' time will be used well. Observing the activity checks if the teacher's predictions were correct by looking for signs that the learning conditions may be occurring. The following is a checklist for observing a meaning-focused listening activity:

1. Were the learners interested in the activity?
2. Did they notice some useful items, and, if so, did they
   - quietly repeat them
   - write them
   - respond appropriately to them?

3. Was there opportunity for repetition to occur?
4. Was there opportunity for recall or retrieval?

Meaning-focused listening can be a very enjoyable part of the language course. This is especially so if the learners work with interesting material and they have some involvement in the activity. An important skill of the teacher is using interesting material in engaging ways.

Tasks

1. Make a listen and draw activity and trial it with a partner acting as the learner. How could you build repetition into the activity?
2. Analyse the listening to stories activity to show how well it fits the MINUS criteria. What guidelines can you suggest for the activity to make it fit the criteria more closely?
3. You want your learners to listen to a text about plastic pollution. You know it will be difficult for them. Suggest three ways of supporting them to make the listening easier.

Further Reading

Read Nation (1990b), which looks at experience, shared, guided, and independent tasks. Nation (2007) looks more closely at experience tasks. Both of these articles are available under Publications among Paul Nation's resources at www.wgtn.ac.nz/lals/resource.

Rost (2016) provides an excellent survey of listening research and practice.

Cauldwell (2013) shows how phonology can help listening.

4 Extensive Listening

What Is Extensive Listening?

Extensive listening involves lots of listening with the right kind of support so that the spoken input is comprehensible. This definition of extensive listening recognises that, unlike extensive reading, where it is much easier to control the language difficulty of written input, extensive listening often requires different kinds of support in order to make the input comprehensible to learners of English as a foreign language.

Nation and Waring (2020: 4) use the following definition of extensive reading: "Extensive reading involves each learner independently and silently reading lots of material which is at the right level for them".

Both extensive reading and extensive listening share the common features of large quantities of comprehensible input. They differ in reaching this goal in that, in extensive reading, at the beginning and intermediate levels, the major way that the input is comprehensible is through control of the language features, as in graded readers. In extensive listening, except when listening to graded readers, the input is comprehensible through various kinds of support being provided, such as pictures and visual accompaniment, repetition, support from the speaker, peer interaction, narrow listening, and support from an accompanying skill, particularly reading. This kind of support is necessary because it is difficult to apply rigorous language control to spontaneous spoken output. However, because listening is often carried out in interaction with others and with visual accompaniment, there are various kinds of support available that are not typically available when reading. A major focus in this chapter is looking at the kinds of support available for extensive listening and looking at how to use the support effectively to ensure comprehensible input.

What Should Be in a Well-balanced Listening Programme?

Extensive listening involves listening to large amounts of reasonably easy material of various types. Intensive listening involves listening to small amounts of material with a focus on the language aspects or strategy aspects of listening. Intensive listening fits into the language-focused learning strand of a course and includes activities such as dictation in its various forms (see Chapter 5 of this book), the listening aspects of pronunciation practice, developing listening strategies, and listening to short texts with accompanying comprehension questions and exercises.

Extensive listening, on the other hand, fits into the meaning-focused input strand of a course and should take up about half of the time in that strand (the other half is extensive reading). A well-balanced extensive listening programme should also include listening fluency development. In listening fluency development, learners listen to very easy material with a focus on fluent listening. The ratio of extensive listening for meaning-focused input to extensive listening for fluency development should be a ratio of two to one. That is, about one-third of the time in a well-balanced extensive listening programme should involve listening to very easy, familiar material with the aim of getting more fluent at listening. It should also include other activities that specifically target listening fluency, such as **Listening to stories, Repeated listening, Quicklistens** (Millett, 2014)**, Speeded listening, easy conversation,** and **4/3/2.**

Spoken language occurs in a variety of forms, and an extensive listening programme should include those various forms. They include informal conversation involving both short turns and long turns, fiction and factual movies and television shows, transactional conversation where speakers work together to complete a task or to learn from each other, formal monologue such as lectures, and listening to text read aloud. These kinds of listening do not occur in equal proportions, and an extensive listening programme should try to take some account of the kinds of listening that the learners will need to do and make sure that they are appropriately represented in the programme. For example, learners in an English for academic purposes programme should practise listening to lectures and note-taking. Because speaking and listening are so closely linked to each other, an extensive listening programme necessarily includes learners doing substantial amounts of speaking.

A major division in these kinds of listening is between material where the learner is not a part of the interaction and material where the learner interacts with the person or persons producing the input. Where there is interaction, the learner has the opportunity to use various strategies to control the input and to negotiate and seek clarification. Where there is no opportunity for interaction, as when watching a movie or listening to a podcast, the learner may need opportunities to prepare for listening, to use accompanying support such as a written transcript or visual support, to repeat a task, and to control of the speed of the recording.

European learners of English as a foreign language especially have many opportunities to learn through listening and viewing (Lindgren & Muñoz, 2013; Peters, 2018). Playing computer games, watching internet shows and movies, and listening to songs and podcasts in English are much more common out-of-class activities than reading in English.

How Can We Support Learners in Extensive Listening?

The challenge to the teacher in an extensive listening programme is how to provide large quantities of comprehensible spoken input. We will look at various ways of doing this, based around the kind of support that can be provided to make the input comprehensible. Technology and the internet have made extensive listening much more practicable in a language course. Let us look first at scripted input, as in recorded graded readers, movies and TV programmes, and songs.

To understand listening input, a learner needs to understand, among other things, the vocabulary in the input. Leonard (2019) provides strong evidence supporting the importance of the bottom–up process of accurately identifying individual spoken words for enabling good comprehension of a spoken text. Learners needed to be able to recognise the spoken forms of more than 93 per cent of the running words to get good comprehension scores. Leonard's study and other studies have found little evidence for the effective use of context clues to compensate for lack of vocabulary knowledge. Knowing most of the words and being able to recognise most of the words are essential aspects of listening comprehension. Thus, for extensive listening, learners need to be working with material where they are familiar with most, but not necessarily all, of the words involved. Pan, Tsai, Huang, and Liu (2018) show that preteaching substantial amounts of relevant vocabulary, including multiword units, can also improve comprehension, especially for lower-proficiency learners.

Quantity through Language-controlled Material and Speed Control

The most obvious way to provide large quantities of comprehensible listening is through listening to graded readers. Many graded readers come with online audio, and learners can listen while reading, read first and then later listen, or just listen. Brown, Waring, and Donkaewbua (2008) looked at incidental vocabulary learning from three conditions—reading while listening to a text, just reading a text, and just listening to a text. Reading while listening was better than just reading, but not by much. Just listening was substantially less effective than the other two conditions. This study was carried out with learners who typically do better at reading than listening, but, putting that consideration aside, reading while listening seems to combine the helpful features of listening and reading. The disadvantage of reading while listening is that it limits the speed of reading to the slower speed of listening. However, if the goal is improving listening, then this is not a disadvantage, and the activity is likely to benefit both listening and reading. The very practical advantages are that such a source of input involves the very considerable benefits of vocabulary and grammar control, and there is a very large amount of listening material readily available.

Instead of continuing with reading while listening, learners can later move to reading first, to gain knowledge of the story and topic-related vocabulary, and then later listen without reading support. Using graded readers and their online audio, learners could explore using this sequence of (1) reading while listening, (2) reading and then listening, and (3) just listening. This could also include repeated listening where the same graded reader is used several times.

Quicklistens (Chang & Millett, 2014; Millett, 2014) involve breaking listening to graded readers into smaller steps by having comprehension questions after each period of listening. Listening to the same continuing story over several weeks builds background knowledge that makes the later listening easier. **Listening to stories** also makes use of graded readers to provide a continuing story read to the learners over many days. However, in this activity, the learners do not read while listening. To a small degree, this activity is interactive in that the teacher reading the story aloud adjusts the delivery to the reactions of the learners. While reading the story aloud, the teacher repeats each clause or sentence, notes words on the whiteboard, and provides quick translations or explanations of difficult words. All the time, the teacher is watching the reactions of the learners. When they seem to be coping better with the spoken input, there are then fewer repetitions, fewer explanations, less noting on the whiteboard, and the story is delivered faster.

The use of graded readers with audio recordings allows the use of speed control so that the playback can be slowed down or sped up. This change in speed could be enough of a challenge to maintain interest in repeated listening to the same material. It certainly provides a clear measure of progress in listening speed. Learners identify the speed of the input as the major factor affecting the difficulty of what they listen to (Renandya & Farrell, 2011), and so being able to control this factor could have a major effect on coping with listening.

Learners may be able to understand listening text with a smaller vocabulary size than they need for written text. van Zeeland and Schmitt (2013) present evidence that 95 per cent coverage of text may be enough for adequate comprehension of listening text, although 98 per cent and 100 per cent coverage provided better comprehension.

Quantity through Visual Support and Written Support

Movies and TV programmes, particularly those where written subtitles are available or that have captioning, are a useful source of extensive listening material. Doing a lot of movie or TV watching is sometimes called "extensive viewing" (Webb & Nation, 2017). The visual support in movies and TV programmes supports a top–down approach to comprehension. This kind of comprehension needs to be eventually related to and enriched by bottom–up, language-based comprehension. Watching movies and TV programmes can support vocabulary learning and comprehension if the spoken language matches the images. Rodgers (2018) looked at the matching of spoken concrete nouns with their visual representation and found that there was much more matching of spoken vocabulary to images in television documentaries than in fiction programmes. Feng and Webb (2019) compared vocabulary learning through listening, reading, and viewing a documentary TV programme, finding that equal amounts of vocabulary learning occurred through all three treatments. As in the Peters and Webb (2018) study, the vocabulary gains were around four words for 1 hour of viewing.

Movie and TV programmes pose a vocabulary challenge to listeners. Webb and Rodgers (2009a, 2009b) examined the vocabulary sizes needed to gain reasonable coverage of the running words (tokens) in movies and TV programmes. They found that a vocabulary size of around 3000 word families plus proper nouns and marginal words was needed to get more than 95 per cent coverage (1 unknown word in every 20 running words), and a vocabulary size of around 6000 words was needed to get more than 98 per cent coverage (1 unknown word in every 50). This means that, without some extra support, learners would already need to have a vocabulary size of at least 3000 words before movies and TV programmes could be used for extensive listening.

Let us, therefore, look more closely at children's movies to see what effort would be required to make them a resource for extensive listening for learners with smaller vocabulary sizes than 3000 words. We have chosen children's movies as these may involve some kind of informal vocabulary control because of their target audience. A typical movie lasts around 110 minutes and is around 9,000 tokens long, with roughly 80 words per minute, although a reasonable amount of time in most movies involves no spoken input. The movie *Aladdin* contains about 1600 different word families. Around 1000 of these are among the most frequent 2000 words of English. Around 80 words are proper nouns (*Aladdin, Jasmine, Jafar, Ali, Iago*), transparent compounds (*birthday, marketplace, forever*), or marginal words (*Oh, Ah, Ha*). That leaves more than 500 words, most of which only occur once in the movie, for a learner with a 2000-word vocabulary size to cope with. A learner with a 1000-word vocabulary size would have to cope with 800 words, because there are just under 300 different word families at the second 1000-word level. From a vocabulary perspective, *Aladdin* is a challenging movie.

The movie *Toy Story* is not such a challenge. It is around 8000 tokens long, contains around 1000 different word families (540 in the first 1000, and more than 700 in the first 2000 words), leaving around 300 different words beyond the first 2000, or 470 words beyond the first 1000 to cope with. *Shrek* is very similar to *Toy Story*. This is still a heavy vocabulary load, but more manageable than *Aladdin* (see Table 4.1).

Webb and Rodgers (2009b), looking at words beyond the 3000-word level, found a similar kind of range.

The vast majority of the different words in the three movies are in the first 9000 words of English, meaning that it would not be a waste of time to learn them. Each movie has its own topic vocabulary—for example, *Aladdin* has *cave*, *diamond*, *sultan*, *genie*—that is very frequent in the movie, but is unlikely to occur often in other movies. Because movies are interesting, learners with a vocabulary size of 1000 words or more may be prepared to do the work that is needed to make a movie comprehensible, so that it could become an opportunity for language learning through extensive listening.

The analysis of the vocabulary of movie or television subtitles can be done using the AntWordProfiler program. Teachers can use such analysis to evaluate movies or TV shows for extensive listening

There are features in commonly used audio and video software that can slow down or speed up the playback speed without distorting the sound. In YouTube, you click on the circular cog icon at the bottom right of the screen and choose Speed. In Windows Media Player, you right-click to open the menu and choose Enhancements, and then Play speed settings. There are also apps that do this.

If a learner decides to use a movie as a source of repeated extensive listening, there are some steps to follow to reduce the work involved and make the learning efficient:

Table 4.1 The Vocabulary Load of Three Children's Movies

	Aladdin	Shrek	Toy Story
Unknown words beyond 1st 1000	800	490	470
Unknown words beyond 1st 2000	500	300	300
Total different words in the movie	1600	1085	1021

1. *Choose a relevant movie with a written script.* Choose a movie on a topic that is not too exotic and that may have some relevance for daily life. This makes it more likely that the unknown vocabulary, especially the topic vocabulary, is worth learning. Make sure that the script of the movie can be downloaded from the web in a form that can be converted to a text file. If possible, choose movies with captions.
2. *Analyse the vocabulary in the movie.* Run the movie through the AntWordProfiler program to produce a text with the frequency levels of the words marked up. This will help you decide what words to skip over and what words to pay attention to. It can also help you decide if you have chosen a movie like *Aladdin*, which has a heavy vocabulary load, or one, like *Shrek* or *Toy Story*, that has a lighter vocabulary load. The difference could involve 200 or 300 different words, so it is worth doing such an analysis. Children's movies need not be easier than other movies, and so it is helpful to analyse the script when making a choice.
3. *Do some language-focused learning on the script and the movie.* The script could be many pages long, so do some editing first to get rid of blank spaces if you are going to print a copy, to avoid printing a lot of pages. Read the script and watch the movie, marking up the words you need to learn and the expressions you need to understand. Write translations on the script. If you do this neatly and in a systematic way, you could lend your script to others in return for them lending you the script of the movie they chose. That would save a lot of work and greatly increase resources for extensive listening. Use word cards or a flash card programme to quickly learn some of the useful words and phrases from the movie. Don't study all of the unknown words. Ignore those that are not really necessary to follow the movie and also low-frequency words that occur only once in the movie.
4. *Choose a speed to play the movie that is slow enough for you.* Listening at a slower than normal speed makes it easier to follow the movie and the script.
5. *Watch the movie several times until the language in it becomes easy to understand.* This is the reason for doing all the previous work on the movie. It is at this stage that watching the movie becomes extensive listening.

As well as movies with separate written subtitles available, there are movies with captions that appear at the bottom of the screen. There are various kinds of caption or subtitle, and the words caption and subtitle are used differently in different parts of the world. If a movie or TV show has open captions, the captions are always visible. With closed captions, the captions can be turned on or off, usually from a menu. For extensive listening, we are most interested in the kinds of captions that are used for people who are deaf or hard of hearing, because these captions are typically an exact copy of what has been said. Thus, reading can provide support for listening (Vanderplank, 2016). By searching on the web, it is easy to find movies and TV programmes with closed captions for the hard of hearing, and it is easy to find how to turn closed captioning on and customise the captions. Research shows that captions with glosses for difficult words are effective for vocabulary learning (Montero Perez, Peters, & Desmet, 2018). Unfortunately, special programmes would have to be written to incorporate this support. The time-on-task principle applies at the word level as well as at the skill level. That is, the more time you spend paying attention to a word, the more likely you are to learn it. Boers, Warren, Grimshaw, and Siyanova-Chanturia (2017) examined the effect of multimodal glosses on vocabulary learning using eye-tracking and found that multimodal glosses caused learners to spend more time on a word. Along with the likely positive effects of dual coding, time spent on the word was clearly a major factor affecting learning. They also noted that:

> It is not necessarily total time spent on an annotation as a whole that matters, but rather the time spent on those components of the annotation that will serve a particular learning purpose (and thus performance on a particular test format) best.
>
> (p. 720)

This involves another principle that says that you learn what you pay attention to (Barcroft, 2015). If you focus on word form, you will learn word form. If you focus on meaning, you will learn meaning. Although this seems such an obvious principle, it is not usually applied well in language learning. Focusing on reading will not be an efficient way of providing help for writing. When we talk about an activity helping vocabulary learning, we need to be clear about what aspect of vocabulary knowledge is being focused on.

Yeldham (2018) looked at several studies to see whether captioning actually improves listening or just develops reading skills. Low-proficiency learners did more reading, whereas higher-proficiency learners paid more attention to listening and reading. Humans are one-channel receivers, and attention to one channel (for example, reading) takes attention away from the other channel (listening). It seems that effective caption use requires good reading skills, so that other aspects of the task (listening and viewing) can receive attention.

Some captions may not be an accurate transcription, even though they convey the same idea as the spoken dialogue. In this way, they are similar to translations in another language for listeners who do not know the language of the movie. Movies with L1 translations can help language learning, but they provide a different kind of support from captions for the hard of hearing because they provide support just for the meaning rather than support for coping with the language of the movie.

For extensive listening, having the script of the movie or TV show provides the strongest support for listening (Chang, Millett, & Renandya, 2019), because this allows study before the movie is watched. Captions provide support while listening, but they require the learner to already know the language used and to be able to read it with some fluency (Montero Perez, van den Noortgate, & Desmet, 2013).

Generally, learners prefer captions and subtitles over transcripts because of their convenience. However, there is plenty of evidence that transcripts provide helpful support for listening and also support language learning (Cárdenas-Claros, 2015; Cárdenas-Claros & Campos-Ibaceta, 2017; Cárdenas-Claros & Gruba, 2012; Danan, 2016; Grgurović & Hegelheimer, 2007; Mohsen, 2015). Transcripts can be used to aid comprehension and to identify and learn words, phrases, and grammatical features. They can also help in the completion of a task that has been set to accompany the listening and help learners maintain confidence that their listening is accurate.

Captions can help language learning (Sydorenko, 2010), benefit comprehension (Gass, Winke, Isbell, & Ahn, 2019; Rodgers & Webb, 2017; Winke, Gass, & Sydorenko, 2013), and are particularly helpful when viewing occurs twice or more. Where learners' L1 uses a different script from the L2, learners' reading skills need to be well developed to benefit from captions. Captions are also likely to contribute to the learning of the written form of words (Sydorenko, 2010).

The *multimedia principle* says that people can learn more deeply from words and pictures than from words alone (Fletcher & Tobias, 2005). However, for foreign language learners, the demands of the listening task must not be high. The higher the demands in terms of unfamiliar content, caption speed, narration speed, unfamiliar language items, and L1/L2 script differences, the more likely learners are to rely on one medium to simplify the task. Viewing with captions is a complex multimedia language task, and there are numerous input and learner variables that can affect success in viewing (Gass, Winke, Isbell, & Ahn, 2019; Wang, 2019). Because of this complexity, it is not surprising that there are often very mixed effects in studies of captions (Rodgers & Webb, 2017; Wang, 2019). To learn from meaning-focused input, the demands of the task must be small. As in extensive reading and extensive listening, extensive viewing needs to be at the right level for the learner. Teachers and learners need to be aware of a range of complementary ways of bringing viewing to the right level for each learner. Repetition of viewing can help bring viewing to the right level (Gass, Winke, Isbell, & Ahn, 2019). Study of transcripts before viewing can help deal with language problems. The ability to control speed, pause, rewind, and replay can help comprehension. To gain the most benefit from viewing, learners need to use whatever means possible to bring the viewing to the right level for them.

The negative effect of captions is that they are a strong distraction. There is a tendency to be drawn to them even when they are not needed.

Quantity through Narrow Listening

Television shows, especially those that involve a series of closely related programmes, also provide useful opportunities for extensive listening. They are also more likely to provide something more like a slice of daily life. Rodgers and Webb (2011) looked at the amount of repeated vocabulary in the "narrow viewing" of each of six different TV programmes—that is, watching a closely related series of about 24 episodes involving the same characters. They compared this viewing with watching unrelated programmes. The results showed that the various series differed a lot in their relatedness. In the most closely related series, called 24, knowing the most frequent 2000 words was enough to get 95 per cent coverage. This series also had 40 per cent fewer word families than an unrelated collection of TV programmes. Having fewer different word families can greatly reduce the vocabulary load of input. The other comparisons between related and unrelated programmes were not nearly as impressive from the point of view of vocabulary, but still largely favoured watching a series. It is also likely that familiarity with the characters, their relationship to each other, and the situations they get into may provide enough supportive background knowledge to make watching a series easier. Webb (2010a, 2010b) has provided evidence for the value of using pre-learning of vocabulary and glossaries to make watching television programmes easier.

There is still a lot of research to be done on using movies and television shows for extensive listening. An important part of this research could involve case studies of individual learners coping with learning from movies. Movies and TV shows are such a great resource for extensive listening that we are likely to see the growth of websites providing material for learners of English as a foreign language to support their use. Such sites could provide analysed subtitles marking word frequency, glossaries, and lists of words for pre-learning.

Quantity through Repetition

Understanding the language in a movie is a lot of work because movies are several thousand words long and contain a large number of different words. Pop songs, however, are much shorter—around 300 words long —and use a much more restricted vocabulary (Romanko, 2017; Tegge,

2017, 2018) and a lot of repetition. More than 6 per cent of the words in songs tend to be marginal words such as *doo, lah, nahh, whoa, oh, ah*. The first 2000 words plus these marginal words cover more than 95 per cent of the running words (tokens) in pop songs. Pop songs are, thus, very accessible for learners of English, and their lyrics are easily available on the internet, along with YouTube recordings of them being performed. In addition, karaoke websites combine the lyrics with the music using captions. The vocabulary in pop songs is clearly useful. Little is known of their effect on speaking, but, as a listening resource, they are well worth using. There is evidence of their positive effect on vocabulary learning, especially when they are listened to several times (Pavia, Webb, & Faez, 2019). There is no difficulty in getting learners to repeatedly listen to pop songs and to memorize them, and, in extensive listening, this is valuable because repetition helps learning and builds fluency. The steps for dealing with pop songs are much the same as those for movies.

Interactive reading (also known as the shared book or "blown-up" book activity) is a way of building repetition into an activity. Although it is a reading activity, it involves a large amount of listening. It is typically used with younger learners and is a standard teaching activity in the early years in New Zealand primary schools. However, there is no reason why it cannot be adapted for use with adult learners, including the same kind of repetition and interaction. In this activity, the teacher reads a book to the learners. Ideally, this book is a blown-up book, which is a very large version of a regular story book or a PowerPoint version of the book for display on a large screen. Having a large book makes it easier for the learners to see the pictures and the text. While reading, the teacher interacts with the learners about the story by getting them to predict what will happen, by relating the pictures to the story, and by asking learners about their feelings about the characters and the story. Any language and comprehension difficulties are also dealt with in an interactive way. In many ways, interactive reading is the classroom equivalent of a parent reading a story to their child. The primary aim of interactive listening is to get learners interested in reading, which is why it was part of Elley and Mangubhai's (1981) book flood research.

So far, we have looked at extensive listening through the use of written or scripted material, such as spoken versions of graded readers, movies and TV programmes, and pop songs, where the learner plays no interactive part in shaping the input. Let us now look at extensive listening where the learner can be actively involved in interacting with the input and, thus, has the opportunity to apply strategies to shape the input and can negotiate understanding and language items. Moreover, the presence of the learner as audience can encourage the speaker to roughly tune the input to the presumed proficiency level of the learner.

Interactive reading and listening to stories are a step towards to this, although they involve a written text.

Quantity through Spoken Interaction

Learners can be trained in strategies that allow them to have some control over the spoken input that they receive. One section of the survival vocabulary involves sentences such as *Can you please repeat that? Please speak more slowly! What does ___ mean?*

The activity **controlling the teacher** (Nation, 1992) is designed to train learners in controlling input. In this activity, the teacher reads a passage aloud to the learners. The learners know that, when the teacher reaches the end of the passage, they will be tested on their understanding of the passage. The learners' job is to stop the teacher reaching the end until they are happy with their understanding of the text. The teacher deliberately reads parts of the text too quickly or mumbles so that the learners are obliged to ask for repetition or clarification. To prepare for the activity, the teacher puts useful sentences on the whiteboard that the learners can use to control the speaking.

This preparation can also include some deliberate training in negotiating spoken interaction (see Chapter 7).

Quantity through Peer Input

Learners of roughly the same proficiency level are likely to speak at a level that others in the class can understand. Because of this, peer activities, such as **oral book reports, issue logs, interviews, problem-solving speaking, prepared peer talks,** and spoken fluency activities, such as **4/3/2** and **headlines** can all be useful sources of extensive listening practice. Listening to peers is a bit like listening to graded readers in that the speakers are providing input that is roughly tuned to the language level of the listener. Robb (2018) suggests getting learners to record a short summary of a TED talk on their mobile phones and then work in pairs to compare and critique their summaries.

Only a very small section of this chapter has focused on extensive listening involving peer input and interaction, but this should be a major source of extensive listening. This is because listening while interacting with others is a very important part of language proficiency. It provides opportunities for learning, for gaining knowledge, for gaining input, for developing relationships, and for coping with daily life in another language. Because listening and speaking are so closely related and dependent on each other, the distinction made in the four strands between meaning-focused input and meaning-focused output becomes difficult to maintain. What it means for the teacher is that speaking activities need to be also seen as listening activities, and the teacher needs to ensure—through the way groups or pairs are formed, through the design of the activity, and through the supports provided in the form of handouts and preparation—that listening is just as well supported as speaking.

Sources of Material for Extensive Listening

The internet is a rich source of material for extensive listening. The Xlistening website provides spoken as well as written versions of graded readers. The ELLLO (English Listening Lesson Library Online) website provides more than 2,500 listening texts for learners of English, with a wide variety of levels and lengths. Randall's ESL Cyber Listening Lab provides a range of materials with accompanying questions and exercises that support the listening. Voice of America (VOA) has a learning English section with broadcasts suited to learners of English as a foreign language, as do many other traditional media providers, such as CNN and the BBC. BreakingnewsEnglish.com is another source of news-focused listening and free lessons designed for English language learners. ESL News New Zealand provides easy listening each month on current topics with an accompanying transcript. The vocabulary load of the VOA texts, however, can be quite demanding, requiring a vocabulary size of around 3000–4000 words (Hsu, 2019). Finally, YouTube offers a variety of channels that have been prepared to provide both audio and audiovisual material that is suitable for language learners at all levels.

Extensive listening supports speaking skills. Huong, a first-year English major student at a Vietnamese university shared that she watched movies and listened to English music on a regular basis to help with her speaking. Here's what she said about how she used this meaning-focused input to learn to link sounds in English, using the example of "it depends on":

> When I first watched movies I heard /dɪˈpendzɒn/ I did not figure out what it was, then I searched and asked my sister, and I came to know that "ah it is the linking of /z/ and /ɒ/". Since then once occasions arise, I just say /dɪˈpendzɒn/ and it has now become a habit!
>
> (Huong, translated from Vietnamese, in Nguyen & Newton, 2020: p. 29)

Extensive listening in its various forms can be a source of vocabulary growth (Pavia, Webb, & Faez, 2019; Peters & Webb, 2018; Rodgers, 2018), as well as a way of improving listening skills. It is an essential part of a well-balanced language course.

Tasks

1. Plan a sequence of five activities based on watching a movie. Be prepared to explain how each activity makes the following activity more manageable.
2. Make a list of sentences that could be used when negotiating language input. They could include sentences like, "Can you spell that? Say that again. What?" Trial them on yourselves when doing the split information activity on pages 235–236 in Chapter 12.
3. Your learners are preparing and practising talks that they will eventually deliver to the whole class. Prepare a model of a PowerPoint that they could use to make sure that their classmates have no major difficulties in listening to the talk.

Further Reading

Renandya and Farrell (2011) is one of the few articles on extensive listening. It contains a useful analysis of the difficulties learners of English as a foreign language face when listening and suggests solutions.

5 Language-focused Learning through Dictation and Related Activities

This chapter has two goals—to explain dictation and its variations, and to show that teaching techniques can be varied to create a large number of different but related activities.

We can describe dictation as a technique where the learners receive some spoken input, hold this in their memory for a short time, and then write what they heard. This writing is affected by their skill in listening, their command of the language, and their ability to hold what they have heard in their memory. **Dictation** is often associated with more traditional teaching methods and with testing rather than teaching (Oller, 1979; Oller & Streiff, 1975); however, it remains a valuable teaching technique, and variations on dictation such as **dictogloss** and **running dictation** are very popular with learners and teachers.

Dictations help language learning by making learners focus on the language form of phrase- and clause-level constructions, and by providing feedback on the accuracy of their perception. There have been no attempts to measure what memory of phrases remains after dictation, and so it is safest to regard dictation primarily as a consciousness-raising activity. The consciousness raising comes from the subsequent feedback about the errors and gaps in perception. Webb and Nation (2017: 121–122) analyse dictation from a vocabulary perspective and see it as a deliberate way of strengthening the connection between the spoken and written forms of words. This learning is helped by varied encounters, repetition (through the delivery and marking of the dictation), and the need to retrieve the written form of the words.

A dictation text is a piece of connected language about 100–150 words long. It is usually chosen so that it is reasonably complete in itself and contains material that suits the level of the learners for whom it is intended. The teacher reads the whole text to the class. Then she reads it again, this time pausing after she reads a group of three to seven words, so that the learners have time to write the words. After the text has been read in this way, and the learners have written it down, the teacher reads it again without pausing after each phrase, but only at the ends of sentences. After this, the writing is checked for accuracy. Here is an example of a dictation text. The lines like this "/" show where the teacher pauses during the second reading so that the learners can write.

> When a person dies/in Bali,/the family and friends/are not usually sad.// For them/death is the beginning/of another life.// The dead person/will come back in the world/in another shape.// Before this happens,/the old body must go.// In some countries,/the dead body/is put in the ground.// In other countries,/and in some places in Bali,/ the body is put/on top of the ground/or in a tree.// The body is then/ often eaten by animals.// But usually in Bali,/the dead body is burned.// After it is burned,/the dead person/can easily come back/ to live in this world again.// Because of this,/the burning of the body/ is a happy time.// When a bad person/comes back to earth,/they may be a dog or a snake.// A good person will have/a better life than the first life.//

The value of a dictation is increased if the learners know what mistakes they made.

Dictation will be most effective when it involves known vocabulary that is presented in unfamiliar collocations and constructions, and when there is opportunity for repetition of the material. The unfamiliar collocations and constructions are the learning goal of dictation. Focusing, holding them in short-term memory, and repetition are the means of learning.

It is easier for the teacher if the learners check their own dictations. The dictation can be written on the whiteboard as a model, or printed material can be used. Each learner can check their own dictation, or they can check their neighbour's, or the learners can compare their versions of the dictation in order to agree on a correct version.

When learners correct their dictations, it is useful to get them to use a different-coloured pen to make the corrections stand out. The teacher should quickly look over some of the learners' corrected scripts to get an idea of the difficulty level of the dictation and what kinds of error the learners are making. In the example from Stuart McLean, a teacher in Japan, shown in the figure, note how the learner has good control of the reduced form *it's* and struggles over two less frequent words.

Choosing Dictation Texts

A dictation text can be taken from material that the learners have studied before or will study, or it can be taken from other books of a similar level. Usually, a dictation text should not contain words that the learners have not met before. Dictation texts should contain useful or interesting content such as that seen in humorous or unusual stories, dialogues, and poems. Thornbury (2001: 120–121) provides a useful range of texts for dictation. An amusing dictation involves dictating a puzzle to the learners. After they have written it down from dictation, they have to solve it. Here is an example:

> There are four people sitting around a table. Three of the people are men—Mr Wood, Mr Williams and Mr Long. One person is a woman—Mrs X. The woman is the wife of one of the men. Mr Wood sits opposite Mrs X. Mr Long sits to the right of Mrs X. Mr Williams sits at one of the longer sides of the table. Mrs X does not sit next to her husband. Who is the husband of Mrs X? Show the positions of the four people around the table.

Pre-dictation Exercises

Dictation can be used after exercises that provide practice in the words or patterns that are in the dictation and that emphasise the language focus of the dictation activity (Brown & Barnard, 1975). This makes sure that there is a strong focus on wanted constructions, and the eventual dictation becomes more like a learning experience than a test. After one or two of these exercises have been carried out, the learners are given the text as dictation. Here are some typical exercises. After one or more of these exercises have been completed, the dictation is carried out in the usual way. Learners should be able to easily get the answers correct in these exercises.

1. Usually, the dictation text is read once by the teacher before the learners write. This reading helps the learners get a complete view of the dictation.

2. Instead of just hearing the text before it is dictated, the learners can be given the text to read and study before it is dictated. While reading it, the learners can be told to pay particular attention to verb endings, plural *s*, and so on, by underlining them. The learners can practise pronouncing the words in the text.
3. Certain types of words from the dictation can be written on the whiteboard in the same order as they are in the dictation. The learners are then asked to write the correct form of the words as they appear in the dictation when the teacher reads it, or to write certain words that come in front of or follow those written on the whiteboard. For example, the nouns in the text are written on the whiteboard. The learners listen to the text and write *a* or *the* or other words that come in front of the nouns. If the nouns are plural in the text, the learners write *s*. Verbs can be written on the whiteboard, and the learners listen to hear if they have *s*, *ing*, or *ed* on the end and they write the correct form. The teacher should pause often while doing the exercise to give the learners enough time.
4. The teacher tells the learners to listen for all the words ending in *s* (or *ing*, *ed*, etc., or with *the* in front of them, etc.) and to write them down.
5. The teacher writes pairs of words on the whiteboard. Each pair is two different forms of a word in the text (e.g., *book—books*, *walk—walked*). The words are written in two columns, a word from each pair in column A and the other in column B. The words are listed in the same order as they are in the text. The learners listen to the text and write "A" if they hear the column A word and "B" if they hear the column B word.
6. The teacher reads the dictation text several times. The learners ask questions about the text, and the teacher checks orally if the learners know all the words. After this, the text is dictated. The questions that the learners ask should be based on their knowledge of the mistakes they made in other dictations—for example, "Is *country* singular or plural in the first sentence?"
7. The learners are given some questions to answer. They listen to the text and try to find the answers to the questions. The questions can ask about both the grammar and the ideas in the text.

Variations of Dictation

Dictation is an easily prepared activity that can become a part of the regular classroom routine. The following variations can add variety to this routine and can refocus the learning goal of the dictation activity.

Running Dictation

A short dictation text typed in a large font is posted on the wall outside the classroom. Students work in pairs or small groups. One learner is the writer, and the other is the runner who goes to the dictation text, memorises a short sentence, returns to the writer, and retells it. If the students are working in groups, the activity takes the form of a relay in which the first runner reads the first sentence of the short text and then runs to another student and tells them what they have read. The second student then runs to a third student and does the same. The third student in turn tells the writer what they have heard.

If the emphasis is on speaking and listening, and not reading and writing, the teacher can sit outside the classroom and say the sentences to the learners. If writing is to be avoided, the sentences can be instructions to draw things spoken by the teacher to the runners—for example, for picture one, draw a man carrying five books and a bag of rice; for picture two, draw two girls kicking a ball and a dog chasing a duck.

One Chance Dictation

When learners make very few mistakes in dictation, instead of reading the text several times, the teacher can read it only once, in short phrases. If the learners know that it will be read only once, it provides a challenge for them to pay attention. If they know that the teacher will read the text several times, they might not listen carefully to the first reading.

Dictation of Long Phrases

During the writing part of the dictation, instead of reading short phrases once, the teacher can read long phrases or sentences several times. Each group can be about ten or more words long.

Guided Dictation

Nouns, verbs, adjectives, and adverbs are written on the whiteboard in the same order as they are in the text. Thus, when the learners listen to the text, they can give their attention to the other difficult words. If the words are written in sentence groups as they are in the text, whole sentences instead of phrases can be read at once during the dictation. The words on the whiteboard help the learners remember the complete sentences. Here is an example of the words on the whiteboard based on the text discussed earlier in the chapter:

person ... die ... Bali ... family ... friend ... usually ... sad
(When a person dies in Bali ... the family and friends are not usually sad.)

death ... beginning ... life.
(For them death is the beginning/of another life.)

Dead ... person ... come ... world ... another ... shape
(The dead person/will come back in the world/in another shape.)

If necessary, the teacher can read each group more than once.

Dictation for a Mixed Class

If the class has some learners who are good at dictation and others who are not very good, the teacher can read the text in a special way. He reads the dictation through once without stopping. Then, when he reads a phrase for the learners to write, he reads the phrase quite quickly so that the good learners can write it, and then he waits a few seconds and reads the phrase again, more slowly, for the other learners. During the second reading, the good learners just check their work. The teacher goes through the dictation, reading each phrase twice in this way.

Peer Dictation

The learners have a copy of the dictation text in front of them. They work in small groups, with one person in the group reading the dictation for the others to write. It may be turned into a competition in the following way: The learners work in pairs. One learner reads a dictation while the other learner writes. They have only a limited time to do the dictation, because, as soon as one pair of learners has finished the dictation, they say "Stop!", and the rest of the class must stop work. The learner who is writing can ask the other to repeat words and phrases and to spell them aloud.

Completion Dictation

The learners are given several printed copies of the text. One copy has a few words missing, the next copy has more words missing, and so on. The learners listen to the text being read by the teacher phrase by phrase and fill in the words missing on their first copy. Then, the teacher reads the text again, and the learners fill in the missing words on the next copy, which has more words missing than the first copy. This continues until the learners are writing the whole dictation. Before the learners fill the words in the second and later copies, they fold their piece of paper so that they cannot see the words that they have already filled in. Here is an example.

1. When _____ person dies _____ Bali, _____ family and friends _____ not usually sad. For them, death _____ _____ beginning of _____ life. _____ dead person will come back _____ _____ world _____ another shape. Before this happens, _____ old body must go.
2. When _____ person dies _____ Bali, _____ family _____ friends _____ _____ usually sad. _____ them, death _____ _____ beginning _____ _____ life. _____ dead person _____ come back _____ _____ world _____ another shape. _____ this happens, _____ old body _____ go.
3. _____ _____ person _____ _____ Bali, _____ family _____ friends _____ _____ _____ sad. _____ _____, death _____ _____ beginning _____ _____ life. _____ dead person _____ _____ _____ _____ _____ world _____ _____ shape. _____ this _____, _____ old body _____ _____.

More and more words are taken out until the learners are writing every word in the text.

Perfect Dictation

After the dictations have been marked, it is usually good for the learners to hear the dictation again while they look at their marked work, so they can pay attention to the parts where they made mistakes. Sawyer and Silver (1961) suggest that, after the dictation has been marked and returned to the learners, it should be dictated again so that they do not make the same mistakes they did the first time. The dictation is then marked again, either by the learners or by the teacher. It is given again on another day, so that, by the time the dictation has been given for the third time, the learners almost know the dictation by heart and are able to write it perfectly. Thus, the first marking is only the first step in the teaching, and learners will finally produce a perfect copy.

Zero-Error Dictation

This activity contains features of dictogloss, but, instead of the teacher reading a whole text aloud for the learners to reconstruct, the teacher reads the text one sentence at a time. After each sentence is read aloud, the learners can ask questions about anything that they are not sure about. The objective is to produce an error-free text. To reach this objective, learners are encouraged to verbalize their conceptions about language and to engage in collaborative linguistic problem-solving. Importantly, it is the learners and not the teacher who initiate the form-focused episodes.

In a quasi-experimental study involving high school learners of French in Canada, Ammar and Hassan (2018) found that learners who had completed zero-error dictations outperformed their peers who had completed standard dictations on tests of four targeted morphological features.

Sentence Dictation

The teacher says sentences, and the learners write them. Tucker (1972) suggests that, after each sentence has been given as dictation, it should be corrected before the next sentence is given as dictation. In this way, the learners see their mistakes immediately and can improve during the exercise. The correction can be done by the teacher or a learner writing the sentence on the whiteboard and the learners checking their own work.

Unexploded Dictation

The teacher records a text at normal speaking speed and without the pauses that would normally occur in a dictation. A spoken copy of the text is sent to learners' mobile phones. Each learner has to make their own transcription of the text, using replay and pause to keep listening to the text until they can make an accurate transcription. There are apps and playback programs, such as YouTube, that allow recordings to be slowed down without changing the pitch. Learners can thus listen to texts that would normally be at too fast a speed for them.

Dictation and the Internet

Dictation can be done as an individualized activity using the internet. There are several websites providing practice in dictation (search for *dictation for ESL*, *dictation for learning*). Learners can, thus, do dictation without a teacher and in their own time. Most websites provide material at elementary, intermediate, and advanced levels. They all provide feedback. The most useful feedback highlights the learner's errors. Some of them, like Daily dictation, allow speed control. It is worth trying several sites to see what form of speed control suits each learner.

Some websites introduce teachers to dictation and provide a range of suggestions for variations of dictation (www.teach-this.com/ideas/dicta tions, https://eslgames.com/esl-dictation-activities/).

Related Techniques

Dictation is related to several other techniques described below (see Figure 5.1). The main difference between the four techniques is the medium of input and output. Dictation has listening input and written output. Delayed repetition has listening input and spoken output. Read-and-look-up has reading input and spoken output, and delayed copying has reading input and written output. They all involve holding language material briefly in memory before producing it. Let us now look at the techniques other than dictation.

In **delayed repetition**, the learner listens to a long phrase, waits for several seconds, and then repeats it. This technique has sometimes been used as a language proficiency test. This is because the length of the phrase that a learner can hold in memory has been regarded as an indicator of language proficiency (Harris, 1970; Lado, 1965). Instead of being an individual test, it can be used as an exercise either with the whole class or in pairs. When it is used as a whole-class activity, the teacher says a phrase, counts to three, and then gets the class to repeat it. The length of the phrase is gradually increased, and the pause between listening and speaking can also be increased.

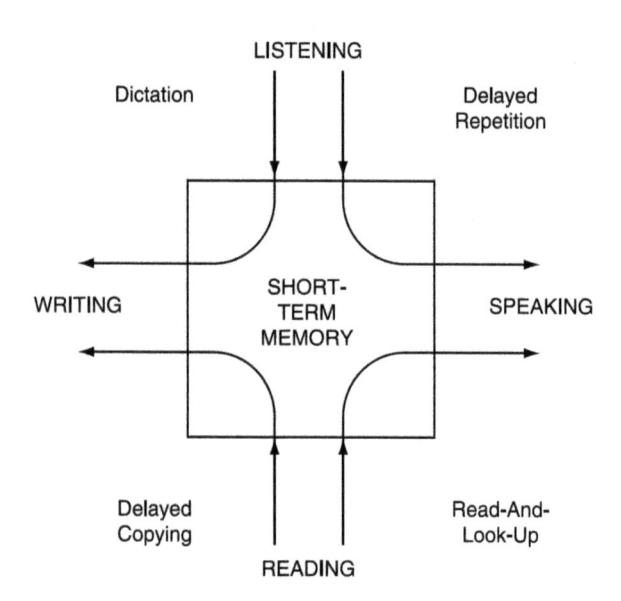

Figure 5.1 Dictation and Related Techniques

The **read-and-look-up** exercise (West, 1960) is a very good preparation for dictation. Remembering a short group of words before reproducing it plays an important part in the read-and-look-up exercise, just as it does in dictation. In the read-and-look-up exercise, the learners work in pairs, and one person speaks, and the other listens. The one who speaks looks at a phrase in the text, tries to remember it, and then looks away from the text and at their partner and says it. They do not speak while reading and, thus, must remember what they have read for a short time before saying it. The teacher can break the text into phrases for the learners, or they can do it themselves. This technique forces the reader to rely on memory. At first, the technique is a little difficult to use, because the reader has to discover what length of phrase is most comfortable and has to master the rules of the technique. It can also be practised at home in front of a mirror. West sees value in the technique because the learner

> has to carry the words of a whole phrase, or perhaps a whole sentence, in his mind. The connection is not from book to mouth, but from book to brain, and then from brain to mouth. That interval of memory constitutes half the learning process ... Of all methods of learning a language, Read-and-Look-up is, in our opinion, the most valuable.
>
> (West, 1960: 12)

Delayed copying does not involve listening or speaking, but is a part of the set of activities related to dictation. It involves copying from a reading text (Hill, 1969)—that is, reading input and writing output. An essential feature of the technique is that the learners try to hold as large a phrase as possible in their memory before writing it. So, instead of copying word for word, the learners read a phrase, look away from the text, and then write it. Unlike dictation, this technique is ideally suited for individual practice.

These techniques can usefully be regarded as variations of dictation, each making use of the same aspect of memory but using different media. There are further variations that can be applied to them. One that can be easily applied to all of them is to provide some written support in the form of the main content words, so that a much longer phrase can be held in memory. For example, the words *person, dies, Bali, family, sad,* are always available for the learner to look at while remembering and producing *When a person dies in Bali, the family and friends are not usually sad.*

Monitoring Dictation

When using these techniques, teachers should look to see that learners are increasing the size of the span that they are using—that is, the number of words that they can hold in one span. A few experiments with short-term memory in foreign language learning have used memory span as a means of measuring second language proficiency. Lado (1965: 128–129) concluded:

1. Memory span is shorter in a foreign language than in the native language.
2. Memory span in a foreign language increases with mastery of the language.
3. The difference between the native and the foreign language memory span is greater when the material in the foreign language contains the pronunciation and grammatical contrasts between the languages.
4. The relation of memory span to foreign language learning is greater for contextual material than for numbers.

Harris (1970) developed a group-administered memory span test. He found that, "the difficulty of the test sentences appeared to be determined very largely by their length and syntactical complexity" (p. 203). Syntactical complexity was determined by the presence of subordinate clauses. Performance on the memory span test "correlated quite highly (from .73 to .79) with performance on standardized listening and grammar tests of English as a foreign language" (p. 203). Research on working memory indicates that people differ in the size of their working memory, and that the size of their working memory is a reasonable predictor of vocabulary 2 years later for young native speakers. There are similar findings for non-native speakers. Typically, working memory is measured by seeing how long a string of numbers or letters can be held in memory (Atkins & Baddeley, 1998; Papagno, Valentine, & Baddeley, 1991; Service & Kohonen, 1995).

Dictogloss and Related Activities

Dictation and its related activities work mainly at the phrase and clause level. The dictation-based techniques described below work with much larger units of language (see Figure 5.2).

In the **dictogloss** activity (Wajnryb, 1990), learners listen to a short text read twice to them while they take notes. In small groups, they reconstruct a written form of the text from these notes. A full description of the steps in the activity is outlined in Table 5.1.

Steps 4 and 5 encourage learners to pay close attention to language form (i.e., word forms, word order, spelling, grammar rules, etc.) within the context of meaning-focused listening and group work. Dunn (1993) cautions that expecting learners to reconstruct a formally identical text may result in strange grammar in the reconstruction as the learners try to fit their notes into the text. This

Table 5.1 Steps for a Dictogloss Activity

Step	Teacher	Students
1 Preparation	Vocabulary study activities to prepare for the text. Discuss the topic (predict vocabulary and content etc). Move into groups	
2 Listening for meaning	Reads the text at normal speed	Listen to the whole text
3 Listening and note-taking	Reads again at normal speed	Take notes listing key words
4 Text reconstruction in groups	Helps groups. Offers guidance	Work in groups to reconstruct an approximation of the text from notes (one learner acts as the writer)
5 Text comparison between groups	Facilitates class comparison of versions from different groups (on OHP or board). Facilitates discussion and correction of errors	Compare group versions of the text. Pay attention to points of usage that emerge from the discussion

problem may be solved through having long texts, encouraging the learners to take non-linear notes, and expecting an interpretive summary rather than an exact reconstruction.

Mayo (2002) also found that learners appeared more concerned with producing a coherent paragraph than discussing specific issues of language expression. To encourage greater attention to form, she suggests that teachers need to pay close attention not only to the choice of task, but also to the way learners interpret and perform the task. Wilson (2003) suggests adding a "discovery" step to the dictogloss activity to improve learners' perception of spoken language. In this step, learners compare the reconstructed text and the original and notice the types of error that got in the way of understanding the text. Learners classify their errors using the following list:

What problems did you have?

(a) I couldn't hear which sound it was.
(b) I couldn't separate the sounds into words.
(c) I heard the words but couldn't remember their meaning quickly enough.
(d) This word was new to me.
(e) I heard and understood the words but not the meaning of that part of the sentence.
(f) Other problems.

(Wilson, 2003: 340)

According to Wilson, by comparing these examples with the original text, learners became aware of four learning points:

1. Recognising common word combinations.
2. Discovering how known words actually sound in context and in unfamiliar collocations.
3. Becoming more familiar with certain grammatical points and words.
4. Discovering how top-down inferencing might have helped resolve specific problems.

Prince (2013) suggests the teacher initially reads a dictogloss sentence by sentence, pausing after each sentence so that learners can check with a partner on their comprehension of each sentence. On a second listening, they can take notes. Prince also tried getting learners to note one key word for each chunk, and getting learners to compensate for unknown or incomprehensible words by using their own words. Prince found value in getting learners to reflect on the strategies they used and the difficulties they faced.

The dictogloss activity has been quite widely researched (e.g. Leeser, 2004; Li, Ellis, & Zhu, 2016; Lindstromberg, Eyckmans, & Connabeer, 2016; Kim & McDonough, 2008; Vasiljevic, 2010).

Dicto-comp

The dicto-comp (Ilson, 1962; Riley, 1972) is similar to the dictogloss, but does not involve group work. In the dicto-comp, the learners listen as the teacher reads a text to them. The teacher may read it several times. Then, the learners write what they can remember without any further help. The main difference between dictation and the dicto-comp is that, in dictation, the learners have to remember a phrase of several words as accurately as possible. In the dicto-comp, the learners have to remember the ideas in a text more than 100 words long and express them in the words of the original or in their own words. The dicto-comp, whose name comes from *dictation* and *composition*, reduces the cognitive load of a task (in this case, a writing task) by preparing the learners well before they do the task. In dicto-comp and its related techniques, the preparation provides the learners with ideas, language items, and text organisation, so that they can focus on the skill aspect, which, for dicto-comp, is writing.

Related Techniques

Figure 5.2 shows how the dictogloss and dicto-comp are related to other techniques.

The input to **retelling** is reading. Different learners can read different texts, or a single text can be divided in half or into sections, with groups

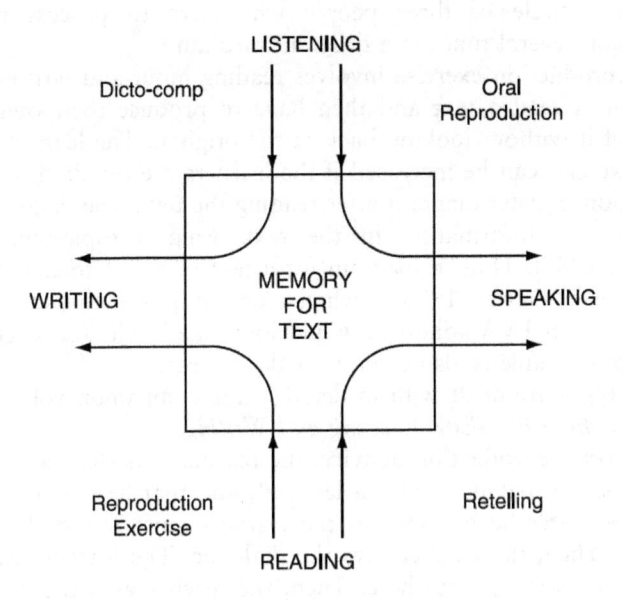

Figure 5.2 Dictogloss, Dicto-comp, and Related Techniques

of learners responsible for reading and retelling their section to the others. For example, in a class of twenty learners, a text can be divided into four sections, with each section read by one of four groups of five learners. These "**expert groups**" read their section of text cooperatively and rehearse their understanding of the text. They then put away the text and recombine into five new groups of four made up of one member from each of the previous groups. In these new groups, each member retells or summarises their section of text from memory, and so the full text is reconstructed orally.

If each learner has a different text, the retelling can be combined with the 4/3/2 technique (Maurice, 1983), where the same information is told by the same person three times. Each time, however, it is told to someone who has not heard it before and with less time (4 minutes, then 3 minutes, then 2 minutes) to retell it. This results in increasing fluency in the retellings (Arevart & Nation, 1991; Nation, 1989a).

Elkins, Kalivoda, and Morain (1972), in an interesting article called "Fusion of the four skills", describe a chain procedure where information is read then spoken then written. This procedure is simply the activities of retelling and dicto-comp chained together and repeated. Elkins et al. intend that there should be a different person in each part of the chain, but there are advantages for the development of fluency if the chain is a circle of three people who have to process the same information several times in a different medium.

The **reproduction exercise** involves reading input and written output. The learners read a text and then have to produce their own written version of it without looking back at the original. The learning benefits of this exercise can be increased if the learners are required to fill in an information transfer diagram after reading the text. The diagram can be based on the information in the text using a topic-type analysis (Franken, 1987). Thus, a diagram for a text of the characteristics topic type (Johns & Davies, 1983), such as a description of contact lenses, the baobab tree, or PVA adhesive, would look like Table 5.2. A completed version of the table is also given to make it clear.

Topic types are dealt with in detail in the companion volume to this book, *Teaching ESL/EFL Reading and Writing.*

In the **oral reproduction** activity, the teacher tells the class that he is going to say a dialogue (with a learner), and that he is going to say it only once. After he has said it, the learners must repeat the dialogue correctly. Then, the teacher says the dialogue. The learners cannot see the dialogue written anywhere. Then, the teacher asks the class to tell him the first line or first word in the dialogue. When someone in the class has told him correctly, the teacher repeats these words and then asks for the next word or line. This continues until the whole dialogue is built up again. As the aim of this technique is to get the learners to memorise the dialogue, the teacher should try to repeat the material the learners have said as many times as he can. If the class has difficulty

Table 5.2 Information Transfer Diagram for the Characteristics Topic Type

Group	
Example	
Features	**Tests or evidence of features**
1	
2	
3	
4	

Group	Glue
Example	PVA
Features	**Tests or evidence of features**
1 water-based	Easy to clean off with water
2 no strong smell	Can use it indoors
3 non-toxic	Safe to use with your bare hands
4 strong bond on wood	

remembering the next word, the teacher can say the word without making any sound, so that the learners must read his lips, or he can pretend that a learner at the back of the class has said the word. This exercise works especially well with a large class. Poems and songs can be used as interesting material for memorisation. They should contain common words and sentence patterns, and should follow the stress patterns of ordinary spoken English (Coe, 1972). The following Robert Frost poem is an example of a poem with these regular features. There are many songs that can be used, but not many poems (Richards, 1969).

Fire and Ice
Some say the world will end in fire,
Some say in ice.
From what I've tasted of desire
I hold with those who favor fire.
But if it had to perish twice,
I think I know enough of hate
To say that for destruction ice
Is also great
And would suffice.

For an easier variation, the teacher reads the complete dictation text once. Then, she reads it again, but this time she leaves out some words. The learners try to replace those words orally.

Disappearing text is a version of **oral reproduction**. The teacher writes a relevant text on the whiteboard. Usually, the text should contain about fifty or sixty words, but this depends on the ability of the class. She asks a learner or two to read it. Then she rubs out some of the words. It is usually best to rub out words such as *a, the, in, of, I, he,* and so on, at the beginning. Then, she asks another learner to read it aloud. The learner must supply the missing words as they read. Then, some more words are rubbed out, another learner reads, and this continues until there is nothing at all on the whiteboard, and the learners are saying the dialogue from their memory. It is best not to rub out too many words each time, so that many learners have a chance to read the text. If someone makes a mistake while reading, the class corrects them (Nation, 1975). The aim of the technique is to get the learners to repeat the material correctly as many times as possible so that it will be memorised. To get more repetitions, the teacher can divide the class in half. As words are rubbed out, one learner from each group reads. So, this gets two readings for each rubbing out. In a beginners' class, this works well with simple dialogues or with substitution tables.

In the **phrase by phrase** activity, the teacher reads the dictation to the learners, phrase by phrase. After reading a phrase, the teacher points to a learner, and that learner has to repeat that phrase from memory. If a learner makes a mistake, the teacher repeats the phrase again. If the learners can do this easily, the teacher says a phrase and then waits for 5 seconds before asking a learner to repeat the phrase. Thus, the learners have to keep the phrase in their memory for a longer time.

Dictation-based techniques such as dictogloss can be designed to suit learners at a wide range of proficiency levels. Aside from the content and language difficulty of the text, the main factors influencing the degree of challenge in the activity are:

- the number of repetitions, speed, or time that the learners have to comprehend and retain the input
- the length of the delay between the input and the production of the output
- the degree of detail and resemblance to the input expected in the output.

These factors can all be played one against the other. So, in a dictogloss, the text may be spoken quite quickly but with several repetitions. Alternatively, the text may be spoken quite slowly and with several repetitions, but the learners are expected to write something that quite closely resembles the original.

The techniques described here have both language learning and skill learning goals. The language learning goal is met when the activity provides opportunities for learners to notice particular language features and to meet these features a number of times. This goal is also met in the dictogloss activity when learners discuss the language of the text they are reconstructing. The skill learning goal is met as learners improve bottom–up listening skills, such as familiarity with the sound of word combinations, and top–down skills, such as making inferences based on deduction, previous information, or background knowledge.

Tasks

1. In groups of three, take turns at practising giving a dictation using the short text below. First, decide where you will pause between phrases and mark the text accordingly. Then, read the whole text aloud once for the learners just to listen. Then, dictate it phrase by phrase, and, then, read the whole text again for checking. Compare two or three ways of correcting the text.

    Everything went well during the first few days of the voyage, but suddenly there was a strong wind and the sky became very dark.

Water began to come into the ship through a big hole in the bottom. In order to save the ship everybody had to throw their things into the sea.

2. Make a list of six phrases and sentences that your learners would need to be able to use to negotiate with their group members to do any dictogloss activity. For example, "What comes after ...?" "How do you spell that?"
3. How could you keep using the same text for a spaced sequence of three different dictation-based activities? Justify the order of the activities.

Further Reading

For more on dictogloss and fun ways to use dictogloss, see http://eal.britishcouncil.org/information/great-idea-dictogloss http://eslcarissa.blogspot.com/2012/09/5-fun-ways-to-use-dictagloss-in-efl.html

6 Pronunciation

When some teachers and learners complain about difficulties in speaking, they are often talking about pronunciation. The amount of attention given to the teaching of pronunciation in language courses varies considerably, partly as a result of teachers' attitudes to error and learners' language learning goals.

The Importance of Pronunciation

Having a good pronunciation of the language can help in normal communication, particularly intelligibility (Derwing & Munro, 2005). However, that is not the only reason for developing stable pronunciation of a new language. There is a very important mechanism involved in working memory called the phonological loop. In essence, the phonological loop is the brain saying a word or phrase over and over to itself in order to keep it in working memory or to help it move into long-term memory. A good example of this is the way we say a telephone number over and over to ourselves in order to keep it in memory while we go about dialling the number. If learners do not have a stable pronunciation for a word, it cannot easily enter long-term memory because it cannot be held in the phonological loop (Baddeley, Gathercole, & Papagno, 1998; Ellis & Beaton, 1993; Singleton, 1999: 148–151). Learners differ in the amount of information that they can hold in the phonological loop at one time. This amount of information correlates reasonably well, both for native speakers and non-native speakers, with vocabulary size a few years later (Papagno, Valentine, & Baddeley, 1991; Service, 1992; Service & Kohonen, 1995). For second language learners, it is likely that the size of their working memory in the second language is affected by their knowledge of patterns of pronunciation and grammar in that language. It is, thus, important that attention is paid to pronunciation in the course so that learners can quickly develop a stable pronunciation and become familiar with the patterns and rules that work within the second language. Although native speakers cannot explain these patterns and rules, they are able to indicate which are permitted within their language and which are not. Second language learners need to develop these same intuitions.

The Place of Pronunciation Instruction

The theme of this chapter is that it is important to have a broad view of what is involved in pronunciation and what is involved in learning a new sound system. This chapter deals with language-focused ways of trying to develop pronunciation. Trofimovich and Gatbonton (2006) show there is value in paying deliberate and repeated attention to spoken features. As will become clear from the first part of this chapter, pronunciation is affected by a wide variety of factors. Being able to consciously perceive and produce the spoken form is only one of these. Some teachers reject any type of form-focused pronunciation teaching, but this is probably short-sighted. Appropriate attention to form for pronunciation is likely to have the same kinds of good effect as attention to form can have for the learning of vocabulary, grammar, or discourse. As with all instruction, it is necessary to find a suitable balance between the four strands of opportunities for learning described in Chapter 1 of this book.

In their review of the status of pronunciation in language teaching, Pennington and Richards (1986) look at a range of factors that should be considered a part of pronunciation. Pronunciation includes the articulation of individual sounds and the distinctive features of sounds such as voicing and aspiration, voice-setting features (Esling & Wong, 1983), and stress and intonation. Attention to these aspects also requires attention to the blending and omission of sounds, and the effect of the various aspects on intelligibility. Thus, although it can be very useful to provide practice with individual sounds, it is also important to pay attention to other aspects of the sound system. Pennington (2019) expanded the range of possible top–down factors.

In trying to change the fossilised pronunciation of advanced ESL learners, Acton (1984) also took account of a wide range of factors. First, he placed much of the responsibility for change on the learners, requiring them to make the best use of their time out of class and to find opportunities for making pronunciation changes in their spontaneous speech. Second, he paid a lot of attention to helping the learners to deal with their attitudes and feelings as these affect their pronunciation. Third, he helped learners with the non-verbal behaviours associated with pronunciation such as facial expression and gesture. Fourth, Acton provided opportunity for the controlled practice of sounds in formal exercises. Fifth, the learners were encouraged to make use of written pronunciation guides in dictionaries so that their pronunciation could be helped by conscious knowledge of the written form. There were other features in Acton's programme, but what is most notable is the wide range of factors that he considered when designing his programme.

In this chapter, we will look at the goals of pronunciation practice, the factors affecting pronunciation, the procedures and techniques that teachers and learners can use to improve pronunciation, and the place of pronunciation in a course.

Goals

There continues to be debate about whether the model for foreign language learners should be native-speaker or non-native-speaker English, and, if native-speaker English, should it be British, American, or some other regional pronunciation (Kung & Wang, 2019; Murphy, 2013; Thaine, 2018; Walker, 2010). Once political issues have been considered, the usual approach is to set up a list of criteria that typify good pronunciation (Brown, 1989). These criteria include intelligibility (Abbott, 1986; to both native speakers and non-native speakers), identity (does the pronunciation identify the speaker with others he or she would like to be identified with?), ease of learning, acceptability by parents and the educational administration, and the availability of teachers and materials to support the wanted pronunciation. In reality, this most often means that local pronunciations of English become the norm for the majority of learners. As we shall see later, Stevick (1978) considers pronunciation and personal identity to be very closely related, and any teacher who ignores this could spend a lot of wasted effort on an unattainable goal. Levis (2005) compares the nativeness principle, which sets a native-speaker goal for learners, and the intelligibility principle, which accepts accents and sets understanding as the goal. Jenkins (2002) argues that intelligibility must be the main criterion and describes what she calls "the Lingua Franca Core", which consists of the phonological and phonetic features that "seem to be crucial as safeguards of mutual intelligibility" in interlanguage talk. These include most of the consonant sounds with some provisos, initial consonant clusters, the distinction between long and short vowels, and the placement of contrastive stress. Jenkins's proposal is a pragmatic approach to setting pronunciation goals and provides useful guidelines for teachers of elementary and intermediate students, although it is controversial (e.g. Swan, 2017).

Factors Affecting the Learning of Another Sound System

There are five factors that have been shown to have major effects on the learning of another sound system. They are the age of the learner, the learner's first language, the learner's current stage of proficiency development, the experience and attitudes of the learner, and the conditions for teaching and learning. All these factors need to be considered in a well-balanced approach to pronunciation.

Age

There is clear evidence that there is a relationship between the age at which a language is learned and the degree of foreign accent (Derwing & Munro, 2015; Patkowski, 1990). Usually, if the learner began to speak in the second language before the age of 6, there will be little or no accent. If the learner began to speak between the ages of 7 and 11, the learner is likely to have a slight accent. If the learner began to speak after the age of 12, then there is almost always an accent (Tahta, Wood, & Lowenthal, 1981a, 1981b). There are two important points to note here. First, this relationship between age and accent does not invariably apply to everyone. A few adult learners do achieve native-like pronunciation. Second, there are several competing explanations of the cause of the relationship. The physical explanation says that there are physical changes in the brain as a result of age that affect the learning of a new sound system and other aspects of the language. Researchers are reluctant to accept this explanation (Flege, 1987; Patkowski, 1990). The intellectual explanation says that learners have already learned the sound system of their first language and this increasingly disrupts their perception of a second and later language. Age affects this perception because the first language system becomes increasingly well-integrated and stable as learners get older (Flege, 1981). The psychological explanation says that pronunciation is a part of our personality and as we become older we become more protective of our personality and unwilling to change it (Guiora, Beit-Hallami, Brannon, Dull & Scovel, 1972a, 1972b; Stevick, 1978). Perhaps the clearest example of this is the unwillingness of many teenagers to publicly pronounce the unusual sounds of a new language, particularly in the presence of their friends. One of the most ingenious tests of this explanation was carried out by Guiora and his colleagues (1972a), who got learners to drink some alcohol to see if its relaxing effect would positively affect learners' pronunciation. They found that drinking a certain amount of alcohol did result in an improved pronunciation. The classroom implications of this are unsettling!

The intellectual and psychological explanations are not in conflict with each other. For a teacher, it means that these factors have to be considered when designing a lesson and a programme.

Stevick (1978) combines these two explanations. Stevick believes that learners are easily able to copy new sounds, but there are three reasons why they might have difficulty:

1. *They overlook some feature.* If this happens, the teacher can help by giving a suitable model that is not too difficult for the level the

learners have reached and by making it easy for the learners to find out how near their pronunciation is to the standard set for the course. This addresses the intellectual aspect.
2. *The learners sound bad to themselves when they copy well.* People are usually sensitive about their pronunciation because it allows others to guess their social background. Also, if learners' pronunciation of a foreign language is very good, others may think it is because they love the foreign culture and want to be like the foreigners. It might also be that the sounds or other features of the foreign language (e.g., tones, stress, phonemes such as /ð/, /f/) sound very strange to the learners and so they may not want to copy them correctly, even though they can. Learners' pronunciation will improve when they feel more comfortable about the way they sound when they speak the foreign language and when they develop positive attitudes towards the native speakers of the foreign language.
3. *The learners become anxious about making the sounds.* If the teacher points out to the students that they are not saying something correctly, they may become tense and nervous and be unable to do it correctly. The teacher, thus, needs to find ways of helping learners find out what their pronunciation is like without making them worried about it.

Stevick's approach sees the learning of pronunciation as only one aspect of a total process, mainly social in nature, that involves the whole learner and not just the speech apparatus or intellectual understanding.

The Learner's First Language

Teachers' experience and research studies show that learners' first language (L1) can have a major influence on learning the sound system of a second language (L2). The type of evidence for this is where speakers of the same first language typically pronounce the second language in the same way, making the same kinds of substitutions and patterns of pronunciation. Another type of evidence is that there is a reasonable degree of predictability in the types of relationships between first language and second language sounds and their relative difficulty for long-term success for second language learners. Hammerly (1982), for example, gives the following list of relationships ranked from the most difficult to the least difficult:

- L1 has an allophone not in L2 (Samoan [t]).
- L2 has an allophone that is not in L1 (dark [l], aspiration).
- L2 has a phoneme that is not in L1 (/ð/).
- The learner has to use an L1 phoneme in a new position (final /t/ for Chinese speakers).

Flege and Port (1981) also found "the most important interference from L1 to L2 occurs at the level of phonetic implementation rather than at an abstract level of organisation based on features" (p. 125). This indicates that, rather than paying attention to general features such as voicing or aspiration, a teacher should be paying attention to the particular sounds where these problems occur.

Teachers can take account of first language influence by being familiar with the sound system of the learners' first language and, thus, gaining some idea of the amount of effort and attention needed to bring about a wanted change. Later in this chapter, a procedure for looking at the difference between wanted and unwanted sounds is described so that this knowledge can be used to help in pronunciation practice. Familiarity with first language sounds can help considerably in this procedure, as unwanted sounds often show a first language influence.

Jenkins (2002) argues that communication activities between learners with different first languages are a good way of encouraging intelligibility, because transfer of L1 features into English is more likely to cause communication breakdown when a person is communicating with someone from a different L1 background.

The Learner's Development and Range of Styles

There is considerable evidence to show that a learner's pronunciation changes as the learner becomes more familiar with the second language (Major, 1987). Just as there is an interlanguage stage for grammatical development, there is a developmental interlanguage stage for phonology. Major (1987: 196) suggests that, as learners proceed in their learning of the second language, interference processes from the first language decrease, but developmental processes increase and then decrease. This means that teachers should not classify learners' pronunciations too quickly as errors, but should look to see if they are stable or changing. If they are stable, there may be value in encouraging change. If they are changing, it may be better just to observe. Change may also be seen by observing learners' pronunciation in formal and informal situations, as different styles of pronunciation may be used. The presence of different styles shows flexibility and that the learners' second language pronunciation is developing. Before beginning intensive pronunciation work, it is, thus, useful to observe learners over a period of time and in a range of situations.

The Experience and Attitudes of the Learner

Each learner brings different life experience and attitudes to the classroom, and these may affect the learning of a new sound system. Purcell and Suter (1980) looked at twenty different factors that might affect learning. These included experience factors such as the number of years the learner had lived in an English-speaking country, the amount of conversation at home in English, the amount of training to speak English, the number of languages the learner knew, and the proportion of teachers who were native speakers. They also included attitude factors such as the type of motivation (economic, social prestige, integrative) of the learner, the strength of the learner's desire to have an accurate pronunciation, the learner's skill at mimicry, and the learner's extroversion or introversion. Purcell and Suter found that the factors most strongly related to success in pronunciation were the number of years the learner had lived in an English-speaking country, the number of months the learner had lived with native speakers, the learner's first language, the learner's desire to have an accurate pronunciation, and the learner's skill at mimicry. In general, it was found that classroom factors, such as the quantity of English lessons and whether the teachers were native speakers, were not important factors.

The Conditions for Teaching and Learning

The ways in which the sound system is taught and learned can affect learning. We cover teaching and learning in the following sections and so offer just two findings here to illustrate how our classroom practice can influence pronunciation learning:

- Sounds that are tested in known words and phrases are mispronounced more frequently than the same sounds in unknown words and phrases (Hammerly, 1982). This means that, when correcting learners' pronunciation, it is better to practise the sounds in nonsense words or in unfamiliar words. If this is not done, there is likely to be interference from previous errors. Similarly, Hammerly (1982) found that problem sounds were more often mispronounced in cognate words than in non-cognate words. This means that, for an Indonesian, for example, using the English word *lamp* to practise /æ/ would cause problems because of the cognate word *lampu* in Indonesian where the first vowel is /a:/. It is easier to pronounce a problem sound if it is in a word that does not bring other sound associations.
- The written form of a word can affect its pronunciation. Hammerly (1982) found that reading aloud was more difficult than imitating for correct pronunciation if the spelling system was misleading. Dickerson (1990) presents evidence that shows that, sometimes, the spelling system may provide a more effective basis for rules of pronunciation—for example, for *-s* and *-ed* suffixes—than the phonological system itself. Teachers need to look carefully at the positive and negative effects of spelling on pronunciation when carrying out a pronunciation activity.

The following checklist summarises the reasons for learners having difficulty with the pronunciation of certain sounds, clusters, or stress and intonation features.

A checklist of reasons for pronunciation difficulty

Learner factors

1. The learner is not a good mimic
2. The learner has little contact with native speakers
3. The learner has never lived in an English-speaking country
4. The learner is not interested in learning English well
5. The learner feels shy or uncomfortable about learning a new pronunciation

Phonological factors

6. The L1 sound system is very different from the L2 sound system

Teaching factors

7. The learner has not had enough English lessons
8. The teacher does not provide good pronunciation models
9. Pronunciation is not taught or is poorly taught
10. The language is not used for real communication

Age factors

11. The learner was too old when learning began

Four Steps for Teaching Pronunciation: Survey, Analyse, Hear, Produce

Teachers often teach pronunciation as production practice, without appreciating the importance of three prior steps that involve: (1) setting priorities by surveying the nature of the pronunciation targets; (2) analysing the nature of a targeted pronunciation feature so that learners become aware of *how* to produce the feature; and (3) providing learners with rich opportunities to process the pronunciation features in input. This is not to say the fourth step of producing the sound only ever happens *after* the first three steps. In fact, practising the feature can happen all the way through the steps. The important point is to realize that conscious awareness of how the feature is produced and perceptual practice focused on distinguishing the feature in input are valuable foundations that need to be in place if production practice is to be effective.

100 *Pronunciation*

In describing the four steps, we will look at techniques and procedures that focus on the articulation of particular sounds. The four steps can equally be applied to prosodic features such as rhythm, stress patterns, intonation, thought groups (tone units), and sentence emphasis. We look at stress and intonation later in the chapter.

Step 1: Survey (Needs Analysis)

Before teaching or correcting a sound, certain information is needed. Then, the teacher can follow several steps to teach the sound. The survey step is a kind of needs analysis and has the objective of setting learning priorities as not every pronunciation feature needs to be taught, and not all features are easily teachable. The following questions can guide the survey process:

(a) What pronunciation feature is a problem?
(b) Does the learner have the wanted feature in their L1? What is the nearest sound?
(c) What sound does the learner put in place of the wanted sound?
(d) Does the learner make this mistake in initial, middle, and final positions?

The following is a list of common pronunciation problems for learners of English:

- Intonation: word stress and sentence stress
- Voiced and voiceless consonants—for example, /p/ instead of /b/
- Free variation of two phonemes—for example, /l/ and /r/, /tʃ/ and /ʃ/
- Consistent substitution of one sound for another—for example, /d/ for /ð/, /b/ and /v/
- Production of final consonants
- Aspiration of voiceless plosive consonants when initial in stressed syllables
- Rhythm and blending
- Vowel length and unstressed vowels.

A particular example: Speakers of some Polynesian languages experience the following difficulties with English because these distinctions are not made in their L1s:

- Voiced and voiceless consonants—the voiced plosives /b/ /d/ /g/ are often made as voiceless sounds /p/ /t/ /k/—for example, /tɪskraɪp/ for *describe*.
- Aspiration—for example, *pen* is pronounced with an unaspirated /p/.
- No clear distinction is made between /iː/ and /ɪ/, /uː/ and /ʊ/.
- Sentence stress is not applied.

Swan and Smith (2001) provide a systematic analysis of the particular pronunciation challenges faced by learners from a wide range of different L1 backgrounds that can help teachers to identify teaching and learning priorities.

(e) Is this item worth spending time on? (see Gilbert, 2001; Jenkins, 2002)

Just because a pronunciation error occurs does not mean that it warrants the time and effort required to correct it. One way to determine teaching priorities is to consider the impact of pronunciation errors on comprehensibility and communication. Errors that have little impact on communication are generally not worth spending time on compared with errors that compromise the comprehensibility of a learner's speech. The important point is that intelligibility rather than accent reduction should, in most teaching contexts, be the teaching priority. In fact, Derwing and (2015) view accent reduction programmes as "highly problematic" "Munro" (p. 173) because of ethically questionable practices and the questionable credibility of claims often made by businesses marketing "accent reduction".

One approach to setting pronunciation teaching priorities is to identify the most frequent and important segmental contrasts (i.e., minimal pairs) that distinguish words in English, or what is known as their "functional load". For example, the /p/–/b/ contrast distinguishes many more words—especially high-frequency words—than, say, the /ð/–/d/ contrast and so has a higher functional load. Consequently, /p/–/b/ errors are more likely to compromise communication than other less frequent contrasts and so deserve more attention in pronunciation teaching. For example, confusing "big" with "pig" is more serious than hearing "they" pronounced as "dey". Munro and Derwing (2006) found that high functional load pronunciation errors made by Cantonese English speakers had a greater impact on the comprehension of native speakers of English than those carrying a low functional load.

(f) What factors are likely to contribute to this pronunciation problem?

We have addressed this question in the previous section and in the checklist on page 99.

Step 2: Analyse the Sound

The focus in this step is on understanding *how* the sound is produced. Teaching involves guiding learners through an analysis of the target feature in order to raise conscious awareness of articulatory settings

(Saito, 2013). Learning about the sound system of English is intended to help the learner to notice the feature more easily in input as well as to produce the sound. It can be especially valuable in cases where a small change in the articulatory settings determines whether the feature is produced accurately or not (e.g., the tongue placed between rather than behind the teeth to produce /ð/).

One way to aid this analytic process when it involves simple segmental contrasts is to ask learners to complete a table like Table 6.1 for the features they are trying to analyse. The table has been filled in for the wanted sound /w/ and the error /v/.

This analysis does not require technical terms such as fricatives or plosives. On the contrary, the terms that learners use to describe the sound differences need to be intuitive to them. Couper (2011) suggests getting learners to describe what they hear using adjectives that are meaningful to them (e.g., loud, soft, big small, strong, etc., or equivalent terms in their own language). His research showed that helping learners to develop the right kind of metalanguage to describe the pronunciation features helped raise their awareness of key elements of the English sound system.

This kind of description of certain sounds can help the learners to hear the sounds correctly. Learners need help *before* they listen, not just correction after they have heard incorrectly (George, 1972). So, for example, before giving hearing practice in distinguishing /ð/ and /d/, the kind of analysis in Table 6.1 highlights that /ð/ is a longer sound than /d/ and is a continuous sound, whereas /d/ is like a small explosion. This description is often best given in the first language.

Seeing a speaker's mouth movements can also have a significant effect on listening (Kellerman, 1990). There are now wide resources available on the internet to show visually how sounds are produced. YouTube is a particularly good source of videos on this topic, such as those produced for the mmmEnglish channel (also available via www.mmmenglish.com/blog/) that provide clear models and descriptions of how vowel and consonant sounds in English are made.

A teacher from Korea had this to say about how they conduct the analysis step:

Table 6.1 Guide for Describing Consonants

Sounds	Voicing	Place (1)	Place (2)	Type
/w/	voiced	top lip	bottom lip	semi-vowel
/v/	voiced	top teeth	bottom lip	continuant

My students struggle with /b/ and /p/ sounds as these are two separate sounds in English but not in Korean. To help with this I demonstrate the position of the lips and tongue, and draw diagrams in the board to help show the position and the flow of air while making the sound. I then have the students practice the sound with me.

Sometimes, **using the written forms** can help with analysing new clusters. Learners can look at the structure of the syllable to help with word recognition and vocabulary learning. The patterns for final consonant groups are much more complicated than the consonant groups at the beginning of the words. The box shows a simple kind of exercise to get learners to find the main patterns at the beginning of words. This kind of exercise also shows the learners some of the connections between spelling and pronunciation.

Make a list of consonant groups at the beginning of these words. Note that qu is pronounced /kw/, and cr, cl, sch are pronounced /kr kl sk/.

through place scale brown sky quality crowd skill grass skin train string break twice try straight spread trust fruit blow trousers travel blood brave pray street twenty smile glory swim strange clever sleep fresh draw squeeze crop steam trade blue splendid square quick glass stop clock spring print smell drop scratch scarce throw proud dry frighten twelve split speed cry queen scrape drink twins true cloud bright brush small slow present strong green dress fly spoon please black stone free stick quite clean plan swam school spell sweet grow clay snake three close play quick grammar front bread glad

---

The learners can make patterns as a result of the listing, and later the teacher can present nonsense words for the learners to decide if they are possible English words or not because of their patterns.

As well as having a group of sounds different from the group of sounds in other languages, English also puts these sounds together according to a certain system (Yasui, no date). For example, a word can begin with /sk/ but not with /ks/, and so on. Three-year-old native speakers seem to know this system. Most native speakers are able to recognise words that are *possible* English words according to the system, such as /skæp/ or /tem/. They can also say which are not words according to the system, such as /ksap/ or /letp/ (this skill has been used as a test of a person's reading ability). Words that are not made according to the system are often very difficult for native speakers to pronounce (Messer, 1967). Teaching learners of English the system or grammar of English sounds could have several good effects. It might be easier for learners to hear, pronounce, and remember new words because they fit in with patterns that the learners already know. Relating these patterns to spelling can have benefits for pronunciation.

Step 3: Hear the Sound

Teaching the sound usually begins with hearing practice, because it is believed that such practice also improves pronunciation (Henning, 1966). A good technique for practising hearing is easy for the learners to understand, tells the teacher quickly and easily if the learners can recognise the sounds, and gives most of the class some practice. The advantage of emphasizing hearing practice in pronunciation teaching is that it is also useful for developing listening skills.

Kissling (2015) focused on using phonetics to improve learners' perception, rather than production, of L2 sounds. Kissling used substantial explanation (sound–spelling relationships, articulatory description, animated vocal tract diagrams, L1 and L2 comparison, and identification tasks) in phonetics training. She found that perception improved regardless of proficiency level. This is a useful finding, because accurate perception is seen as being a necessary step towards production.

Hearing practice can involve either distinguishing activities in which learners compare the target sound with the sound the learner usually puts in its place, or identifying activities in which the learner identifies other sounds that are like it both in L1 and L2. Distinguishing should come before identifying.

To help learners to **distinguish sounds**, the teacher says a pair of words (they can be nonsense words). Sometimes, the two words are the same, *pa—pa*. Sometimes, they have one sound different, *pa—ba*. The learners listen and, if they think that the two sounds are the same, they say "the same". If they are different, they say "different". Learners answer individually when the teacher points to them, or the learners can move their right hands when the two sounds are the same and do nothing when they are different. Briere (1967) found that learners preferred to answer "the same" rather than "different" when they were not sure of the correct answer. Thus, in such exercises, many of the correct answers should be "different".

In the **identifying sounds** activity, the teacher writes two words on the whiteboard and draws a hand next to one of the words.

fa (picture of a hand)
pa

Whenever the teacher says a word that begins with the same sound as the word with the picture of the hand next to it, all the learners must move their right hand. If the teacher says a word that begins with the other sound (the one that does not have the picture of a hand next to it), the learners do nothing. This gives all the class practice, and the teacher can easily see who can hear the sound. Later during the exercise, the learners can shut their eyes so that they do not copy others but give all their attention to hearing. One of the most important parts of hearing practice is telling the learners whether they are correct or not. The teacher should give plenty of examples first and move her hand herself in the beginning to help the learners. The learners should practise hearing the sound in all positions in the syllable. There are various ways of responding in this activity. Instead of moving their hands, the learners can say, write, or point to a number:

1 fa
2 pa
or a letter f or p.

In **identifying sounds using pictures**, the learners see two pictures—for example, one showing a sheep and another showing a ship. When the teacher says "a sheep", the learners must point to the correct picture. This exercise is used with pairs of words that are the same except for one different sound—for example, *watching—washing, chair—share, live—leave*, and so on. In order to give all the class some practice, the teacher should put the two pictures far apart, at opposite ends of the whiteboard. Then, the teacher can easily see who is pointing to the wrong picture.

The pairs of words can be put in sentences: "I see a ship. I see a sheep". It is often difficult to make matching pairs of sentences like this, but it makes an amusing classroom exercise. Learners can give answers to the sentences to show that they hear them correctly.

| "I see a ship." | Answer: "It's in the port." |
| "I see a sheep." | Answer: "It's eating grass." |

When the learners are trying to hear the difference between sounds, it is best for the sounds to be alone or in nonsense words (Jones, 1960). In each pair of sounds, one sound can be from the first language and the other from English, or they can both be English sounds. Words that are already known to the learners or that have a meaning for them should be avoided. The meaning of the words may take the learners' attention away from the sounds, and their past failure to make the sounds correctly in those words could increase difficulty (Wintz & Bellerose, 1965). During some hearing exercises, learners can close their eyes while they listen, or the teacher can hide her mouth with a piece of paper.

In **don't be tricked**, some words are written on the whiteboard. A learner points to one of them. The teacher pronounces it. Sometimes, the teacher pronounces the wrong word. The learners must say if the teacher is right or wrong. So, *pa* and *fa* are written on the whiteboard. The learner points to pa. If the teacher says *fa*, the learners say "no". The learners listen carefully because they know that the teacher will sometimes try to trick them.

In **keep up**, some words that are only a little different from each other are written on the whiteboard:

fa
pa
ba

While the teacher says the words quite quickly, a learner tries to point to them. Or, each word has a number in front of it. The teacher says the words in a different order, and the learners write the numbers in the same order as the teacher says them.

Multiple-choice sounds involves the learners seeing a list of groups of five words:

1   heat hit eat hat it
2   can kin ken gone Kim

The teacher says one word from each group, and the learners draw a circle around the word that the teacher said. The same list can be used several times. When the teacher has gone through the list once, she can say to the learners, "Now we will start at number 1 again. This time draw a square around the words that I say". Then, the teacher says words that she did not say the first time.

In **triplets**, the teacher says three sounds or words one after the other —for example, "fa pa pa". The learners must answer 2, 3, because 2 and 3 are the same. If the teacher says "fa pa fa", the learners must answer 1, 3, because 1 and 3 are the same. The learners can write their answers or say them. If all the sounds are the same, the learners answer 1, 2, 3. Briere (1967) found that, if the two sounds that are the same are next to each other—fa fa pa (1, 2) or fa pa pa (2, 3)—it is easier for the listeners than if they are not next to each other, fa pa fa (1, 3). Denham (1974) also found that the arrangement had an effect on the difficulty, although her results were slightly different from Briere's. It seems that, in this exercise, memory is also important.

The same technique can be used for four sounds or words, but then memory becomes even more important.

For **sound dictation**, the teacher says nonsense words or new words, and the learners write them. If the learners write them correctly, it shows that the learners can hear the words correctly. Another way is that the vowels are given numbers. When the learners hear a word containing a vowel, they write the number of the vowel. The different vowels can be given with the same consonants to make hearing easier (Allen, 1972).

Pronouncing to hear works on the idea that learning to produce new sounds may improve the learners' ability to hear them correctly. The learners may experiment in pronouncing the sounds with the teacher guiding them. They can be shown the position of the tongue and copy the teacher's pronunciation. There is no rule that hearing practice must come before speaking. Teachers should experiment to see what way is best for certain learners and certain sounds. Learners can be taught to pronounce some sounds correctly before they can hear the difference between these sounds and others (Briere, 1968).

Step 4: Produce the Sound

Celce-Murcia, Brinton, and Goodwin (2010) distinguish between **controlled practice** (e.g., oral reading of minimal-pair sentences), **guided practice** (e.g., structured communication exercises such as information-gap activities), and **communicative practice** (e.g., fluency-building activities such as role play). In this section, we describe a range of activities that mostly fall into the first two categories of controlled and guided practice. Communicative practice is covered in the next chapter.

Controlled practice often involves practising the sound by itself or in easy syllables. The first step is for the learners to repeat the sound, copying the teacher. If this is not successful, learners can be helped to pronounce sounds if the teacher explains the position of the tongue and

---

/f/, /v/	/f/ is a voiceless continuant. /v/ is a voiced continuant. The bottom lip touches the top teeth. Push a pencil against the bottom lip to bring it forward to touch the top lip. Bring the top teeth down to touch the bottom lip. Make a long sound. If the two lips touch each other, lift the top lip with your own hand. This stops the two lips from touching.
/r/	/r/ is a voiced continuant sound. The end of the tongue is near the top of the mouth. The tongue should not touch the tooth ridge. Put a finger or a pencil *under* the tongue. Push the tongue back and up. The pencil should go about 5cm into the mouth. Be sure the tongue does not touch the top of the mouth. The pencil stops the tongue from touching the tooth ridge. Make a long sound.

lips and explains what type of sound it is. If the learners still cannot make the sound after trying to copy the teacher and listening to the explanation, there are several techniques that they can use to force their mouths to the correct position. The technique that is used often depends on the type of mistake that the learners make. For example, if a learner says /f/ instead of /v/, the teacher has to make the learner voice the sound. If a learner says /w/ instead of /v/, the type of correction is different: the teacher has to get the learner to push their lips into the correct position. So, the teacher should look carefully at the type of error before deciding what technique to use for forcing. Here are some examples of simple descriptions and forcing procedures.

When the teacher pronounces a sound, the learners should watch the teacher's mouth carefully. Then, they can practise using a small mirror so that they can see their own mouth.

It is valuable to let the learners experiment with sounds. By changing the position of their tongue, they can change the sound. (This is useful for /s/ and /š/.) If the position of the lips and teeth is changed, the sound can be changed. Activities such as these may help learners to be able to feel where their tongue is in their mouth. This is a useful ability when learning a new language.

Learners also need opportunities to practise the sound in other positions. Consonant groups should come last of all.

In the **repeating sounds** activity, the teacher says the new or difficult sounds. The learners listen and repeat. Locke (1970) found that, after a learner had copied a model to pronounce a new sound twice, there was very little further improvement. That is, after repeating the sound for the second time, the learners did not usually make any more improvement, even though they heard the same model and tried to copy it several times. This means that repeating after the model is only useful for a short time. If the teacher wants the learners to make further improvement, she must either explain to the learners how to make the sound, show the written form of the sound, or use some "trick", such as forcing, to help the learners make the correct sound (George, 1972). As well as giving a model for learners to copy, a teacher thus needs to be able to provide other help when teaching pronunciation.

Once the learners can make the sounds well, the teacher can give a written model or show pictures or objects to get the learners to pronounce the sounds. Carr (1967) suggests that, for a difficult sound, the teacher should have a box containing objects that have the difficult sound as a part of their name. In this way, quick practice can easily be given.

Difficult vowel sounds can often be made by using the exercises that Pike (1947) calls **slurring and bracketing**. In slurring, the tongue or another part of the mouth is slowly moved from one position to another. This is done several times, with the learners copying the teacher. Then, the movement is stopped a part of the way between the two sounds, so that the wanted sound is produced. So, for example, the first sound is /i/, and the last is /æ/. By stopping halfway, /e/ is produced. Bracketing is almost the same, except that the vowels are pronounced clearly and separately, one after the other—for example, /ɪ æ/. The learner copies the teacher in order to do this and then tries to make the vowel halfway between the first two that were practised. The result will be /e/.

In **testing the teacher**, some of the exercises that are used for hearing practice can be used to practise pronunciation. The learners take the teacher's place, and the teacher takes the learners' place. So, for the same/different exercise, the learners individually pronounce pairs of words, and the teacher says "the same" or "different".

Tongue-twisters such as "Round the rugged rocks the ragged rascal ran" or "She sells sea shells on the sea shore" are very difficult for native speakers of English. For learners of English as a second language, they are a cruel and unusual punishment. The technique of **shadowing** is growing in popularity in Japan and more widely, and there is a body of research (Hamada, 2016, 2019) supporting its value for improving pronunciation and listening comprehension. Shadowing involves repeating exactly what the teacher says while the teacher is saying it, without the help of a written model. The learner's repetition lags less than 1 second behind the teacher's production so that both are speaking at the same time, though not exactly in sync. de Guerrero and Commander (2013) investigated shadow-reading by pairs of Spanish-L1 learners of English shadowing each other reading aloud. The researchers showed how shadowing encouraged the learners to "chunk" speech units rather than articulating every word separately. They conclude that shadowing provided valuable opportunities for "persistent, meaningful imitation and internalization of second language (L2) exemplars as well as story comprehension and retention" (p. 433). Tim Murphey provides practical examples of students participating in conversational shadowing on YouTube (www.youtube.com/watch?v=Bri4tpCbjR4). One way for teachers to gauge the usefulness of shadowing is to try it themselves, shadowing a speaker of a language that they do not speak fluently.

The four steps for teaching pronunciation described above can be usefully compared to a **communicative framework for teaching English pronunciation** proposed by Celce-Murcia, Brinton, and Goodwin (2010: 45). This framework has five stages:

Stage 1: Description and analysis. Here, the teacher shows and describes how the feature is produced and how it is used in communication.

Stage 2: Listening discrimination. The teacher provides focused listening practice and feedback on how well the learners have discriminated the target feature.

Stage 3: Controlled practice. The learners practice the target feature in controlled activities that emphasise accurate production such as oral reading of minimal-pair sentences or short dialogues.

Stage 4: Guided practice. The learners use the target feature in structured communication activities such as split information activities in which they can monitor their production of the target feature during communicative use.

Stage 5: Communicative practice. Learners put the target feature to use in more open communication activities such as role play or problem-solving tasks.

As with the four steps for teaching pronunciation described in the preceding section, the five stages in this framework move through a sequence of analysis and consciousness-raising, then listening discrimination, and finally production. Both approaches reflect the four strands principle that, for effective learning, language items met in one strand need to also be met in the other strands.

Correcting Pronunciation Mistakes

When a learner makes a pronunciation mistake and the teacher wants to correct it quickly, the teacher can do any of the following things.

- The teacher repeats the word correctly several times with ordinary stress and intonation until the learner self-corrects by copying the teacher.
- The teacher repeats the word correctly, giving extra stress and length to the part where the learner made the mistake.
- The teacher compares the mistake and the correct form: "Not *lice* but *rice*".
- The teacher writes the word on the whiteboard correctly and underlines the part where the learner made a mistake. The teacher also says the word correctly.
- The teacher just says "No" and lets the learner find the mistake without help. The teacher can make a certain signal, such as hitting the desk softly, when a learner makes a pronunciation mistake. This technique is used when the learners can make the correct sounds but forget to do so while talking.

Stress and Intonation

Languages can be classified according to whether they are stress-timed or syllable-timed. It used to be thought that, in a stress-timed language (such as English), the stresses were equal distances apart, even though the number of syllables between each stress was not the same. This would mean that some syllables would have to be said very quickly if there were several between two stresses, and some would be said slowly if there were few between two stresses. In syllable-timed languages, the syllables occur at regular intervals (as in Spanish and Indonesian). Research indicates that the spacing of stresses is by no means equal in stress-timed languages, although there is a tendency towards regularity (Dauer, 1983). The main differences between stress-timed and syllable-timed languages lie in syllable structure (syllable length varies more in stress-timed languages than in syllable-timed languages), vowel reduction (stress-timed languages are more likely to use centralised vowels in unstressed syllables and vowels may be shortened or omitted), and lexical stress (stress-timed languages usually have word-level stress). When speakers of a syllable-timed language such as Chinese or French learn English, they may need help to observe and copy the rhythmic patterns of speech. The following techniques may help. George (1990) very usefully discusses a range of features involved in the way different languages sound and suggests gradual shaping to the wanted type. Aufderhaar (2004) found that getting learners to listen to and perform texts recorded by native speakers was viewed positively by some learners as a way of improving their control of pronunciation, particularly prosodic features. Some, however, felt it was rather time-consuming, although this objection could be dealt with by more careful class planning.

Teaching Word Stress

In English, one part of a word is usually said with greater strength, stress, than another part. Strong stress often goes with an increase in the length of the syllable and a change in intonation. There are no easy rules to find which syllable should be stressed in a word. The stress pattern of each word just has to be learned. A common mistake is to say words with the stress in the wrong place. Stress can be taught in the following ways:

- The teacher taps the stress pattern of a word, with a hard tap for the stressed syllables and soft for the others. The learners say the word.
- When the teacher provides a model, she can make the stressed syllable longer than usual and the unstressed ones very short.
- When the learners say a word, they make a gesture to go with the stressed part of the word. This gesture can be a hand movement.
- The teacher says a sentence and she stops before a word that gives the learners problems with the stress. Instead of saying the word, she taps the stress pattern on the table. The learners must guess the word by listening to the context and stress pattern, and then say it.

"Very well, I'll come tap TAP tap tap." (immediately)

If the learners need extra help to guess the word, the first letter can be given.

- The learners are given a list of words. The teacher reads them, and the learners underline the stressed syllables.
- The learners are given a list of words and they put them in groups according to their stress pattern. The teacher can give them some model words to represent each stress pattern. When practising stress, the teacher can present words with the same stress pattern for practice.

Teaching Sentence Stress

The place of stress in an English sentence depends on the relative importance of the different words in the sentence. Usually, nouns, adjectives, certain pronouns, main verbs, and adverbs are given strong stress (Jones, 1960). Learners can be given practice in looking at the meaning of sentences to decide where the strong stress should be (Halverson, 1967). One sentence can be spoken in many different ways to give different meanings (Jones, 1960; Robinett, 1965). Allen (1972) suggests using a simple situation where a person is asking for something, but the other person keeps giving him the wrong thing: "Give me a SMALL bottle of medicine". George and Neo (1974) point out the close relationship between stress and information distribution in a sentence, with the stressed parts conveying the least predictable information.

In English sentences, the stressed syllables are roughly the same distance from each other. So, if there are many unstressed syllables between the stressed syllables, the unstressed syllables are said very quickly. A very common mistake, especially by speakers of Asian languages, is to make every syllable, stressed or unstressed, the same length. Learners can be helped to avoid this mistake in the following ways. When providing practice, it is important to pay attention to the unstressed syllables as well as the stressed syllables. The unstressed syllables will be shorter and will probably contain a centralised vowel such as /ə/. Weakening the unstressed syllables gives prominence to the stressed syllables.

It is worth checking that learners use weak forms of common words such as *a*, *and*, *can*, *will*, *had*, *is*, *was*, and *not* in connected speech. For some learners, it may also be necessary to practise leaving out sounds (elision) and assimilating adjacent sounds, to help keep the flow and rhythm of normal speech.

- The teacher taps the rhythms of sentences with his finger on the table. The learner practises saying the sentences while tapping in time with the teacher (Jones, 1960).

- The teacher explains the way rhythm works in an English sentence and gives models for the learners to copy.
- The teacher says a short sentence with two stresses, and the learners repeat it. Then, the sentence is built up in several steps into a long sentence that still has only two stresses and is repeated in almost the same length of time as the short sentence:
- The boy's in the house.

The boy's in the old house.
The little boy's in the old house.
The little boy's not in the old house (Robinett, 1965).

- Reading poetry aloud can help to teach learners the rhythm of English sentences.

Teaching Intonation

Learners can practise intonation in the following ways:

- The learners can copy the teacher.
- The learners can make gestures to go with changes in intonation. The rise at the end of a yes/no question can go with the speaker raising her eyebrows or lifting a shoulder (Robinett, 1965).
- The learners say the last word of a sentence by itself with the correct intonation, rising or falling. Then, word by word, they build up the sentence from the end to the beginning while keeping the correct intonation (Robinett, 1965):

  "tea. or tea. coffee or tea. want coffee or tea. and so on."

- The learners can be shown drawings of intonation patterns to help them understand what they should try to do.

Fitting Pronunciation into a Course

Several possibilities are available for making pronunciation improvement part of a course:

1. A special time is regularly set aside for direct attention to pronunciation for the whole class. Typical activities might include distinguishing sounds, identifying sounds, repetition drills, and monitored speaking activities.
2. Pronunciation is focused on occasionally, perhaps to set goals and activities for individual work.

3. Pronunciation errors are dealt with as they occur, usually on an individual level, or in a small group while others do other work.
4. Pronunciation is not given any special attention, but meaning-focused speaking activities that can affect pronunciation are part of the listening and speaking programme. These activities might include split information activities; formal talks, poems, and songs; read-and-look-up activities; and the whiteboard reproduction exercise.

The type of attention given to pronunciation will depend partly on whether the teacher sees it as more useful to regard pronunciation as a skill to be developed through language-focused learning using repetition and practice, or as a system of knowledge that evolves and develops with appropriate help through meaning-focused use.

Learners need practice in transferring what they have practised in controlled situations to unmonitored spontaneous use. Situations for speaking can be ranked on a continuum from careful and highly monitored to spontaneous. Table 6.2 shows such a range, starting from the most careful.

Learners can gradually move through the range of activities with a focus on bringing about change in particular sounds or aspects of pronunciation. In the careful activities, the learners prepare, monitor, and receive feedback. In the spontaneous activities, only feedback is provided.

It may also be useful for learners to have physical reminders to help them monitor a particular sound to bring about change. This physical reminder can be something like crossing your fingers before starting to speak to remind you to say /θ/ as correctly as possible.

The way correction and pronunciation practice is done can affect the learners' attitude to changing their own pronunciation. Stevick (1978: 146) suggests three approaches to teaching pronunciation that take account of learners' feelings:

Table 6.2 Types of Control and Techniques for Speaking

Degree and type of control	*Techniques*
Prepared reading aloud	Giving dictation
	Read and look up
Unprepared reading aloud	Chain story
Rehearsed formal speaking	4/3/2
	Read and retell
Formal speaking with no time pressure	Peer talks
One-way information gap activities	Listen and do
Split information activities with time pressure	Find the difference
	Same or different

1. The teacher hardly speaks but guides the learners to find their own criteria for the sounds of the language. This is the approach followed in the silent way.
2. The pronunciation is given gently but clearly from a point outside the learners' view but within their personal space. This often creates the illusion that what the learners hear is coming from inside their own heads. This is the approach followed in community language learning.
3. The learners speak first, not the teacher. Then, no matter whether the learners are right or wrong, "the teacher gives the same word or phrase correctly, using a tone of voice that conveys interest and support, but that does not say 'right' or 'wrong'". The student, in turn, may or may not repeat after the teacher. In this informative but non-evaluative atmosphere, students pick up most of what they need to know. The non-evaluative aspect of this technique reduces the alienation between student and teacher. Whatever information the students do not pick up in this way is provided from time to time by the teacher, in brief, matter-of-fact statements addressed to no-one in particular.

An effective way of showing learners the importance of an intelligible pronunciation is to get them to meet communication difficulties with peers (Jenkins, 2002). In his research on split information activities involving the relabelling of diagrams, Newton (1995) found that at least 25 per cent of the negotiation between learners focused on the spoken form of words. This resulted in the learners repeating the words, often with altered pronunciation, or spelling the words. It is not difficult for a teacher to design split information activities that focus on wanted sounds and increase the learners' awareness of the importance of pronunciation. Information gap activities involving the labelling of diagrams or plans are particularly useful.

Diagnostic Testing

There is a noticeable lack of any diagnostic testing of pronunciation in most teachers' classroom practice. And yet this can be a useful source of information for the teacher and a valuable way to raise learners' awareness of the quality of their pronunciation. A simple diagnostic assessment needs to be easy to use and fast to implement. Getting learners to make a recording that the teacher can listen to and analyse is a useful form of assessment. One part of the recording can involve each learner in reading a passage aloud, followed by some unrehearsed talk based on topic prompts. These recordings provide a useful baseline so that, by getting learners to make the same recording again at the end of a course or at set points over the duration of a course, there is a basis for mapping progress.

The Rainbow Passage, which is freely available online, is often used for speech diagnosis purposes as it is designed to ensure the production of a wide range of segments and prosodic elements. However, its primary purpose is for diagnosis of speech issues rather than as a second language learning resource, and so the vocabulary in the text is not suitable for low-level learners, and it is quite long (332 words). The following passage on the topic of intercultural communication from Gerhiser and Wrenn (2007)[1] provides a shorter alternative:

> *A Passage for Read-aloud Pronunciation Diagnostic Assessment*
> *Instructions*: Read the following passage to yourself once or twice to understand the meaning. Then, read it aloud and record it.
> *Intercultural Communication*
> Have you observed the ways people from different cultures use silence? Have you noticed that some people interrupt conversations more than other people? All cultures do not have the same rules governing these areas of communication. Many Americans interpret silence in conversations to mean disapproval, disagreement, or unsuccessful communication. They often try to fill silence by saying something even if they have nothing to say!
> On the other hand, Americans don't appreciate a person who dominates a conversation. Knowing when to take turns in a conversation in another language can sometimes cause difficulty. Should you wait until someone has finished a sentence before contributing to a discussion, or can you break into the middle of someone's sentence? Interrupting someone who is speaking is considered rude in the United States. Even children are taught explicitly not to interrupt.
> (Levine & Adelman, 1982: 23)

For teachers in contexts where all the learners share the same L1, identifying problematic aspects of pronunciation is easier because the same errors are likely to be made by many students. However, we should not assume that this will always be the case; there can be considerable variation, even among speakers of the same L1. As noted earlier, Swan and Smith (2001) provide a comprehensive and systematic analysis of the particular pronunciation challenges faced by learners from different L1 backgrounds.

Monitoring Pronunciation

The most effective way of testing a learner's pronunciation is to observe and record the learner performing in a variety of situations. This is not always possible, and there have been ingenious suggestions to test groups of learners. For groups that are not too large, learners can record a passage using their best pronunciation. They are allowed to practise the passage as much as they like, but they can only record it once (Whiteson, 1978). Another way that learners find enjoyable is for the teacher to hand out a sheet with minimal pair sentences on it (Hole, 1983). Here is an example of part of a sheet:

1. I asked him for a ship a sheep
2. The pen is in my pocket pin
3. John was said to be going sad

The learners write their names at the top of the sheets. Then, they draw a circle around one word in each minimal pair. They can choose either member of a pair of words. Then, the teacher calls on the learners one by one to say each sentence containing the words they circled. The teacher writes which member of each pair they say. The learners' papers are collected, and the teacher's notes are compared with what the learners circled.

Dobbyn (1976) devised a test for quite large groups. As in the test procedure devised by Hole (1983), the teacher does not know what the learners are trying to say. Ten different sheets are prepared, all based on the same minimal pairs. Here are three such pairs:

1. (a) She couldn't be heard in class.(b) She couldn't be hard in class.
2. (a) He guards his gin carefully.(b) He guards his shin carefully.
3. (a) Give him his tie back.(b) Give him his toy back.

One of the ten sheets will contain these sentences and the key:

1. She couldn't be heard in class.
2. He guards his shin carefully.
3. Give him his tie back.
   1a, 2b, 3a
   Another sheet may have these sentences and the key:

1. She couldn't be heard in class.
2. He guards his chin carefully.
3. Give him his tie back.
   1a, 2a, 3a

The sheets are distributed so that the teacher does not know who has which sheet. As each learner is called on to pronounce the sentences on their sheet, the teacher writes a or b under their name for each number. Then, the teacher gets the learner to read the key aloud, and the teacher marks what they wrote.

118 *Pronunciation*

It is useful to see improvement in pronunciation as fitting into the four strands of a course. An intelligible pronunciation can be encouraged by meaning-focused input and meaning-focused output during communication activities where learners with different first languages are trying to get their meaning across (Jenkins, 2002). Pronunciation can also be helped through a deliberate focus on individual sounds, consonant clusters, and suprasegmentals. Fluency activities may also have a role to play in the improvement of pronunciation. Because fluency and accuracy affect each other, working on very easy tasks to improve fluency may also have a positive effect on pronunciation accuracy, although this remains to be researched.

The intelligibility of a speaker's pronunciation is also dependent on the attitude of the listener. If the listener wants to understand, is sympathetic to the speaker, and makes an effort to understand, intelligibility will be greater. Pronunciation practice can take learners so far, but communication is a two-way process, and some responsibility for understanding also lies with the listener.

Tasks

- List three pronunciation difficulties that your learners have. Use your list to do the following tasks:
    1. Suggest which pronunciation features could be modified to make comprehension easier, and which could be considered part of the range of individual differences among speakers of English.
    2. If you were teaching this person, choose one area of difficulty you would work on. Say why you chose this point.
    3. Use a checklist of reasons for pronunciation difficulty and tick off those that are most likely to apply here. (Use 1, 2, or 3 to indicate the possible rankings among these reasons.)
    4. Invent details about the students' language learning situations—for example, attitude towards the target language. Indicate how these details are likely to affect their pronunciation goals.
    5. Set some immediate and some long-term goals based on your analysis of the feature and on the information you have invented.

- How would you respond to these comments about pronunciation?
    1. All my learners have a problem with /θ/. I teach them how to say it, and they can. But they don't do it in normal speaking.
    2. The teachers are really nice to us and they say they can understand us easily, but I know that other people can't understand me easily, so I practise by myself with a recorder.
    3. I don't know if I should teach my learners American pronunciation or British pronunciation.

- Work with a partner. One of you is the learner and one is the teacher. Choose a pronunciation difficulty to work on, such as the pronunciation of /f/ or /Θ/. Go through the following steps:
    1. Give practice in hearing the sound.
    2. Get the learner to copy a model.
    3. Show the learner what to do.
    4. Explain what to do.
    5. Use a procedure to "force" the sound.

    Steps 3, 4, and 5 are only used if a previous step is not successful.

Further Reading

Derwing and Munro (2015) provide a comprehensive, accessible, and practical discussion of research on L2 pronunciation teaching and learning by two leading scholars in the field, who have a strong commitment to helping teachers.

Note

1 http://teachingpronunciation.pbworks.com/f/Pronunciation+assessment+packet+.pdf

7 Learning through Task-based Interaction

This chapter examines interactive activities that bring listening and speaking together. This integration of listening and speaking emphasises learning collaboratively and listening actively, with the listener negotiating and shaping the spoken message. Part of the skill of listening is learning how to take an active role in providing feedback to the speaker (Brown, 1986). This feedback may involve pointing out problems with the comprehensibility of the message and specifying where the problem lies. This feedback and questioning is called *negotiation* and is part of what are more broadly called *language-related episodes*, where there is a focus on language features during language use. Here is an example of a group of learners negotiating successfully with each other during a speaking task:

L3	"All enclosures should be filled" (reading from task sheet).
L2	"Enclosures should be filled." *Enclosure*, do you know?
L1	What means *enclosure*? Do you know?
L3	Close ah—"should be filled".
L2	No I don't know enclos- enclosed.
L1	*Filled* what means *fill*? Oh oh all enclosed, I think that all enclosed that means enclosed.
L2	Fill.
L3	Filled, filled.
L2	Ohh.
L1	Every every area yes should be filled.
L2	Should be filled.
L3	Should be put put something inside.
L1	Yes because yes yes because you know two? the-
L2	I see. No empty rooms ahh.
L3	No empty rooms yeah.
L2	Two is the empty I see.
L1	Yeah empty so we must fill it, okay?

Negotiation is a part of interactional feedback. There are three main kinds of interactional feedback (Nassaji, 2016): (1) Reformulations provide corrected versions (recasts) of the learner's errors. (2) Prompts include clarification requests, repetitions, and metalinguistic clues to indicate an error, encouraging the learner to self-repair. (3) Metalinguistic feedback provides information such as grammatical explanations that can guide correction. Interactional feedback provides opportunities for improvements in accuracy, negotiation thus increasing comprehension, pushed output, scaffolding, and a deliberate focus on language features (focus on form), all of which help learning.

One of the main ways that negotiation helps the listener learn is by clarifying unknown items. As Michael Long (1996) claims,

> tasks that stimulate negotiation for meaning may turn out to be one among several useful language-learning situations, in or out of classrooms, for they may be one of the easiest ways to facilitate a learner's focus on form without losing sight of a lesson's (or conversation's) predominant focus on meaning.
>
> (p. 454)

Negotiation also plays other roles in assisting language development, such as the following, which are based on Long's detailed discussion of interaction (Long, 1996: 445–454). Negotiation:

- makes input understandable without simplifying it, so that learnable language features are retained
- breaks the input into smaller digestible pieces
- raises awareness of formal features of the input
- gives learners opportunities for direct learning of new forms
- provides a "scaffold" within which learners can produce increasingly complex utterances
- pushes learners to express themselves more clearly and precisely— "pushed output"
- makes learners more sensitive to their need to be comprehensible.

Overall, interaction can help language learning by providing opportunities to learn from others, often through negotiation and by speakers having to adjust their output to communicate with others. This interaction helps learning by providing plenty of comprehensible input, by encouraging pushed output, by making learners aware of what they do not know, and by helping learners develop the language and strategies needed for interaction. Susan Gass (1997: 131–132) sums up the value of negotiation in the following way:

The claim is not that negotiation causes learning nor that there is a theory of learning based on interaction. Rather, negotiation is a facilitator of learning; it is one means but not the only means of drawing attention to areas of needed change. It is one means by which input can become comprehensible and manageable, [and] ... it is a form of negative evidence [helping] learners to recognize the inadequacy of their own rule system.

Negotiation is a form of corrective feedback and as such has positive effects on learning (Ellis, 2016), especially where the feedback is explicit. It is, thus, useful to point out learners' errors in communication.

Encouraging Negotiation

Most of the techniques in this chapter encourage negotiation. The extent to which negotiation helps language learning depends on what is negotiated and how far the negotiation takes the learner through *comprehending, noticing, comparing,* and *using* unfamiliar or partly unfamiliar language items.

Several studies of negotiation have shown the range of reasons for negotiation (Aston, 1986; Larsen-Freeman & Long, 1991). These include keeping the group together by "celebrating agreement", clarifying poorly presented items, clarifying because of inattention, clarifying unknown items, and clarifying the task procedure. Only a few of these are likely to contribute directly to language learning. When the teacher monitors tasks involving negotiation to judge their effectiveness, the teacher should look carefully for negotiation of lexical and grammatical items and should notice whether form or meaning is being negotiated. Direct training of speaking strategies can have a positive effect on learners' development of speaking skills (Sayer, 2005). Training can involve: (1) explanation of discourse strategies such as "holding the floor", negotiating meaning, providing feedback to the speaker, and managing turn-taking; (2) observing conversations using a checklist and later providing feedback; and (3) learners transcribing recordings of their own speech and critiquing them.

Using Written Input to Encourage Negotiation

Newton's (1995, 2013) research on the effect of written input on negotiation showed that, in the tasks he used, *all* of the negotiated vocabulary was in the written input sheets used in the activity. That is, the learners did not negotiate vocabulary that they incidentally brought into the activity. If this finding is true across a variety of activities and texts, it means that, by careful choice or rewriting of texts, teachers can set up wanted vocabulary to be negotiated (Joe, Nation, & Newton, 1996; Nation, 2013a: 190–199).

Let us take the **agony aunt column** activity as an example. Some magazines and newspapers print letters from readers in which they describe their relationship problems or other personal problems. An answer giving advice about how to solve these problems is printed next to each letter. These letters and their answers can be used for class discussion. The following steps are adapted from Hall (1971):

1. Read the letter to the learners, but not the answer. Unknown vocabulary and other difficulties should be explained. The learners can take notes as they listen to the letter, ask questions, repeat it aloud phrase by phrase, or write it as dictation.
2. The learners discuss the letter in small groups and suggest advice of their own.
3. Each group reports their advice to the class.
4. The teacher presents the advice given in the newspaper and discusses and compares this advice with the advice suggested by the learners.

In order to encourage negotiation, in Step 1 the learners are simply given the written version of the letter. Before doing this, the teacher checks that the letter contains about six to eight language items (words, multiword units, grammatical features) that may be beyond most of the learners' present level but that are appropriate for them to learn. The teacher may wish to simplify the other vocabulary that is not worth spending time on. There is nothing wrong with adapting the text, providing the teacher is confident that the adaptations represent normal language use. Steps 2 and 3 provide helpful repetition of useful language items through discussing and comparing the group's advice with advice from the newspaper.

Here is a typical letter. Some of the underlined vocabulary is in the Academic Word List (Coxhead, 2000) and is the learning goal of the activity:

> Dear Belle,
>   My boss keeps inviting me to <u>participate</u> in various sporting activities with him, such as playing golf and <u>squash</u>. I am quite good at the sports and enjoy them. However, it is <u>affecting</u> my <u>relationship</u> with my wife. The time that we would usually spend together is now <u>devoted</u> to keeping my boss happy. I don't know what decision to make. Should I refuse my boss and risk my <u>promotion</u>, or should I continue with golf and squash and risk my marriage?
>   Confused sportsman

Tsui (2012) offers an alternative version of this activity that incorporates group writing. Here is an adapted version of Tsui's activity:

1. The class read and discuss a number of sample agony aunt letters, focusing on both content and genre and language features.
2. Each group is given a letter to reply to. They discuss the problem and how to solve it, and write their response letter on a poster.
3. The posters are displayed for a **poster carousel/gallery walk activity**.
4. In new groups, students write an agony aunt letter asking for advice.
5. Each letter is distributed to another group who write a response (on posters).
6. The posters are displayed for another poster carousel activity.

Throughout these steps, there are many opportunities for learners to interact and negotiate. Equally, there are many opportunities for the teacher to provide feedback and brief instructional interludes to raise awareness of language points.

There are many activities involving written input that could encourage negotiation. These include **completion activities, ordering activities, split information activities, ranking, problem-solving,** and **modifying the statements** and are described later in this chapter.

The nature of the task will determine the kind of language use that occurs. As Newton and Kennedy (1996) show, strongly focused two-way tasks such as split information, where each learner has different information, can result in the use of almost telegraphic language because this is the most efficient way of getting the message across, particularly when there is a time limit placed on the task (see also Newton, 2013). Similarly, the way in which the learners take turns in a task is largely determined by the nature of the task. For this reason, teachers need to monitor tasks well and use this feedback to redesign tasks to suit learning goals. But it is important to keep in mind that, ultimately, it is the learners who determine how they will interact within a given task (Coughlan & Duff, 1994; Nakahama, Tyler, & van Lier, 2001). And so teachers need also to foster in learners an appropriate orientation and awareness of how to participate in group interaction in ways that maximise learning benefits. Crabbe (2007) offers the following simple example of how to do this. The teacher carries out a short communication task with a student or small group of students in front of the class. She does this to model how to go about negotiating for meaning when something is unclear. For example, the teacher models asking for clarification and checking comprehension. In a follow-up communication task, negotiation for meaning is made an explicit learning focus.

Using Information Distribution to Encourage Negotiation

It is possible to distinguish four kinds of group work according to the way the information needed in the activity is distributed among the learners (Nation, 1989b). These four ways are:

1. All learners have the same information (a cooperating arrangement).
2. Each learner has different essential information (a split information arrangement) (Nation, 1977).
3. One learner has all the information that the others need (a superior–inferior arrangement).
4. The learners all see the same information, but each one has a different task.

The term "information gap activities" is sometimes used in the literature. These can include split information tasks and superior–inferior tasks. The term information gap will be largely avoided here to preserve the distinction between cooperating and split information tasks.

The first two types of information distribution are the ones that most encourage negotiation, and there has been considerable research into their effects. **Split information activities** have been called two-way tasks, or jigsaw tasks, and cooperating tasks have been called one-way tasks. The clearest example of a split information task can be seen when the learners work in pairs. For example, in the task in Figure 7.1, each learner in a pair (Learner A and Learner B) has a similar task sheet with 30 simple, numbered pictures on it. About half of the pictures on Learner B's sheet are the same as Learner A's, and the other half are not the same.

Learners A and B sit facing each other. They must not be able to see the information on each other's sheet. Because there is a cross next to Item 1 on A's sheet, Learner A begins by describing the first picture. Learner B listens carefully to this description, asks Learner A any questions that they need to, and looks at the first picture on their sheet to decide whether or not their picture is exactly the same as Learner A's. If Learner B thinks it is the same, they say "the same" to Learner A, and they both write S next to Item 1 on their sheets. If, after listening to the description given by Learner A, Learner B thinks their picture is different, they say "different", and both learners write D next to Item 1 on their sheets. When the first item has been completed, Learner B begins describing Item 2, because there is a cross next to Item 2 on B's sheet. Each pair works through the items in this way. After five or ten items have been completed, the learners change partners. When all the items have been completed, Learners A and B in each pair put their two sheets next to each other and compare the pictures to see if their answers were correct. Anderson (2019) looks at a range of uses of jigsaw activities.

The essential feature of the split information arrangement is that only by working together in combining their material can the learners find the required answers. A learner cannot find the answer simply by looking at their own material.

One weakness of these tasks where they require labelling and completion of diagrams with words is that learners can resort to spelling out words to each other and, in so doing, reduce the quality of meaning-focused talk.

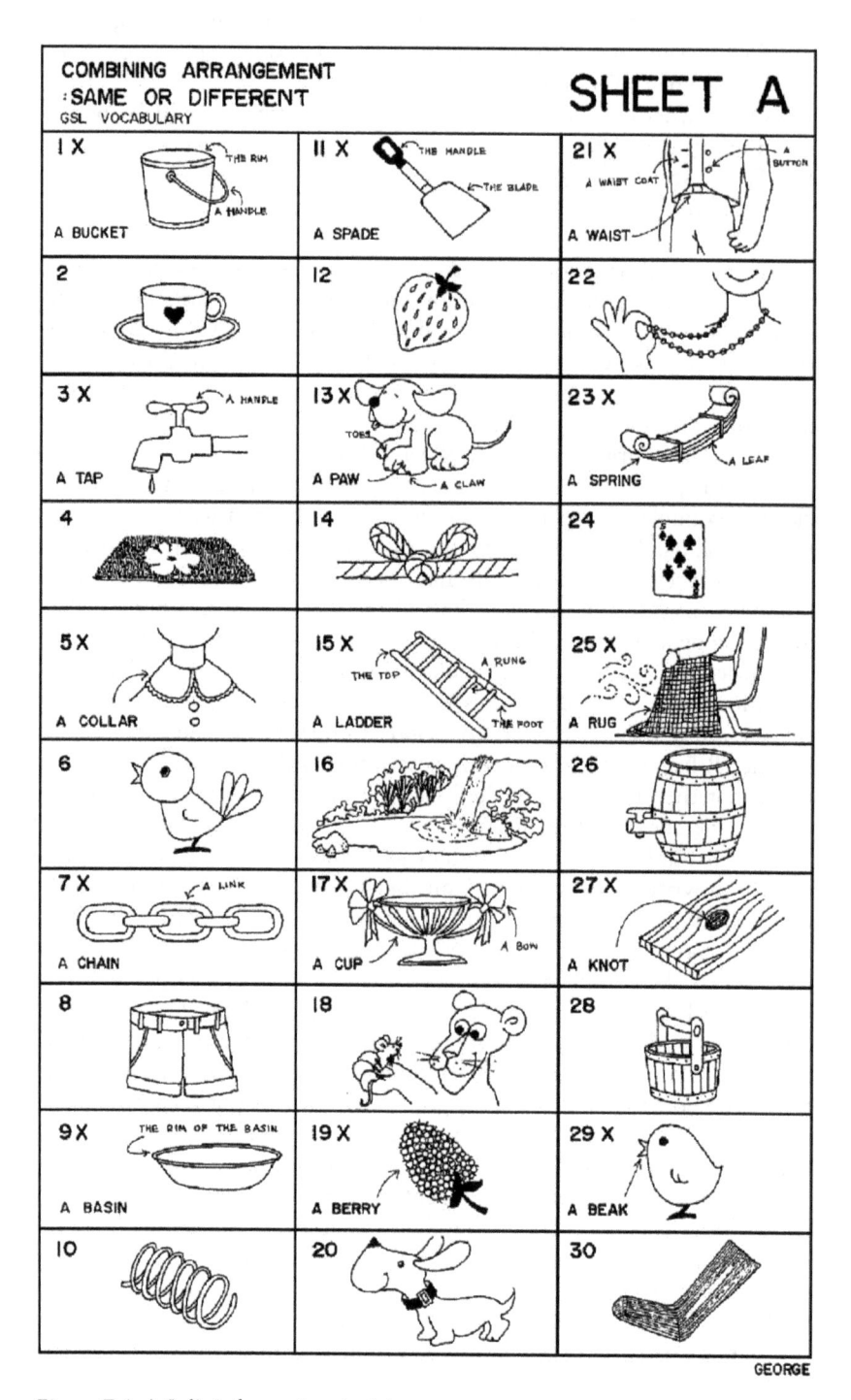

Figure 7.1 A Split Information Activity

Figure 7.1 (Cont.)

Split information tasks can be used with learners at any level, from beginners to advanced students, if appropriate materials are employed (Nation, 1977). Following is an example of two young learners in a Grade 4 primary school EFL class in Vietnam doing a split information activity from Newton and Bui (2017: 271). In the activity, the learners are exchanging information about subjects in a school timetable. The example illustrates collaborative scaffolding and negotiation for meaning in which learner L2 seeks clarification of the word "draw" from L1. When L1 is unable to supply the correct word, L2 offers a suggestion that L1 takes up.

L1: I have Science, Math and draw
L2: draw há? [Is it "draw"?]
L1: Um
L2: draw hay Art? ["draw" or "Art"?]
L1: Art

Cooperating tasks involve all the learners having the same information. For example, in a **ranking** task, the learners are given a list of items and a criterion for ranking or choosing among the items. They must arrange the items according to the criterion or choose the top three and the bottom one (Green, 1975; Thomas & Nation, 1979). Here is an example:

> You are alone and lost in the jungle; put the following things in order of importance for your survival:
>
> a sleeping bag
> a radio (for listening only)
> an axe
> a gun and ten bullets
> matches
> a tent
> a torch
> a map of the area
> a cooking pot
> three cans of food
> three metres of rope
> a story book

This type of problem-solving activity can be done by moving through a variety of group sizes. This is called a pyramid procedure (Jordan, 1990). First, the learners are presented with the problem and are then asked to think individually about the problem and choose a possible solution. In the second step, the learners work in small groups to reach an agreement. The third step involves whole-class work in which groups compare their rankings and the teacher facilitates discussion of the rankings and of language issues that came up in the task. Activities such as ranking with a strong focus on reaching consensus can encourage negotiation of language items. If you want to reach agreement, then there must be understanding. There follow some techniques that require a consensus.

In **modify the statements,** the learners are given a set of controversial statements, such as "Every child needs at least one brother and sister". They work in groups to make changes to the statements so that everybody in the group can agree with them (Gower, 1981).

In the following kind of **problem-solving,** the learners are given a problem to solve. They must do this by reaching an agreement among themselves. They should not do this by voting but by discussion. The work is done in small groups of up to six people. When they have reached an agreement, they report the result of their discussion to the class. Here is an example from Cole (1972):

> A teacher sees a student cheating in an examination. He is the student who manages the student website. He is a good student, but because of his outside work his marks have not been very high. If he gets to law school, he will probably become a very great lawyer. What should the teacher do?
>
> 1. Pretend not to see the cheating.
> 2. Quietly ask him to stop cheating.
> 3. Tell the class that someone has been cheating and if it happens again that person will be sent out.
> 4. Send the student out of the room and tell the class the reason.
> 5. Do the same as (4) but also tell the head of the school so that the student is forced to leave the school.
>
> The learners must choose one of the five possibilities.

In **complete the map,** each learner has an incomplete version of a map or diagram, and each learner has information that the other(s) do not have. By combining this information, each learner can make a complete map. They do this by keeping their map hidden from the others and by describing what is on their map for the others to draw on theirs.

In the **strip story,** the teacher chooses a story that has roughly as many sentences as there are learners in the group. The teacher writes each sentence from the story on a different piece of paper. The story should be one that the learners have not met before. It should contain known vocabulary and sentence patterns. Each learner is given a different sentence from the story to memorise. If there are not enough sentences for each learner to have one, it does not matter, because they can still participate in ordering the sentences. If there are more sentences than learners, then some learners can have two short sentences to memorise. So, each learner sees only one sentence and does not see the other sentences in the story. After each learner has memorised their sentence, the pieces of paper with the sentences on them are collected by the teacher. Then, each learner tells their sentence to the others in the group, and, without doing any writing at all, the learners arrange themselves to solve the problem of putting the sentences in the right order to tell the story (Gibson, 1975). The teacher takes no part in the activity. The technique allows the learners to communicate with each other in the target language to solve the problem. The solving of the problem is less important than the communication that needs to take place in order to solve the problem.

In a beginners' class, the strip story activity can provide an excellent way of practising key phrases related to the students' lives that have been previously learned in class. For instance, during a lesson, the following recount was constructed on the whiteboard by a class of adult beginner-level learners in a community ESL class, guided by their teacher:

> In the morning I get up at 7 o'clock. First, I have a shower. Then I eat my breakfast. After breakfast, I do the dishes. I leave home at 8 o'clock. I catch the bus to class. I get to class at about 8.45am. In the evening, I help to cook dinner. Then I do the dishes. After dinner, I watch TV. I go to bed at about 11 o'clock.

The next day, the teacher handed out strips of paper with each of the eleven sentences written on it. Each learner had to memorise their sentence and then circulate around the room to find the people with the sentences on either side of them. This involved a lot of talk and interaction. Once they had ordered themselves in a line according to the sentence that each had memorised, they retold the recount in sequence enough times to do so fluently. Similarly, the strip story activity can be used with short, set dialogues that learners have been learning. It can also be used with picture stories.

Factors Affecting Negotiation and Language-Related Episodes

Working in pairs or groups helps learning in a variety of ways. It can provide more opportunities for learners to use the language. It can provide opportunities for types of language use that are usually assigned to the teacher, such as asking questions, or that otherwise do not occur in the classroom. It can provide learners with opportunities to receive and provide feedback. It can provide opportunities for learners to collaboratively construct meaning, thus raising performance (Foster & Ohta, 2005). It can provide a less threatening environment for language use.

Several factors affect the amount, type, and effect of negotiation.

1. Pair work usually produces more negotiations on the same task than work in a group of four (Fotos & Ellis, 1991). However, Fernández Dobao (2014) found that, although using groups provided less time for each learner to use the language compared with pairs, groups provided more instances of negotiation and more successfully resolved negotiations that resulted in vocabulary retention.
2. Storch and Aldosari (2012), Leeser (2004), and Kim and McDonough (2008) found that not only proficiency level, but also the pattern of participation affected the number of language-related episodes (LREs) produced. Pairing learners of different proficiencies works best (more LREs) if learners genuinely collaborate and the high-proficiency learners do not dominate. However, Storch and Aldosari caution that the kinds of pairing also need to take account of the purpose of the group work. If the goal is fluency development, then pairing learners of equal proficiency may be useful. If the goal is proficiency development, then pairings of mixed proficiency may be more effective. Nguyen and Newton (2019) came to slightly different conclusions in research on LREs in pair work by Vietnamese high school EFL learners. They found that pairs of low-proficiency learners engaged in significantly more LREs than mixed-proficiency pairs. However, more of the LREs in the low-proficiency pairs were unsuccessful or resolved incorrectly. In contrast, when low-proficiency learners were in mixed-proficiency pairs, they did not produce as many LREs, but the LREs that did occur were much more successfully resolved. These LREs also led to significantly more learning as measured in uptake of the target language items in subsequent repeated performance of the same task in front of the class. In the following example (Nguyen & Newton, 2019: 11), the learners engage in an LRE in the task rehearsal focused on the term *charity auction*. Then, later in the same lesson, S2 is able to use this item fluently.

Rehearsal	Performance
S2: Hi Tú[1] [laugh]. Last night did	S2: Hi Tú
S1: you watch ah (.) the programme?	S1: Hi
S2: the auction	S2: ahm did you watch er the charity did you
S1: huh?	watch the *charity auction* on TV last
S2: auction	S1: night?
S1: option? ghi răng?(*how to spell it?*)	S2: yeah I think that's a great programme.
S2: a-u-c-t-i-o-n. auction a!(*auction!*)	after watching the programme I hope
S1: Rồi, chi auction chi?	I can do charity, too. Erm if you if you
(*Ok, what auction what?*)	have 500 million VND, what (.) how
S2: charity auction	will you spend it on do … doing charity?

3. Cooperating tasks produce more negotiation of the meaning of vocabulary than split information tasks (Newton, 2013). Split information tasks produce a lot of negotiation, but not all of it is negotiation of word meaning or, indeed, language features.
4. The signals that learners make affect the adjustment of output during a task. In a study of output in activities involving native speakers working with non-native speakers, Pica, Holliday, Lewis, and Morgenthaler (1989) found that the most important factor determining whether learners adjusted their output was the type of signal made by their partner. When their partner asked for clarification ("What? I still don't know what the word is."), the learners were more likely to adjust what they said than if their partner asked for confirmation by repeating what the learner had just said, by changing it (**NNS** house has three windows? **NS** three windows?), or by completing or elaborating on it (**NNS** there is a car parking ... left side **NS** of the picture, right?). The researchers caution, however, that confirmation checks that do not lead to adjusted output may still have an important role to play in language acquisition in that they provide models for input.

Using Learner Training to Encourage Negotiation

In order to negotiate, learners need to know the language features necessary for negotiation and to develop negotiation strategies. Anderson and Lynch (1988) reviewed studies with young native speakers on the effect of training on the use of negotiation while listening. The training can involve telling learners the importance of asking for more information, watching others ask, and providing simple plans of what to do when there is a comprehension problem. Anderson and Lynch conclude: "The successful methods [of training young native speakers] seem to depend on the listener already possessing the requisite skills, but not realising their relevance to the current listening task" (p. 30). Encouraging second language learners to negotiate can involve learning the appropriate language items and procedures to negotiate and providing opportunities for practice. If these steps are not successful, the simple training procedures described above may be useful.

When taking part in a conversation, a learner may find that there are unknown words or structures, or that what the speaker said was not clear. If this happens, one strategy is to ask for clarification. The simplest language needed to do this includes phrases such as "Pardon?", "What?", or even more colloquially "Eh?". Sentences such as "What does ___ mean?" and "How do you spell ___?" are useful for getting information about words. Another possibility is to repeat the part just before the unclear part and add "what", as in "He what?" or "He agreed what?". These phrases can usefully be taught before learners do activities like the following, in order to practise the phrases and the strategy.

Clennell (1999) describes a useful procedure for making learners aware of the linguistic and sociolinguistic features of interactive spoken language. Stage 1 involves preparing for an interview and then carrying out the interview. The preparation can involve focusing on appropriate ways of addressing the interviewee, different ways of requesting an interview, and so on. It can also involve ways of managing the discourse by asking the interviewee to repeat or slow down. Stage 2 involves transcribing the recorded interview and coming to an understanding of what happened during the interview. Stage 3 involves presenting the analysed transcription to the class in the form of a seminar presentation with accompanying discussion. Lynch (2001) found plenty of evidence that transcribing their own spoken interaction resulted in learners finding plenty to improve and being able to make substantial corrections to the language of the transcription. There was also a useful follow-up role for the teacher in providing helpful corrective feedback, especially in vocabulary choice. Mennim (2003) found that the teacher's feedback on learners' written transcription of a taped rehearsal of a presentation had substantial positive effects on the grammatical accuracy of a subsequent presentation.

Listen and do activities can also give rise to negotiation if they are at the right level of difficulty. Picture drawing in pairs has often been used in research on interaction and negotiation (see, for example, Mackey, 1999). For example:

> "Draw a circle. Draw a cross in the circle. Draw a line under the circle. Draw a square around the circle ..." or "Draw a circle. This will be a person's face. Draw an ear on each side. The left ear is bigger than the right ear ..."

Sometimes, communication is difficult because the speaker is going too fast or is not being considerate of the listener. If this happens, the learner can try to control the speaker. The language needed to do this consists of phrases such as, "Please speak more slowly" and "Could you say that again?".

In the **controlling the teacher** technique, learners gain control of the listening material. When the learners have this control, listening exercises can become learning exercises. The teacher makes sure that the learners know the following sentences and, if necessary, writes them on the whiteboard so that they can be seen during the exercise:

> Please say the last word (sentence/paragraph) again.
> Excuse me, please speak more slowly.
> Excuse me, what was the word in front of king?
> Could you tell me the meaning of convince?
> Excuse me, how do you spell apply?

Then, he tells the learners that he is going to read a text aloud for them to listen to. He tells them that, after they have listened to the text, he will check their answers to some questions about the text. The teacher gives the learners copies of the questions or writes the questions on the whiteboard. He also tells the learners that, at any time during the reading of the text, they can ask him to stop, read more slowly, repeat, go back to the beginning, spell a word, explain the meaning of a word, or read more quickly. Then, the learners look at the questions and listen. However, the teacher deliberately reads the first two sentences of the text too quickly for the learners to follow. Then, he stops and looks at the learners for instruction. He does not do anything further until the learners give him instructions. When the teacher finally reaches the end of the text, and the learners have no further instructions for him, he asks the learners for the answers to the questions. As an alternative to questions, the teacher can divide the text in two and make copies. The learners then work in pairs, each reading their part of the text while the other learner interrupts with clarification questions as required.

Could you repeat that? (Folse, 1991) involves a learner or group of learners dictating to someone writing on the whiteboard while they are facing the other way. Therefore, the people dictating cannot see what is being written on the whiteboard. This can be done with two teams and similar, but not the same, sentences.

Discover the answer is another technique to encourage learners to question the speaker. The teacher asks the learners a question that she is sure that they cannot answer; for example,

"How many kilometres is it from here to Paris?"

When one learner tries to guess the answer, the teacher says things like,

"No, it's less than that" or
"No, it's less than half of that" or
"Take away a few kilometres", and so on

By the things that she says, the teacher guides the learners to the correct answer. This is an amusing technique because, in the end, by listening to what the teacher says about the answers, the learners are able to give the correct answer to the question, although they really did not know the answer before. The technique helps learn phrases such as "more than that", which guide learners towards the answer.

All of these activities increase the need for negotiation between the learners in a group. They all involve an information gap that may be there because of split information or a superior–inferior information distribution.

Monitoring Negotiation

Group work can have a variety of learning goals, and monitoring should reflect these goals. If the goal is the learning of language items, then the amount of support that learners provide each other during the activity will be of major interest. This support can take the form of negotiating the meaning of language items, encouraging all group members to contribute, valuing each other's contributions by commenting positively on or picking up others' ideas, co-constructing the discourse (Foster & Ohta, 2005), and the modelling and supplying of needed items.

Teachers or learners acting as observers can look for these kinds of support and comment on them to the group as a way of bringing about the development of group support skills that will help language learning.

If observation shows that there is a need for increased support, there are several ways of arranging this:

1. Parts of group work sessions are recorded and used as case studies to show learners how to increase support.
2. Each learner in the group is assigned a different role to play during a group work activity. Thus, one person could have the role of encouraging each person to contribute to the discussion. Another person could have the role of commenting positively on good ideas put forward by others, and so on.
3. The teacher should consider redesigning the activity to include an information gap, a series of well-defined steps for the learners to follow, or a different outcome such as ranking, completion, or distinguishing.
4. It may be necessary to rearrange the assignment of learners to groups so that, for example, learners of a similar proficiency level are in the same group, or so that there is not a gender mix.

As well as monitoring the dynamics of group work, it is also useful to monitor learners' focus on the task. This monitoring can involve looking at the amount of discussion of how to do the task, the amount of time spent focused on the task, and the amount of use of language items from the written input used in the task.

Learning through Non-negotiated Interaction

Although negotiation is an effective way to encourage learning through interaction, it probably does not account for most of the learning through interaction. Learning will also occur through guessing from context that is not overtly signalled and noticing language features even when these features have not been negotiated (Nation, 2013a: Chapter

4; Newton, 2013). Sometimes, there may be overt signs of this noticing. In his study of units of oral expression, Bygate (1988: 74–75) provides examples of how "the flexibility of oral discourse can make it easier for the learner to pick up a lexical item or structure offered by a colleague ... before proceeding to weave it into a phrase or clause".

S9: on yours you have a clock and I have a
S10: a picture
S9: a picture
S3: I think there are more than three differences
S1: yes
S2: yes
S1: more than three differences

Small group activities also provide an opportunity for learners to get better at putting language items they have learned receptively into productive use, supported by interaction with peers. It is likely that the design features to encourage this production include the use of split information tasks that contain a large amount of shared information.

The **find the differences** activity is a good example of this. In this activity, a pair of learners have a similar picture each, but they have to find the differences by describing and not showing their pictures to each other (see Figure 7.1). In this activity, the support comes from the common features of the two pictures. Support may also involve some kind of support during the task such as notes, pictures with annotations, or objects. Breitkreuz (1972) suggests a sequence of speaking activities starting with a set of pictures. The learners are shown several pictures that tell a story. Usually, there are about four pictures. First, the learners must describe the pictures and tell the story in their own words. Then, they retell the story as a dialogue. After this, they can act it. Questions can be used to help the learners. The pictures can be taken from books of picture stories or joke books, or they can be made of stick drawings drawn by the teacher.

In this procedure the teacher may simply rely on group cooperation to produce the wanted vocabulary and constructions. If monitoring the activity shows that this does not happen, then it may be necessary for the teacher to write words and phrases on the pictures for the learners to use. This gives the first activity something of a focus on form, and so the follow-up activities of turning it into a dialogue and then acting it may serve to bring back the meaning focus. Fowles (1970) suggests using humorous cartoons in a similar way. This has the learning goals of cultural understanding and language development.

All these kinds of support allow learners to draw on explicit knowledge of the language in their spoken production.

Monitoring Learners Beginning to Speak

Some learners may be reluctant to speak. It is important to find out the causes for this and to deal with the causes. Table 7.1 outlines some possibilities.

Each of the possible causes for reluctance to speak is accompanied by a way of checking the cause. A vocabulary of 1000 words is easily enough for substantial spoken production. Where learners have a very small vocabulary, very controlled activities may need to be used.

It is important to be aware that reluctance to speak may not be only because of language difficulties. Day (1981) found that some learners possessed adequate language skills, but had not received enough encouragement to speak in a classroom. When they were taken out of the classroom for short periods of time with one or two other learners and given lots of encouragement to speak, they were soon speaking a lot. After several sessions of such speaking, they seemed more willing to contribute to speaking in the larger class.

Observing learners in speaking activities can provide important information for the teacher about the learners' control of developmental linguistic features such as forming questions and using verb forms. This information can indicate to the teacher where language-focused instruction could usefully be directed. The presence of a feature in the learners'

Table 7.1 Causes and Solutions for Learners Who Are Reluctant to Speak

Possible causes	Way of checking the cause	Solutions
Inadequate vocabulary	Use the updated vocabulary levels test or the picture vocabulary size test	Use activities where the learner can study the vocabulary beforehand
Inadequate control of grammar	Use sentence completion tests to see areas of strength and weakness	Use controlled activities such as **substitution tables** and **What is it?** Use guided or creative techniques to develop control of grammar
Lack of fluency	Provide a long "wait time" to see if the learner is able to construct a spoken sentence	Do repetitive activities such as **4/3/2**
Shyness	Compare how the learner talks to the teacher with how the learner talks to peers	Start the learner with safe, small group activities, gradually increasing the risk
Lack of encouragement	See if the learner will speak with friends in English in the playground or in pair activities	Work in a small group with the learner giving a lot of encouragement

Source: (Day, 1981)

speaking is a sign that formal teaching could have a positive effect on expanding and refining its use (Pienemann, 2003).

Tasks

1. Classify these ten activities into (1) split information, (2) cooperating, (3) superior–inferior, and (4) individual performance tasks: 4/3/2, ranking, same or different, agony column, strip story, twenty questions, dictogloss, controlling the teacher, interview, listen and do.
2. Work in small groups to make a problem-solving task. (1) Choose a topic: For this task the topic will be "Helping a visitor who is coming to stay with you and who wants to see your town". (2) Choose one outcome from these three: suggest, choose, rank. (3) Think of two restrictions or challenges that will make the task more difficult to complete. For example, the visitor might be afraid of heights, or might not have much money. Choose two different challenges. (4) Write up the task as a handout for your learners. Include the topic, outcome, and restrictions.
3. Work in groups of three to do the split information task in Figure 7.1 of this chapter, with one learner in your group acting as an observer. Comment on the strengths and weaknesses of the activity.

Further Reading

Nation (2013b: Chapter 3) covers the steps for creating problem-solving group discussion tasks and provides a wide range of topics and examples.

Nation (1989b) distinguishes different kinds of group work according to the way information is distributed among the members of the group. It shows how other features of group work such as seating arrangements need to match the distribution of information.

Jane Willis provides a practical description of six main types of language learning task on this BBC/British Council sponsored site: www.teachingenglish.org.uk/article/six-types-task-tbl

Note

1 The real name of the student has been changed.

8 Learning through Pushed Output

The comprehension approach suggests that speaking should not be encouraged until learners have substantial receptive experience and knowledge of the language system. Some researchers, however, argue that the knowledge that is needed to speak will not come unless the learners are "pushed" to speak. Swain (2005) argues that learners can comprehend input without having to look closely at the grammar. If, however, they are "pushed" to produce output, then the attention that they give to the grammar changes. The idea behind pushed output is that receptive knowledge of the L2 is not always sufficient for production. Comprehension processes involve semantic decoding focusing on turning language items into meaning. Production additionally involves syntactic processing, that is, deciding on the language items needed to express meaning.

Biber's (1989) research on the various clusters of syntactic items in different text types suggests that learners might be made aware of gaps in their productive knowledge of language features if they are required to speak in unfamiliar genres. The aim of setting demanding tasks, then, is to encourage learners to extend their use of grammatical features and words. There are other ways of making tasks demanding, including getting learners to talk on unfamiliar topics, speaking where high standards of performance are expected, speaking without the opportunity for planning or preparation, and speaking in formal situations without the interactive support of others.

Learners are "pushed" when, through encouragement or necessity, they have to produce spoken language in unfamiliar areas. These areas may be unfamiliar because the learners are more used to listening than speaking, or are not accustomed to speaking certain kinds of discourse, or are now expected to produce a higher standard of spoken language in terms of accuracy, precision, coherence, and appropriateness. Pushed output extends speakers and, in doing so, heightens their awareness of the importance of particular grammatical features in productive use of the language.

Without pushed output, learners mainly acquire language features that are necessary for comprehension. Givon, Yang, and Gernsbacher (1990) argue that, because language learners can only give their attention to one demanding task at a time, they initially learn vocabulary. Once vocabulary recognition is largely automated, they can then give their attention to grammar. Swain suggests that, if learners are not pushed to produce output, then there is little reason for them to pay attention to the grammar needed for production. Pushed output can result in the learner moving "from a purely semantic analysis of the language to a syntactic analysis of it" (1985: 252). This analysis could result in the learning of new grammar or in making "fuzzy" grammar more precise.

Pushed output does not mean that learners have to be pushed to produce as soon as an item is introduced. There is value in building up receptive experience, but this needs to be seen as only a first step. Learners need to be pushed to turn their receptive knowledge into productive use.

The time-on-task principle says that the more you perform a skill, the better you will be at it. If you want to learn to speak, do a lot of speaking. If you want to be good at writing, write a lot. Skehan (1998: 16–19) provides a wide-ranging set of justifications for the value of oral output for language learning. It helps get better input, it forces the learners to use syntactic processing, it allows learners to test their speaking skills, it helps develop fluency, it helps learners learn discourse skills and it helps them develop a personal voice. Although there is now plenty of evidence for the value of output in language learning, we need to consider not only participation, but also the nature of that participation. Quality of participation can be enhanced through, for example:

(a) allowing time for planning
(b) using split information tasks (two-way tasks) where each learner's contribution is essential for the completion of the task
(c) adding an audience
(d) helping learners understand the value of pushed output for language learning
(e) providing opportunities for teacher feedback on performance.

Note that the factors accounted for in this list include task conditions (a) and (c), task types (b), learner training (d), and teacher guidance (c). These and other factors are discussed in the next section.

Pushing Output

When planning for a variety of speaking tasks to push learners' output, there are several factors to consider. These include covering a range of topics, a range of text types, and a range of performance conditions.

Topic

Learners should be pushed to speak on a range of topics. van Ek and Alexander (1980) provide a categorisation of topics. West (1960: 113–134), in his classification of the minimum adequate vocabulary, also provides a range of possible topic areas. Topic is most likely to have an effect on the vocabulary that is used, because each topic is likely to have its particular technical, topic-related vocabulary. Covering a good range of topics in a course ensures that a wide range of vocabulary is used. Topic will also have a relationship with amount of background knowledge, as learners may be familiar with the content of some topics and not that of others. There could be strong gender difference effects in relation to background knowledge of topics, which can make some topics much more demanding than others for male and female learners.

A useful way of preparing learners for language use outside the classroom is to prepare for typical encounters in the classroom. Lilja and Piirainen-Marsh (2019) used a three-step format of (1) preparing for the encounter by watching a video, observing language use and then planning the encounter, (2) participating in the encounter outside the classroom while a partner records it on their mobile phone, and (3) back in the classroom, reflecting on the encounter while watching the recording and perhaps re-enacting and improving it. This final step could be done while working in a group of four with another pair of learners. This activity sets up the useful learning conditions of repetition, varied use, analysis and elaboration, and deliberate attention. It also has the considerable advantage of being strongly focused on the learners' needs. Riddiford and Newton (2010) provide a classroom resource for teaching communication in the professional workplace that draws on these learning conditions.

Text Type

Biber (1989) distinguished eight major spoken and written text types on the basis of the clustering of largely grammatical features. These text types included intimate interpersonal interaction, "scientific" exposition, imaginative narrative, and involved persuasion. Although most of these were written types, many of them do have spoken equivalents. The most useful distinctions to consider when ensuring that learners are pushed to cope with a range of text types are:

1. Involved interaction versus monologue. Is only one person speaking, or are speakers interacting with each other?
2. Colloquial speech versus formal speech.
3. Short turns versus long turns. Do speakers make short contributions to a conversation, or is there opportunity for longer, largely uninterrupted speech?

4. Interactional versus transactional speech. Is the goal of the speaking to establish a friendly relationship or is it to convey important information (Brown, 1981)?
5. Narrative versus non-narrative.

Learners should have the opportunity to speak across the range of these types of speaking. Just as we distinguish extensive listening and extensive reading, it is also useful to think of extensive speaking, where learners have plenty of opportunities to speak across a wide range of types of speaking. Extensive speaking should make up around half of the meaning-focused input strand of a course, with the other half focused on extensive writing.

Performance Conditions

When learners perform speaking tasks, they can do this under a variety of conditions. One set that has received a reasonable amount of attention in research is the opportunity for planning before speaking.

Planning

Planning involves preparing for a task before the task is performed (Ellis, 2009; Nielson, 2014). Typically, it involves having time to think about a given topic, having time to prepare what to say, and making brief notes about what to say. The task may involve being given a set of pictures that represent a story to talk about, describing a Lego model, preparing a small talk, making a decision, or providing personal information (Ortega, 1999).

Planning is useful because speaking is stressful. In addition to the social and interpersonal demands of communicative speaking, it puts pressure on the learner's limited attentional resources; it requires the learner to simultaneously work on the complexity of their language (grammatical and lexical), avoid mistakes (accuracy), and speak smoothly and coherently (fluency). These demands require learners to make trade-offs in what they pay attention to. For example, if a learner is concerned about accuracy and not making mistakes, their fluency will suffer (Skehan, 2015). Planning helps with pushed output because it allows part of the work to be done before the task so that there are fewer things to attend to while the task is being performed. In other words, planning gives learners experience with a task before they have to do it. In research studies, it has been found that about 10 minutes' planning time is usually enough to give good results. The effects of planning are usually measured by looking at the effects on fluency, grammatical and lexical complexity, and grammatical accuracy. In several studies, planning had positive effects on fluency and grammatical complexity, but had mixed effects on accuracy (Ellis, 2009).

Rehearsal and Task Repetition

Although repeated practice is typically associated with traditional lock-step teaching approaches, its value in communicative settings is now widely recognised (Gatbonton & Segalowitz, 2005). For example, in three separate studies described in Skehan, Xiaoyue, Qian, and Wang (2012), task repetition had huge effect sizes for the accuracy and fluency of language production by tertiary EFL students in Mainland China and Hong Kong SAR. Similarly, in the context of Vietnamese high school EFL classes, Newton and Nguyen (2019) show that, when pairs of Vietnamese high school EFL students were given the opportunity to rehearse a task prior to performing it in front of the class, they engaged in a lot of language-related episodes (LREs) during rehearsal to fill gaps in their language resources. Their subsequent public performances of the task were not only more confident and fluent, but much more linguistically accurate, reflecting the hard work they had invested in resolving language issues in rehearsal. This point is illustrated in the following example of a task rehearsal by a pair of learners followed by them doing the same task again as a brief performance in front of the class. Notice how dramatically the learners' language use improved from rehearsal to performance.

Rehearsal Phase

S1: I'm erm mình nói kinh doanh have business à? (*I want to say "do business". Should it be "have business"?*)
S2: I do business thôi! (*I do business!*)
S1: I do business and erm I gain kiếm được … kiếm được là chi? (*earn … how to say "earn money"?*) raise (.) uhm kiếm được là chi hè (*how to say "earn"*)
S2: (.) earn (.) earn!
S1: and I earn a lot of money

Performance Phase

S1: Hi Linh. How are you doing?
S2: I'm fine. And what's your job?
S1: I *do business* and I *earn* a lot of money and I want to take uhm part in volunteer work
S2: Ok. That's a good idea and erm what are you going to do with this money?

(Newton & Nguyen, 2019: 49)

Two other points are worth making about the value of rehearsal in this lesson. First, during rehearsal, the students used their L1 (Vietnamese) a lot in order to *resource* the upcoming performance. As in the example, L1 played a valuable role in solving language problems and in building up the language resources in English needed for the upcoming public performance. Teachers are often concerned that, in group work, L1 will replace English. But, in this case, the upcoming performance ensured that L1 was used productively in rehearsal.

The second closely related point is that the rehearsals involved frequent LREs in which the learners talked about talk. The example above contains two LREs, one focused on "do business" and the other on "gain money". These two LREs show how rehearsal provides space for generating ideas and formulating these ideas into English sentences, so that, when the learners subsequently perform the same task in front of the class, their focus is on clear and smooth articulation, and on communicating clearly to others.

Getting learners to use new language items while their attention is focused on the meaning that they are conveying is a challenging part of designing speaking activities. As we have seen, planning time and rehearsal are two ways to help with this challenge. Another is to make use of techniques that involve **retelling**. This retelling may be retelling of a written text or of spoken input. Here is part of a retelling of a text (Joe, 1998: 375):

> *The written input*
> One of the greatest human problems is chronic pain—continuing, often severe pain caused by such disorders as lower-back problems and cancer. Chronic pain is so severe that people are incapacitated by it.
>
> *The retelling*
> The chronic pain ... I don't understand exactly what mean ... what is it. But I think it is a severe pain very: severe: ... disease it ... always happened when: the human have ... severe pain at ... the back in the lower part of the back ... or cancer ... something like that—it make people strengthen less.

In this particular example, the learner was tested on the underlined vocabulary some days before, and the test indicated that these items were unknown. However, the retelling task pushed the learner to make sense of the items from the input and to use them productively. Clearly, there are a variety of ways in which the items could be used, ranging from an exact repetition of the input context to very creative use resulting from generalisations based on analogy.

Giving learners a chance to prepare for tasks can increase their chances of success. Such preparation could involve the **retelling of** a previously studied written text (Joe, 1998), as described above, group members helping in preparation and rehearsal before the task, or research and planning on an assigned topic. In **class judgement**, preparation is an essential part of the task. Two learners are chosen to be the competitors in a quiz. They are given a text to read that they will later be quizzed on. The rest of the class also have the text and the questions that the competitors will be asked. The competitors do not see the questions. Then, the competitors are asked the questions orally, and the rest of the class note whether they think the answers are right or wrong (Picken, 1988).

In an **ask and answer** activity (Simcock, 1993), the learners work in pairs. One learner has a text to study, and the other has a set of questions based on the text. The learners may work together on the text. Then, one learner questions the other to get them to display their knowledge of the text. They practise this for a few times and eventually do it in front of the class. The performance is done without looking at the text. Many variations of this technique are possible, particularly in the relationship of the questions to the text and the type of processing required to answer them.

Time Pressure

The second major performance condition affecting speaking is time pressure. Researchers have distinguished pre-talk planning and online planning (Yuan & Ellis, 2003). We discussed pre-task planning in an earlier section. It is useful for allowing learners to focus on the range of ideas to cover and the organisation of these ideas, as in **prepared talks**. In contrast, online planning involves not setting a tight time limit for the task so that learners can pay careful attention to turning ideas into speech *while* they speak. This is more likely to have a positive effect on accuracy. Giving learners plenty of time to perform a speaking task allows them to access both their implicit and explicit grammatical knowledge and, thus, increase the quality of their spoken output.

Amount of Support

Supported or guided tasks allow learners to operate under the most favourable conditions for production. An important design feature in such tasks is the presence of patient, understanding, sympathetic, and supportive listeners. There are several ways to achieve this. One way is to train the listeners in supportive listening strategies. These can include providing plenty of wait time while the speaker prepares what to say, using the **you said ...** strategy to periodically summarise what the speaker has said, asking easy questions to direct the speaker, as in the **ask and answer** activity described above (Simcock, 1993), and, after sufficient wait time, supplying needed phrases and vocabulary if the speaker is struggling. An important requirement in supportive listening is giving the speaker the chance to find the language items needed without being overwhelmed by support. Using three learners in a speaking activity can be a useful way of training supportive listeners. One learner is the speaker, one is the supportive listener, and one is monitoring the supportive listener with a checklist.

Checklist for Monitoring Supportive Listening

- Did the listener wait long enough before giving help?
- Did the listener provide positive comments on well-produced sentences?
- Did the listener provide useful words and phrases?
- Did the listener keep the main focus on the message?

The three learners discuss the monitor's findings at the end of the speaking task. Another way to get supportive listening is to give listeners the chance to experience the difficulties of speaking and to reflect on these difficulties.

Standard of Performance

The fourth major performance condition affecting speaking is the standard of output expected. The pressure on learners to perform well is increased if they have to speak in public, and if they are aware that some judgement is going to be made on their performance. We saw this in the discussion of rehearsal and public performance of tasks above (pp. 143–144). Doing transactional speaking with others when important information has to be conveyed and where it needs to be conveyed accurately is also a way of pushing output. Speaking with others can be supportive, and it can also be demanding.

Learner Factors

All too easily, we can treat teaching speaking mechanistically and impersonally and without regard to the complex ways in which a learner's identity and emotional life affect their willingness to participate in speaking practice in the classroom (Swain, 2013). The effective language teacher is sensitive to these factors and cultivates a positive atmosphere in the speaking class and positive learning opportunities. One could imagine a classroom where plentiful learning opportunities are provided by the teacher, but in which the learners are anxious or unmotivated or experiencing psychological pressures, all of which make them ill-disposed to take up the opportunities provided.

When learners are required to speak, especially in face-to-face interaction, much more is at stake than the language they produce. Having to communicate in a second language in front of others is often a stressful experience for learners, and this stress can produce emotional or psychological effects that cause the learner to be unwilling to speak. These effects include apprehension, nervousness, and low self-efficacy. Research shows that anxiety has a negative effect on the language learning process. The weight of research evidence suggests that one of the speaking teacher's most important jobs is to create a positive atmosphere and environment for learning, an environment in which learners feel a sense of belonging to a community, in which cooperation and empathy are extended to all by all, and in which learners can make mistakes and take linguistic risks without fear. If learners do not feel emotionally safe and secure in the classroom, the learning experience and learning outcomes will inevitably be compromised. The human brain functions quite differently when a person feels threatened and fearful compared with when they feel safe and secure. Some of the practical steps that teachers can take to build a positive learning environment include:

1. Modelling respect and regard for all in their own behaviour and responses to learners
2. Knowing how to use small group work and cooperative learning effectively for learning and for enhancing engagement and well-being
3. Agreeing on a set of classroom behaviour expectations, especially focused on how to support one another and what are and are not appropriate ways to work alongside and respond to others
4. Including short activities that involve humour, movement, collaboration or friendly competition, and/or creativity, and that all learners can complete successfully.

Below are two classroom speaking activities that are designed to strengthen positive emotions and the sense of classroom community.

Activity 1: I Really Appreciate

I really appreciate

This simple activity created by Marc Helgesen offers learners the chance to connect with something of value in their life and to talk about it in English (or a mix of English and L1 if necessary). The point is to cultivate positive feelings and, through talking about this topic in English, to create positive associations with English.

Brainstorm three things you really appreciate.

1. Choose one and draw a picture of it.
2. Stand up, walk around, and find a partner.
3. Show your picture to your partner. Say at least five sentences about it. Then listen to your partner talk about their picture.
4. Move to a new partner and repeat step 3. (Do this three times.)

Language support:

Questions	Comments
Can you tell me about this?	Tell me more.
What is this?	That's really nice.
Why do you appreciate it (them/her/him)?	I think so, too.
When? Where? Who? What? How?	Thanks for telling me.
	Cool! Awesome! Fantastic!

© 2016 Marc Helgesen, www.ELTandHappiness.com

Variations

- The teacher can model the activity by talking about a picture of something that they really appreciate. This can also be used as a simple comprehension activity in which learners are then asked to recall the five things the teacher said about the topic.
- To reduce the risk of chaos, in Step 3 the class can be arranged using the **donut arrangement** in which half the class (the A group) spreads out and forms an outer circle, standing around the classroom and facing inwards. Once they have done this, the other half of the class (the B group) pairs up with members of A facing towards their partners. Thus we have two circles of learners, one outer circle (A) and one inner circle (B). When the learners are ready to move to a new partner, this arrangement allows for orderly and efficient movement. Group A is instructed to stay where they are for the whole activity. Group B simply moves one "click" clockwise to face a new partner, and so on for as many times as the activity needs to be repeated.
- Lower proficiency learners can be given time to write out five sentences about their topic, but should be discouraged from reading these sentences aloud when talking about their pictures. This planning time allows them to access a dictionary or the teacher for help with language gaps.
- Alternatively, the learners can be asked to write a short description of their chosen topic after they have finished talking about it. This way, the talking steps can be thought of as generating ideas and rehearsing in preparation for writing.

- The teacher may ask for one or two volunteers to talk about their picture to the class for the purpose of further modelling and also to highlight learnable language points, perhaps through corrective feedback to the presenters.

Activity 2: Class Happiness Poem

The class happiness poem is deceptively simple but can produce some inspired performances from groups of learners when they are asked to perform their poem in front of the class. The activity described below is a variation of the activity from Clare (2016: 53).

The activity starts with the teacher introducing the topic of happiness and then asking learners to close their eyes and think of something that makes them happy. They then each write a simple sentence about one example of what happiness is for them. The teacher can provide an example such as:

> Happiness is ... walking barefoot on a windy beach

To strengthen the language learning dimension of the activity, learners can be required to use a particular feature of grammar such as the gerund (as in the example above). Learners are then put into groups of four to six learners and asked to rehearse their five sentences as a poem that they will then present to the class as a performance (i.e., standing at the front of the class, and with consideration given to how their poem will sound and what their bodies will be doing). This requires them to think of language in relation to bodily movement, voice quality, and aesthetic qualities such as the sound and flow of their five voices and how they will make this into a simple but seamless performance.

Another learner factor is "engagement", a term widely used in education to refer to student interest and participation in learning activities and in learning communities such as schools and classrooms. Schlecty (1994: 5) describes engagement as the extent to which students are "attracted to their work, persist in it despite challenges and obstacles, and take visible delight in accomplishing their work". It covers four dimensions: behavioural (e.g., being on-task), cognitive (e.g., being attentive), social (e.g., mutuality and willingness to collaborate), and emotional (e.g., enthusiasm and enjoyment). Philp and Duchesne (2016) argue that observing all these dimensions of engagement can help us better understand learning through task-based interaction in language classrooms.

Let us look at an example of engagement that illustrates part of Schlecty's (1994) definition, "visible delight in accomplishing their work", from Newton and Bui (2017: 272). This example is of two young learners in an EFL class at a Vietnamese primary school as they come to the end of a split information activity. In the activity, they had to exchange information from two versions of a school timetable about when different subjects are scheduled without looking at each other's copy of the timetable. In line 1, L1 expresses her satisfaction in completing the task, and then, without prompting from the teacher, the two learners engage in a small piece of genuine communication in English (lines 3–5), before reverting to Vietnamese to again tell the teacher they have finished the task.

S1: Cô ơi xong rồi, cô ơi. [Teacher, we've finished]
S2: Crazy ...
S1: ... What subject do you like best?
S2: Uh ... I like Math. What about you?
S1: I like Vietnamese. Xong rồi cô ơi. [We've finished, teacher]

This is a simple piece of interaction, but one in which these beginner level EFL learners effortlessly move from a structured communication task to natural communication in English. We found no evidence of learners engaging in communication like this in traditional lessons in the same school that followed the PPP approach (presentation, practice, production; Bui, 2019). Here's what one of the learners said about the experience of the split information activities (translated from Vietnamese):

> I like to exchange information about the timetable with my friend. I tried to help my friend understand using the language I knew. This helps me speak English more naturally.
> (Bui, 2019: 181–182)

The teachers who participated in the research in which they adopted task-based lessons instead of PPP agreed. Here's what one of them said (also translated from Vietnamese):

> When involving themselves in the task-based lessons [...] students had to mobilise their vocabulary resources to help them express their ideas. Because they were not provided with the target language items necessary for their communication, they had to make every effort to help their friends understand what they want to say. This could enable a lot of vocabulary words to be mobilised.
> (Bui, 2019: 169)

Let us now look briefly at how learners can be helped in informal speaking before looking in more detail at formal speaking.

Informal Speaking

Informal speaking typically involves tasks where conveying information is not as important as maintaining friendly relationships. Brown (1978) calls this interactional speaking as opposed to transactional speaking. Interactional speaking can be supported in the following ways. This support enables learners to produce what they would not normally be able to produce.

1. Learners can be taught conversational strategies that can help keep the conversation going (Holmes & Brown, 1976). A very useful technique for doing that is called **Q → SA + EI**. What this formula means is a question (Q) should be followed by a short answer (SA) and then some extra information about the answer (EI). So, if someone asks, "How long have you been here?", the reply may be "About 6 months, but I found it very difficult at first". This extra information then provides an opportunity for the person asking the question to continue the conversation, typically by taking up the point raised in the extra information: "What were the difficulties you had?". This very useful strategy deserves quite a lot of practice in class, particularly in guiding learners in the kinds of extra information that they can provide. It is also a good way for the person being questioned to take control of an interview or conversation by using the extra information to guide the direction of the conversation (Nation, 1980).
2. Having a supportive partner in a conversation can make speaking much easier. Learners can be trained to provide support for other speakers. This support can involve supplying unknown words, completing sentences that the speaker has begun, and asking helpful questions to provide language and content support.
3. Repeated tasks can also be a good way of providing support. Initially, the speaking may be difficult, but with repetition it can become easier. Techniques such as **retelling** can provide this kind of repetition. Another useful technique is **pass and talk**. In this activity, each learner has a card with a task on it. The tasks can involve describing something in a picture or in the classroom, saying something about another person in the group, mentioning an item from the current news, or expressing an opinion on something. Each learner in the group has to perform the task aloud. After each learner has completed their task, the cards are passed around from hand to hand until the teacher says stop. Then, each learner must perform the task on the card that they are holding. The passing around should happen several times, meaning that the same tasks are repeated several times.

4. Informal speaking can be prepared for. As people typically speak about their lives, a good way to prepare for this is to get learners to write a diary describing what they did each day. Every few days, the learners get in groups and are asked questions by the others in the group about the content of their diaries.
5. Spoken language uses many more multiword units than written language. It is worthwhile memorising some of the more useful sentence stems, such as, *I see, That's right, Are you sure?, Really?, I haven't seen you for ages, What have you been up to?* (McCarthy & Carter, 2003).

Because most of our speaking tends to be informal speaking, this deserves attention within the classroom.

Formal speaking is affected by all the performance conditions of planning, time pressure, support, and standard of performance described above. We will now look at formal speaking in detail to see how learners can be helped with such speaking. Focusing on formal speaking also provides an excellent opportunity for learners to become aware of what is involved in speaking effectively and can lead to the development of useful planning and delivery strategies.

Formal Speaking

Formal speaking helps language learning in the following ways. It may represent a new use of English for most learners and thus requires them to focus on language items that are not as well represented in other uses of the language (Biber, 1989). Formal speaking requires control of content, awareness of a largely passive audience, and being the focus of attention (a rather unsettling experience). It thus requires learners to use language under difficult and demanding circumstances, which will stretch the boundaries of skill development.

In a study of first language speakers of English, Brown, Anderson, Shillcock, and Yule (1984) identified the following ways of getting learners to develop their skill in taking a long turn:

1. Learners should experience the task from the listeners' point of view. This enables them to notice things that they should avoid in their own spoken presentation and helps develop a sense of having an audience.
2. The learners should have the opportunity to work through a series of spoken tasks that gradually increase in complexity. There are several aspects that affect complexity. These include the amount of preparation available; whether the task involves describing a "static" display or "dynamic" process; and the number of items, characters, or points to deal with in the information they are presenting. The performance conditions described above also affect the complexity of the task.

The Nature of Formal Speaking

Some of the most valuable resources available for helping learners understand the nature of formal speaking are TED talks, and especially the set of talks provided on the TED website under the title "Great TED Talks for language practice".[1] Although TED talks are only one kind of formal speaking, and their purpose is equally to inform and entertain, they nevertheless provide valuable models of how to structure and pace a talk; how to use movement, gesture, and facial expression; and how to use slides to support a talk.

Speaking as a part of work or academic study may involve presenting reports or presenting a viewpoint on a particular topic. This type of speaking has several important features (Brown, 1981):

1. It is transactional. That is, its purpose is to communicate information rather than to maintain social contact as is the case with most interactional speaking.
2. It involves taking a long turn. That is, it is not usually presented as a dialogue but requires speaking for several minutes in a comprehensible and organised way.
3. It is influenced by written language. Often it will involve speaking from notes and will involve academic vocabulary.
4. The speaking is done in the learner's "careful" style in a clear and deliberate way with opportunity for the speaker to monitor the production.
5. It often needs to be taught as it is a skill that is not a part of typical language use.

These features have implications for teaching. Let us look at each of them in turn.

Teaching Formal Speaking

The transactional nature of formal speaking means that the effectiveness of the learners' performance should focus on the successful communication of information. Formal speaking opportunities in the classroom should, therefore, be done with an obvious audience who are interested in the speaker's message. The physical arrangement of the room can affect this. The speaker should face the audience, who are sitting in rows or perhaps a horseshoe arrangement. The learners can present **prepared talks** that they give in front of the class or in their group. It is a good idea to have a time limit for the talk, but then to let people ask as many questions as they wish. If the other learners know the subject of the talk, they can prepare questions before the talk begins. To help learners develop strategies and skills for responding to audience questions, the **unpredictable audience activity** can be used. Before a student gives a talk, the teacher distributes four or five question cards around the class, with each card specifying the kind of question to be asked. The cards reflect the difficult kinds of question that sometimes get asked, such as the following:

- Ask a question about an implication of the topic
- Ask a question in a quiet voice so that it is difficult to hear
- Ask a question about information already covered in the talk
- Make a critical comment on some aspect of the talk
- Ask a question that is on the topic of the talk but is not relevant to the purpose of the talk.

This activity gives learners the chance to develop strategies for responding politely to inappropriate or misguided questions.

If the learners are working in small groups, the members of the group can help each other prepare their talks. During each class, one or two people can give their talks. The talks may be used as a way of reporting outside reading. Two people may talk on the same subject. One talks in favour of that subject, and the other talks against it, somewhat like a small debate (Deyes, 1973). It is best if the learners do not write out their talk and read it, but use short notes to remind themselves of what they want to say. If the class consists of adults in the workforce, they can talk about their jobs or some aspects of their experience.

Formal speaking involves taking long turns. Many native speakers find this difficult, and so learners need to be aware of the ways of organising a long turn so that it most effectively achieves its goals. This gives a high priority to planning the turn. This planning can be done in several ways:

1. The speaker can look at the ideas that will be presented and find an effective way of organising them. This will usually require very good knowledge of the content matter of the talk.
2. The speaker can use a standard rhetorical framework for organising the ideas. For example, when presenting a description of something, the speaker can present a feature followed by two examples, the next feature and two examples, and so on. If the speaker is defending a viewpoint, the speaker could proceed by systematically eliminating the arguments against that point of view.
3. The speaker can use a standard information framework, such as topic type (see Appendix B). Thus, when describing how to do something, the speaker describes the materials needed, the tools needed, the steps to go through, with cautions and conditions mentioned at some steps, and then the final result, as in the instruction topic type.

4. Group planning activities can be very useful in providing help for a speaker. **Moderation** is an interesting way of doing this. The teacher writes a topic for discussion on large sheets of paper and distributes one to each group of learners. The learners write their ideas about the topic on post-it notes and then discuss and organise their ideas by clustering the post-it notes on the sheet of paper. If a person disagrees with an idea, that person says "Objection!", and that objection is written on a different coloured piece of paper and placed next to the idea. Then, the learners think of headings for each cluster. The headings are written on pieces of paper and are added to the large sheet. The next step is for the learners to work on the relative importance of the clusters of ideas. Each learner is given two or three stickers to put on the headings they think are most important. Instead of clusters, a scale or a matrix can be used (Purvis, 1983). This could be done as a **poster carousel** activity, with each group posting its sheet of paper on the wall, and the groups circulating to look at the ideas produced by other groups. This information is then used as the basis for planning a talk.

Formal talks may be scripted. That is, they may initially be in a written form. It is not usually desirable for the talk to consist of simply reading a written paper aloud. Learners thus need to get practice in preparing notes and speaking from brief notes. To encourage this, it may be necessary to use a **pyramid procedure** (Jordan, 1990). This means that the learner works alone to prepare the notes for a talk. Then, the learner presents the talk to one learner using the notes, and gets feedback from that learner about the talk. Then, using a shorter form of the notes, the learner presents the talk to a small group of three or four learners. Finally, the talk is presented to the whole class, using only brief note cards. The practice before the class presentation reduces the need for the notes.

Learners need unthreatening opportunities to speak carefully on topics they know well. They need feedback on what aspects they need to monitor.

Learners need graded tasks, the chance to be listeners in order to get a consumer's view of formal speaking, and a systematic approach to planning and presenting formal talks. These are nicely combined in the **serials** activity. The learners work in groups to prepare a story that will be told part by part over several days. Each group prepares a different part of the story, and the other groups respond to each part of the story, saying whether it is interesting, well presented, and so on (Hirvela, 1987). The starting point for the story can be a picture (tell the life story of this person), a personal account, a folk tale, a story from a graded reader, or a dramatisation of a newspaper story. Because the learners have the opportunity to be both speakers and listeners, they can develop their understanding of what is involved in making a spoken presentation.

Student mini-podcasts[2] are a useful activity for developing learners' ability to deliver semi-formal sustained talks that require academic vocabulary and critical thinking, and so are particularly good for teaching academic English. The following steps are involved:

1. The teacher and class decide on a range of issues related to a topic the class has studied (e.g., on the topic of work–life balance, issues might include workload, gender differences, a minimum wage, etc.). The teacher may want to provide guidelines to help students structure their talk (e.g., agree/disagree plus two reasons).
2. Each student, in their own time, uses their mobile phone to rehearse and record a brief talk giving an opinion on the topic.
3. They upload their talks to a shared platform such as Blackboard or Google Docs.
4. Students listen to and comment on each other's talks.
5. The teacher also listens and comments or gives feedback.

Table 8.1 summarises the main points covered in this section and can act as a checklist for ensuring that a suitable range of activities has been covered to help with formal speaking.

A Process Approach to Formal Speaking

Because formal speaking is usually a planned activity, it is possible to take a process approach to it. This means dividing the task into parts such as taking account of the goals and the audience, gathering ideas, organising ideas, making a set of speaking notes, designing PowerPoint slides, and presenting and monitoring the talk (see the companion volume to this book, *Teaching ESL/EFL Reading and Writing*, for a process approach to writing using very similar parts of the process).

An important part of the formal speaking process is taking account of the audience and the suitability of the information that is to be conveyed

Table 8.1 Features of Formal Speaking and Their Implications

Features	Implications for teaching
Transactional	Focus on successful communication to an audience
Long turn	Give a high priority to planning
Written influence	Practise making and using notes
Careful style	Provide well-prepared opportunities to speak carefully
Needs to be taught	Use graded tasks and give learners the chance to be listeners

to them. This involves considering questions such as: Which parts of my information will be the most useful for the audience? Which parts will be difficult for them to understand? What do I want them to gain from my talk? Speakers can gain an awareness of the audience by having experience of being part of the audience, by getting questions and feedback from the audience, and by observing the audience's reactions during a talk. Table 8.2 relates activities and supports for the various parts of the formal speaking process. Taking a process approach is effectively encouraging learners to develop a strategy for dealing with formal speaking. Thus, when a teacher takes this approach, learners should be made aware of the parts of the process and how they can take control of them.

It is useful for members of a language class to present talks to each other so that they experience both the roles of speaker and listener. It is also useful to take part in tasks where there is immediate evidence of whether the speaker understands or not. This can be done with extended **listen and do** type tasks, or with a restatement type of activity such as

Table 8.2 Tasks for Learning the Parts of the Process of Formal Speaking

Parts of the process	Tasks
Goals and audience	Be a listener
	Analyse good models of formal talks, such as TED talks
	Talk and get audience feedback
	Perform **listen and do** tasks where there is an observable outcome of the talk such as something drawn or made from Lego
Gathering ideas	**Brainstorm** and **What is it like?** in groups
	Follow schema such as topic type or discourse plans to gather information systematically
Organising ideas	Use rhetoric plans
	Discuss and evaluate model outlines
	Use guiding checklists
Making speaking notes	**Information transfer**
	Note-taking
Presenting and monitoring	Talk on your speciality
	4/3/2
	Prepare, talk to a partner, talk to a group, then talk to the class
Designing slides	Compare examples of well-designed and poorly designed slides and draw up guidelines for good slide design

triads. In triads, A and B have a conversation. C is the referee. One topic for discussion is chosen from a list of fairly controversial topics, such as: "Learners should be paid to go to school" or "Money spent on space travel is a waste". A speaks for a short period of time, expressing two or three ideas. B listens carefully, then paraphrases what A said. Both A and C, the referee, listen carefully to B's paraphrase. If B simplifies or changes A's ideas, then either C or A can correct him. If both C and A agree that B's paraphrase is correct, then B may give a few ideas of his own on the discussion topic. A must listen carefully, then paraphrase what B said before she can give more opinions of her own. B and C listen and correct A's paraphrase, and so on. After 5 or 10 minutes, depending on the teacher, the members of the triad change roles, that is, B becomes the referee, and A and C discuss, and a new discussion topic is chosen.

A speaker may have difficulty with a talk because there is little to talk about or the topic is poorly understood. A high level of familiarity with the content of a talk is likely to lead to quality in other aspects such as the presentation, formal correctness, and awareness of audience. So, good preparation for a talk can involve using group work activities to gather and elaborate the information that will be presented. **Brainstorming** is an effective way of doing this. In this activity, learners suggest ideas that are listed uncritically, the main goal being to get as many ideas as possible. Later, the ideas are organised and evaluated. An advantage of brainstorming is that it can result in a very diverse collection of ideas. A much more focused way of gathering ideas involves using information schema or self-questioning scales to gather information systematically. Appendix B lists one such set of schema (see *Teaching ESL/EFL Reading and Writing*, Nation & Macalister, 2020b, for more on topic types). So, for example, if the talk was about an exciting event, the state/situation topic type could be used. This involves these questions:

- Who are the people involved?
- When and where did it happen?
- What were the background causes?
- What happened?
- What are the things likely to happen as a result?

Organising ideas clearly relates closely to awareness of the audience and the getting of ideas, and, in preparing a talk, there could be continual movement between these parts of the process. Is it best to begin the talk with a complete overview, or is it most suitable to begin with an example? Should the talk be divided into quite separate sections? In making such decisions, it is useful to look at how others have organised their talks, or rhetorical models such as description by exemplification or argument by the elimination of alternatives.

Most people speak using written notes as a guide, either written on paper or in the notes section of a slide presentation. These probably offer a feeling of security as much as they offer guidance. Learners should practise being able to prepare and present from brief notes. For any particular talk, this may mean starting from quite elaborate notes and, with practice, reducing them. Even very experienced speakers welcome the opportunity to practise their talks with a supportive audience.

The **pyramid procedure** and procedures involving a changing audience such as **4/3/2** can provide opportunities for repetition, with the speaker using an increasingly reduced form of notes each time. **Information transfer** grids and diagrams are useful forms of notes to guide speaking. Owing to their structured nature, they give the speaker a systematic route to follow and allow the audience to predict what will come.

Presenting and monitoring the talk, like all the other parts of the formal speaking process, can be planned for and practised. Repeated opportunity to present is important here. Tactfully designed and used checklists are also useful. Feedback on presentation should lead learners to reconsider other parts of the formal speaking process.

Guidelines for Presenting a Formal Talk

The following guidelines for presenting a formal talk take account of the importance of monitoring the attention of the audience and communicating a clear message.

1. The message should be limited to three or four major pieces of information. For example, if the talk is about the speaker's country, the speaker could limit the main points to three or four features that are most striking about the country. In the case of Singapore, these may be: (1) the importance of its location, (2) its multiracial nature, and (3) its strong social policies. These three or four pieces of information should be emphasised by presenting them in a written form as well as a spoken form, by numbering them or signalling them in some other way ("The first important feature is …"), and by repeating them in a final summary.
2. The speaker should present a *simple* outline of the main points of the talk at the beginning and work through it. This helps the audience keep up with the talk and allows them to anticipate what comes next.
3. There should be three or four changes of the focus of attention during the talk. This means that the whole talk should not consist of the speaker talking to the audience. The changes of focus of attention provide a rest for the audience, and the speaker, and thus help to keep their attention. Here are some different foci of attention:

(a) The speaker talks to the audience.
(b) The speaker asks the audience questions.
(c) The audience question the speaker.
(d) The audience talk to each other in pairs.
(e) One of the audience talks to the rest of the audience.
(f) The audience study a slide, see a short film or watch a demonstration.

If there are too many changes, the audience may lose track of the main message. Here are some examples of the changes in focus of attention used during a complete talk on the sound system of English:

(a) The audience listened to the speaker.
(b) The audience worked on transcribing a few items and reported back to the speaker.
(c) The audience listened to the speaker again.
(d) The audience questioned the speaker.

Note in this example that there were two opportunities for the speaker to talk to the audience, but there was a change in the focus of attention between these two opportunities, so that the second opportunity to talk to the audience was regarded as another change in the focus of attention.In a talk on his work as a drug enforcement officer, the following changes occurred:

(a) The audience listened to the speaker.
(b) The audience worked in pairs preparing questions.
(c) The audience questioned the speaker.
(d) The audience listened to the speaker.

Note, in both examples, the sessions began with the audience listening to the speaker. There are two reasons for doing this. At the beginning of the talk, the audience is likely to be most attentive and rested, and so this is a good time to get the main points across. Second, the audience are there to listen to the speaker, and so the speaker should show that he has interesting and useful information to present and thus establish credibility with the audience. Note in the second example how the speaker made sure that he would be asked questions, by getting the audience to work in pairs to prepare questions. He introduced the working in pairs by saying this:

> Many people have seen films about the work of drug enforcement officers. The films usually only show the most exciting and often unusual parts of their work. Talk to your neighbour about what you think my work might involve and prepare a question to ask me about it.

4. The audience should be involved in the talk by having a chance to participate through asking questions, providing feedback, and responding to tasks. There are three reasons for this. First, it keeps the attention of the audience. Second, it provides feedback for the speaker about whether the learners are following the talk, where they have difficulty, and what any are interested in. Third, it improves the quality of the information, particularly if some of the audience are already well informed on the topic.

Presenting a formal talk is a worthwhile skill, and it is one that many native speakers have difficulty in learning. It is, however, an important skill and also an important source of language learning opportunities.

Monitoring Formal Talks

The process division of the formal speaking task (shown in Table 8.2) provides a useful basis for monitoring and providing helpful formative feedback. When listening to formal talks, both teachers and learners can look analytically to see where the strengths and weaknesses of the speaker lie.

Goals and Audience

- Is the speaker showing awareness of the audience through the use of appropriate language, pace of presentation, and shared experience?
- Is the speaker's goal clear?

Ideas

- Has the speaker enough relevant things to talk about?
- Is the speaker trying to present too much information?

Organisation

- Is the talk well organised?
- Is the organisation of the talk clear to the listeners?

Notes

- Is the speaker talking to the audience?

Presentation

- Is the delivery fluent?
- Does the speaker keep the attention of the listeners?

- Are there enough changes of focus of attention?
- Are the slides well designed?

Learners should be encouraged to reflect on their own formal speaking, noting what they do well and where they need to make improvement.

Another kind of long turn is conversational story-telling (Jones, 2001) where, during a conversation, someone tells of an incident that happened to them.

Formal speaking pushes learners in their output. It is worth remembering, however, that formal monologue is typically only a small part of most people's speaking.

Speaking with others, as we have seen, can push learners in their output and make them notice gaps in their knowledge. In Chapter 7, on learning through task-based interaction, we saw how negotiation can push learners to change their output and can provide encouragement for speaking skills to develop. Many of the activities described there are very useful for pushing learners' output. Thus, although this chapter has largely focused on formal speaking, this is only one part of a balanced programme in helping learners to learn through speaking.

Tasks

1. In groups of three, practise supportive listening (use the checklist on page 146).
2. Practise using the Q → SA + EI strategy.
3. Here is the beginning of a list of topics that could be used in informal speaking. Add at least five topics to the list to suit your learners' needs:

    The weather
    A movie you have just seen
    A friend who just left to live in another town
    ...

4. Choose one of the TED talks that TED recommends for language learners. Watch it and identify ways you could use this as a resource in a lesson on formal speaking.

Further Reading

Eslbase provides a valuable guide to using role plays, along with many other ESL resources: www.eslbase.com/teaching/esl-roleplay

Hughes and Reed (2016) is a useful guide to research and teaching on speaking.

Nation (1980) looks at the Q → SA + EI procedure and how it can be applied in interviews.

Marc Helgesen is a professor in the Department of Modern Business at Miyagi Gakuin Women's University, Sendai, Japan. His website provides a wealth of communicative activities that draw on principles from positive psychology: https://helgesenhandouts.weebly.com/john–marcs-jalt-2016-presentation-handouts.html

Notes

1 www.ted.com/playlists/655/great_ted_talks_for_language_practice
2 Thanks to Alison Hamilton-Jenkins and Ha Hoang, teachers in the Victoria University of Wellington English Proficiency Programme, for sharing this idea.

9 Teaching Using a Course Book

Many teachers of English as a foreign language work from a course book, often because they are required to do so. Unfortunately, a course book cannot provide enough material to let learners develop their language proficiency to a high enough level. This is mainly because a course book cannot provide the large quantities of extensive reading and extensive listening within a controlled vocabulary that are needed to get enough repetitions of the vocabulary, word groups, and grammatical features that learners need to learn. Deliberate learning can help, but this needs to go with lots of opportunities to use the language across the four skills of listening, speaking, reading, and writing. Course books also cannot provide enough fluency development material, especially for reading fluency, to strengthen knowledge and to help learners make the best use of what they already know. McLarty (2019) provides a useful list of the positive and negative aspects of course books, including the types of additional material that teachers use.

In this chapter, we look at how a teacher can use the material in a course book, and we look at what needs to be done in addition to course book work. We will focus mainly on listening and speaking, but we will also look briefly at the role of the course book in teaching reading and writing, and in relation to vocabulary and grammar. Finally, in this chapter, we look at the importance of repetition in learning and suggest a variety of ways in which the teacher can build repetition into a course, particularly when using a course book.

The most important job of the language teacher is to plan a good language programme with plenty of opportunities for learning; with a good balance of the four skills of listening, speaking, reading, and writing; and with a good balance of studying the language and using the language. Each of the four skills should get about the same amount of time in a language programme. In each of the four skills, about three-quarters of the time should involve using the language as in extensive listening, extensive reading, speaking, and writing, and one quarter of the time should involve studying the language, such as learning vocabulary, studying grammar, doing intensive listening, including dictation and listening to sounds, and doing exercises in the course book. Figure 9.1 is designed so

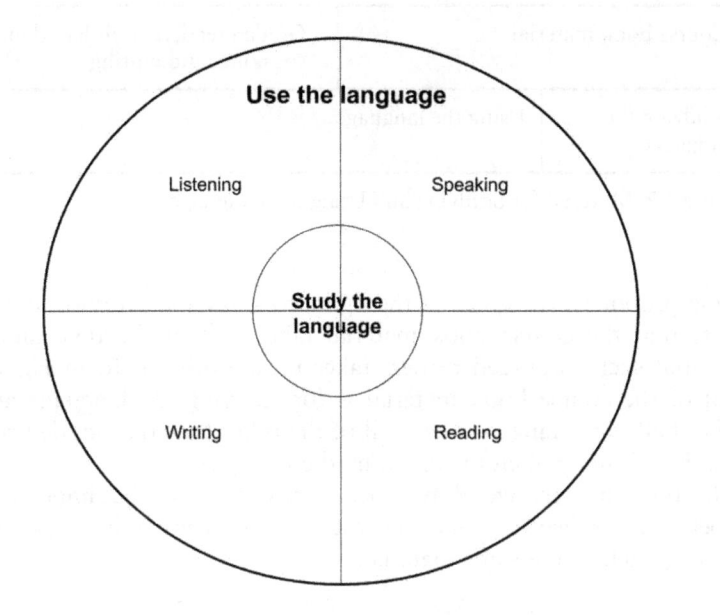

Figure 9.1 Proportion of Time to Spend on Using and Studying the Four Skills

that the amount of space given to each part of the figure represents the amount of time that should be given to each skill of listening, speaking, reading, and writing, and to using and studying the language. Note that equal time is given to listening, speaking, reading, and writing, and studying the language gets much less time than using the language.

Most language courses and course books have too much of studying the language and not enough of using the language. Teachers do too much teaching and not enough letting their learners listen, speak, read, and write.

It is not necessary to have a good balance of the four skills in every lesson, and it is not necessary to have one quarter of the time in each lesson for studying and being taught and three-quarters of the time for using the language. However, if we look at all the lessons for 2 weeks or a month or more, over all of those lessons there should be a balance of the four skills, and there should be about one quarter study and teaching and three-quarters using the language.

A lot of the work in the course book involves studying the language, but, in a good course book, at least half of the material can involve language use. If the course book contains most of the material for study and teaching, then about half of the class time should involve the course book, and the other half should involve other material such as graded readers for extensive reading, extensive listening material, and opportunities for communicative speaking and writing. Figure 9.2 shows this

Course book material		Graded readers, web-based material, speaking, and writing
Studying the language	Using the language	

Figure 9.2 Material for Studying and Using the Language

using proportion of space in the figure to show the proportion of time. Note that the course book material takes half of the time and other material such as graded readers takes up the other half. In Figure 9.2, half of the course book material is for studying the language and the other half is for language use. All of the other material (graded readers, web-based material etc) is for using the language.

In this chapter, we draw special attention to the importance of repetition for learning and suggest ways of getting learners to keep coming back to the same material.

Listening and the Course Book

Most course books for beginners include some of the survival vocabulary, especially greetings and talking about yourself. Often, this material for listening and speaking is in the form of a conversation. Box 9.1 shows an example from Nation (2019: Book 1).

Box 9.1 A Course Book Conversation Activity

A Listen

Parker: *Hi.*
Morgan: *Hi.* I'm Morgan. Morgan Harris.
Parker: My name is Parker Leeds.
Morgan: *Nice to meet you,* Parker.
Parker: *It's nice to meet you, too.*
Morgan: *What's your last name again?*
Parker: It's Leeds. L-E-E-D-S.
Morgan: Leeds. Got it.

B **Practise the conversation with a partner.**

How can you use this material for listening? The first step is to make sure that the learners understand this conversation. Briefly talking about it in the first language is a quick and useful way to do this. The second step is for the learners to listen to it at least three or four times. During the first times, the learners should try to understand it. If you have a recording of the conversation and you can change the speed of the playback, let the learners listen slowly first and then go a bit faster the next times. If you do not have a recording, read it aloud slowly and clearly for the learners. The third step is to get the learners to say the conversation. Get two or three learners to individually repeat after you. Correct any pronunciation errors. When you think the learners can say each sentence clearly enough, get them to practise in pairs.

Notice that this practice does not involve the learners all saying the conversation together after the teacher. All the practice involves individuals or pairs. There are several reasons for not doing group speaking. In individual speaking, the teacher and the other learners can clearly hear what the learner says. In group speaking, mistakes are hidden. Also, in individual speaking, the speaker needs to speak carefully because others are listening.

The goal of the teacher is to get the learners to listen to the conversation at least ten times during the lesson. This is because repetition helps learning. The more repetitions, the more likely learning is to occur.

The fourth step is to help the learners memorise the conversation. After they have worked in pairs looking at their course books, get them to write one or two words from each line of the conversation on a piece of paper (or you write them on the whiteboard). They close their books and then use their memory and what is written on the piece of paper to repeat the conversation in pairs. When this is easy, they put away the piece of paper and then say the conversation in pairs from their memory. After the whole class has worked in pairs for a while, the teacher should ask two or three pairs to say the conversation, while the rest of the class listens.

A course book does not usually contain enough opportunities for extensive listening practice. Learners need to know where they can get more listening practice, and teachers need to provide activities in addition to the course book. There are many websites that provide listening material for learners of English. You can get the learners to search for them by searching for *EFL listening* and *easy ESL listening*. With most of the listening materials on the internet, the learners should be able to control the speed of the material. In YouTube, you click on the circular cog icon at the bottom right of the screen and choose *Speed*. In Windows Media Player, you right-click to open the menu and choose *Enhancements*, and then choose *Play speed settings*. Learners should keep a brief list of the listening that they do on the internet and should tell the teacher and their classmates about listening material that they really liked and found useful.

Repeated listening is one way of increasing the quantity of listening. It involves listening to the same material over and over again until it is well understood. Learners can do this on their mobile phones. Such listening can include popular songs in English. The lyrics are usually available on the internet; just type in the name of the song, followed by the word *lyrics*. The lyrics can be studied before listening and can be read while listening. Movies are also good for repeated listening, but, if learners do not have a vocabulary size of at least 2000 words, there may be too many unknown words for the learners to deal with. Movie scripts and scripts of TV programmes may be available on the internet. There are also websites that present talks intended for learners of English. Listening Spotlight presents short texts in easy English spoken very slowly. Ted Talks are more difficult but use subtitles to help listening. The Voice of America presents news material using a controlled vocabulary.

If your learners have English for 4 hours a week, then, for a month, there will be 4 hours of listening. About half of the material in a course will come from the course book and about half from graded readers and other material. So, 2 hours of the 4 hours for listening will involve the course book, and 2 hours will involve other material. Of the 4 hours of listening each month, 3 hours should involve extensive listening, and 1 hour should involve intensive listening. You might decide that, twice a week, at the beginning of the class you will do the extensive listening activity of listening to stories. Your learners are likely to enjoy this activity, and it may help to get them to class on time. For almost the whole of a 1-hour class, you might decide to do extensive listening, getting the learners to find listening material on the internet or doing listening while reading. This hour is largely to train the learners how to find and do such listening so that they can do it by themselves later, outside class time. So far, that has used about 2 hours of listening time for the month—that is, 1 hour of listening on the internet and eight short periods of listening to stories.

Around 2 hours can be spent on listening material in the course book. About half of that should be intensive listening, and the other half extensive listening. In Figure 9.3, in Row 2, we can see that work in the course book makes up half of the 4 hours. In Row 3, we can see that half of the course book work involves studying the language and half of the course book work involves using the language through extensive listening. In Row 4, we can see the activities that might be used.

The course book work for studying the language for listening might involve memorising conversations, answering questions based on listening, dictation, filling the blanks while listening, and intensive listening led by the teacher explaining the listening texts. The course book work for using the language might involve listening to texts, repeated listening, and practising memorised conversations.

The extensive listening work outside the course book might involve regular listening to stories, listening on the internet, and listening while reading a graded reader. The activities for extensive listening work outside the course book need a little preparation at the beginning, but largely involve the teacher making sure that the learners do the work.

1	2	3	4
Course book		Graded readers and other material	
Studying the language	Using the language—extensive listening		
Answering questions Dictation Filling the blanks Intensive listening	Listening to texts Repeated listening Conversations	Listening to stories Listening on the internet Listening while reading	

Figure 9.3 Four Hours of Listening Using Course Book Material and Other Material

Speaking and the Course Book

Most course books contain useful conversations that learners can memorise and practise. It is important to help learners achieve clear pronunciation of the sentences and words in the conversations. The most useful ways of doing this are to get the learners to listen to the conversations several times and to guide them in what to listen to. Guiding the learners involves getting them to focus on individual sounds and on the stress and intonation of phrases and sentences.

Most course books have useful conversations for the learners to memorise. Box 9.2 contains an example from *Fast Track* (Nation, 2019: Book 1, Unit 3).

Box 9.2   A Conversation Activity from a Course Book

Listen

A: Our group thought of three famous _movies_.
B: What are they?
A: They are _The Matrix, La La Land,_ and _Coco_.
B: Have you _seen_ all of those?
A: Yes, I have. In fact, I've _watched Coco three times_.
B: Is that your favorite _movie_?
A: No, it's not.
B: What's your favorite _movie_?
A: That would be _Pacific Rim_.

Practise the conversation with a partner.
Use the given ideas in the conversation above or use your own ideas.

When the learners first meet this conversation, they need to understand it, listen to it two or three times (there is a recording of it), and then practise it in pairs with a partner. This practice should involve saying the conversation two or three times. The next part of the lesson involves saying the conversation, changing some of the ideas in it. The places to change are underlined. The teacher should leave this part for another lesson. When doing the next unit, the teacher should come back to the same conversation. The learners can practise it in pairs again and then they can do it again, changing some of the underlined parts, but keeping to the topic of movies. The teacher should get one or two pairs to perform for the rest of the class to listen to, so that it is clear what they have to do. After a few minutes of pair work on this, the teacher then moves on to the parts of the new unit, Unit 4 (see Figure 9.4). About a week or more later, when the learners are working on Unit 5, the teacher should come back to the same conversation from Unit 3 again. This time, the learners can make new substitutions, talking about TV shows rather than movies. After a few minutes of this, the learners carry on with Unit 5. A week or two later, when they are working on Unit 7, the teacher should come back to the same conversation from Unit 3 again. This time, the learners make substitutions based on video games or board games, as suggested in the course book. Now, the learners have met the same conversation four different times—first in Unit 3, next when they are up to Unit 4, again when they are up to Unit 5, and again when they are up to Unit 7. It would be good to practise it again when the learners are up to another unit such as Unit 10, making a total of five spaced repetitions. Also, during each of the five spaced meetings with the same conversation, the learners practise it two or three times. This means that the learners practise the same or a very similar conversation at least 15 times.

The reason for having these many meetings is because repetition is very important for learning, and spaced repetition is particularly important. Notice also that, although there are many exact repetitions, there are also repetitions where the learners change what they are saying in small ways. This adds quality to the repetitions by varying them. Varied repetitions are particularly useful for learning. We will look at repetition again at the end of this chapter.

Speaking activities involve learners working together, and so, usually, speaking activities need to occur in class time. But, by utilising technology,

Unit 3 (first meeting)	Unit 4	Unit 5	Unit 7	Unit 10
2 or 3 repetitions	2 or 3 repetitions	2 or 3 repetitions	2 or 3 repetitions	2 or 3 repetitions

Figure 9.4 An Example of Massed and Spaced Repetitions of a Course Book Conversation

the teacher can create opportunities for speaking practice outside the classroom. For example, the teacher can compile a set of short speaking activities such as those described earlier in this book and upload them to the class website. Learners pair up or get into groups outside class time and record themselves completing a set number of activities each week. Where students live on or near their school or campus, the tasks can be completed face to face. In other situations, they can be completed online using video and audio conferencing such as Skype or Zoom, or via a social media app. The recordings are uploaded to the class website, where the teacher can check completion and give feedback, and where learners can listen to each other's performances. To build on learning from a course book, the topics for these talks can be set to reflect course book topics.

Most course books provide a good variety of speaking activities, and the teacher just needs to make sure that the learners have repeated opportunities to revisit speaking activities from previous parts of the course book so that they do not forget what they have studied and so that they get fluent at using what they have learned. A simple way to keep a record of revisiting old parts of lessons is for the teacher to tick each part of a unit in the course book each time that the learners have a chance to redo it. The aim should be to revisit each important part around five times during a year.

Learners need to prepare their personal record of speaking material, both in class and for homework. These sheets should contain sentences and phrases that they are likely to use often. They need to keep adding to them and changing them as their needs for language use change. Spoken fluency in the early stages of language learning will largely depend on the amount of material that learners have understood, memorised, and repeatedly practised. As learners' knowledge of the language increases, they can move from memorised material to freer production of language.

Wolf (2013) found a motivation and confidence advantage for learners choosing their own topics for discussion compared with using topics suggested by the course book. There thus seems to be value in getting learners to choose their own topics for discussion, as long as this does not have negative effects on recycling course book material to enhance learning through repetition.

Reading and the Course Book

Course books typically contain small amounts of reading, involving short passages that are followed by various related activities, including comprehension questions.

Course books cannot deal with extensive reading because the amount of extensive reading that learners need to do is much too large to fit into a course book, and ideally learners should have some choice in what they read. In addition, the learners in a class are likely to be at a range of proficiency levels, and, in extensive reading, each learner needs to read at the level that is right for them.

Similarly, reading fluency development requires several thousand words of reading material, and this is too much to easily fit into a typical course book that covers the four skills. There are fluency development course books that consist largely of fluency development material. There is also free reading fluency material available on the internet (see Sonia Millett's speed-reading material on LALS resources page at https://www.wgtn.ac.nz/lals/resources).

Course books usually focus on vocabulary, grammar, and comprehension in relation to reading. Teachers may wish to add to the intensive reading activities in the course book, for example, by translating the reading passages. For most course books, it is usually not a good idea to do this, because course books usually already spend enough time on intensive reading. It would be much more useful to spend the extra time on extensive reading.

Very few course books provide training in reading strategies, and this training would be a useful addition to a course book. An important part of this training would involve making learners aware of the value of extensive reading and how to do it. Strategy training could also involve guessing word meanings from context, and dictionary use.

Writing and the Course Book

Writing activities in course books usually focus on guided writing, where the topic and framework for the writing are already provided, and the learners have to make changes within the framework. Box 9.3 has an example from *Fast Track* (Nation, 2019: Book 1, Unit 5).

Box 9.3 A. Study the writing example. Then fill in the blanks with the correct information

What I really like to eat is spicy rice cake. That is a kind of snack food from Korea. Some restaurants make it, but I prefer to get it from street carts. My favorite place to eat it is near the subway station. They cook other things there like soup and grilled chicken. Those aren't as good as the spicy rice cake in my opinion.

bakery   cheese   pastry   bakes   favorite   recommend

One of my _____ foods is called pirozhki. This is a kind of _____ made in Russia. There is a _____ near my home that makes them. My favorite kind has _____ in it. That bakery also sells all kinds of special breads. If you're looking for really good bread, I _____ Good Grains Bakery.

In guided activities, some of the work is already done for the learners. In the example from *Fast Track* in Box 9.3 (Nation, 2019), the model is provided with the necessary grammatical constructions, and the learners have to put the given vocabulary in the right place. This activity has a correct answer and so is easy to mark.

A well-balanced writing course includes opportunities for writing across a range of purposes and text types. These could include taking notes from written text or lectures, writing academic assignments, writing stories, texting, writing in social media, writing friendly letters and emails, filling in forms, and writing business letters and emails. These kinds of writing all involve the strand of meaning-focused output. They also contain chances to do careful writing and to do extensive writing.

A well-balanced writing course also includes deliberate attention to the language features of writing and skills and strategies in writing. These can involve doing copying and guided writing, analysing written texts, learning procedures for checking the grammatical accuracy of written work, and getting feedback on writing. A well-balanced writing course also involves the chance to become fluent in the most useful kinds of writing.

Vocabulary and the Course Book

Most course books are written with some idea of vocabulary control, so that most of the words in the books are useful words. The problem words in course books are the words that are closely related to the particular topic of each unit in the course book. These words are usually very important for understanding the content, but often do not occur in any of the other lessons. For example, in a unit of work on people you might be related to, there will be words such as *ancestors*, *descendants*, *related*, *roots*. These words are important in that unit, but do not occur again in the book. If these words are useful, then the teacher needs to make sure that they are repeated. If some of the words are not so useful for the learners at their present level, the words should be dealt with quickly, perhaps using translation, and no further time should be spent on them.

You can find out if words are useful or not by looking at word lists. You can find carefully prepared word lists on the LALS resources page at https://www.wgtn.ac.nz/lals/resources. If your learners know fewer than 1000 words, then the words from the first 1000 and second 1000 words are the ones they need to learn. If your learners know about 2000 words, then the words from the third and fourth 1000 are the most useful ones for them.

You can measure your learners' vocabulary size by using parts of the updated Vocabulary Levels Test or the new Vocabulary Levels Test. If you teach young learners, you may wish to use the Picture Vocabulary

Size Test. These tests are available free from Paul Nation's website (www.victoria.ac.nz/lals/staff/paul-nation.aspx).

When choosing a course book, it is important to see what level of vocabulary it focuses on. You can check this by using the Vocabprofiler on the Compleat Lexical Tutor website (www.lextutor.ca; choose BNC-COCA 1–25k). Type about thirty of the words that are focused on in the course book into the program, and the program will show you the frequency level of those words.

Multiword Phrases

Just as there are useful high-frequency words, there are also high-frequency multiword phrases, such as *I see, you know, good morning, thank you, at last, as well as, last night*, and *out of the blue*. Most of these multiword phrases can be understood by looking at the meaning of their parts along with their use in context. For a small number of phrases, there seems to be little connection between the meaning of the parts and the meaning of the whole phrase—for example, *as well as, by and large, so and so, out of hand*, and *the Big Apple* (New York). These just have to be learned as whole phrases, but there are only a few of them.

There is a large and always growing and changing group of items where each multiword phrase has a literal meaning and also a figurative meaning. Here are some examples:

- tighten one's belt
- the light at the end of the tunnel
- get the green light
- at the end of the day
- the ball is in your court
- two sandwiches short of a picnic

The literal meaning of *tighten your belt* is to pull the belt around your trousers tighter. The figurative meaning is that you do not have enough (food), but you have to just carry on without worrying about it. The literal meaning of *the light at the end of the tunnel* is the light in the distance that you see when you are walking through a dark tunnel. The figurative meaning is that the end of a piece of work is near. Here is a joke based on both the literal and figurative meanings: "I thought I could see the light at the end of the tunnel, but it was just someone with a torch bringing me the next job to do". The meanings of figurative expressions can be worked out using context and the meaning of the parts. The teacher can help learners to see the connection between the literal and figurative meanings, and talking about this connection and where the figurative expression comes from helps learning. Talking about the connection increases the quality of processing of figurative expressions.

The largest type of multiword phrases is where the meaning of the whole is related to the meaning of the parts. Within this type, there is a range of difficulty where some multiword phrases, such as *fish and chips* and *a lovely day*, are little more than the meanings of their parts, but there are other multiword phrases where the meaning of the whole is not fully clear from the meanings of the parts. Here are some examples of these less clear phrases—*last night, you see, going to, a number of, take place, each other*. These less clear phrases need some explanation when they are first met, and the most frequent ones are well worth memorising using flash cards (see Martinez and Schmitt (2012) for a useful list).

Grammar and the Course Book

Most course books are organised around topics or situations of language use, but some course books follow a grammatical syllabus or also include a grammatical syllabus. The teacher should look for this syllabus in the front or back of the book and make the learners aware of it.

Course books pay attention to grammar through grammatical explanation and identifying parts of speech, and through exercises such as blank filling, joining sentences or parts of sentences, substitution, transforming, and putting words in order. Because important examinations such as entry examinations for universities often pay special attention to grammar, course book writers, teachers, and learners see grammar as being an important part of a language course.

Paying deliberate attention to grammar can have benefits for learning. So, when learners do the grammar-focused activities in course books, the teacher should point out the grammar pattern or rule that lies behind the exercise so that learners are aware of what they are supposed to learn from the activity. One way to do this is for the teacher to go through the answers for the activity with the whole class, explaining the reasons for each answer and dealing with learners' questions about the answers. Another way is to briefly write the grammatical pattern on the whiteboard before the learners do the exercise.

Course books often include lists of useful multiword phrases, called collocations, for learners to memorise. These collocations are easier to remember if learners understand their parts and can see how the words add to the meaning of the whole collocation. Learning collocations is really memorising short pieces of grammar, because the learners do not have to construct the collocation each time they need to produce it or understand it. In the very early stages of language learning, memorising phrases and sentences such as the survival vocabulary is the first step in learning grammar.

Deliberately focusing on grammar is one part of the language-focused learning strand of a course, and it has to share the limited time in this strand with focusing on guided skill activities such as guided listening and guided writing, pronunciation, spelling, vocabulary, collocations, and strategy training. Most of the grammar that learners need to focus on will be covered by a course book, and so the teacher's problem will be making sure that there is not too much time spent focusing on grammar, and that there is plenty of time for meaning-focused input, meaning-focused output, and fluency development. Studying grammar should make up much less than one quarter of one quarter of the total course time. Figure 9.5 uses the four strands to show how much deliberate focus on grammar there should be in a course.

A deliberate focus on vocabulary provides knowledge that is immediately available for language use. A deliberate focus on grammar does not usually do this. Because of this, teachers should limit the time spent focusing on grammar and should make sure that focusing on grammar has clear purposes, such as producing correct sentences, correcting errors, or understanding unfamiliar constructions.

Building Repetition into a Course

Repetition is essential for learning, and one of the main goals that a teacher should have when using a course book is to make sure that there are repeated opportunities to meet the same language items again. One of the easiest ways to do this is to make sure that the same content is repeated several times in the course. This repetition can be **verbatim repetition**, where the same content is repeated with little or no change, or **varied repetition**, where the same content occurs again in a different form.

Teachers need to realise the importance of repetition for learning and need to see that a very important part of their job as a teacher is to make

Meaning-focused input	Extensive listening		Extensive reading	
Meaning-focused output	Speaking		Writing	
Language-focused learning	Sounds & spelling	Vocabulary	Grammar	Strategies and metacognitive awareness, discourse and pragmatics
Fluency development	Listening	Speaking	Reading	Writing

Figure 9.5 The Place of the Study of Grammar in a Well-Balanced Course

sure that new material in the current lesson is repeated, and that the old material from previous lessons keeps coming back, preferably in slightly different ways, so that it has a very good chance of eventually being learned. A large proportion of the time in any lesson should involve working on previously met material again.

Verbatim Repetition

Verbatim repetition involves doing the same task again. It is involved in activities such as repeated reading and 4/3/2, and in these activities the repetition occurs immediately within a single task. Verbatim repetition also occurs when exactly the same task is done again several days or weeks later, as, for example, when re-reading a graded reader, when delivering the same talk again, or when coming back to the same activity in a course book again.

When coming back to the same material in a course book again, the repetition can be kept interesting by doing the activity more quickly, by demanding a high level of accuracy, or by making learners recall much of what they met before.

Varied Repetition

Varied repetition involves meeting or using the same language items again but in different contexts from previous meetings or uses. Varied repetition has also been called *generative use* (Joe, 1998) and *creative use* (Nation, 2013a). Varied repetition within a task occurs in tasks such as linked skills activities, where the learners focus on the same content three times, one after the other, each time using a different skill. For example, they may read a text, then listen to a version of it, and then talk about it with a partner (Nation, 2013c: Chapter 15). Varied repetition of language items can also occur when the content of a task is not repeated—for example, when learners do extensive reading or extensive listening or engage in conversation activities. In this chapter, however, we focus on activities where the content is largely repeated.

The problem facing the teacher is to find ways to vary the repetition of the content enough to encourage varied meetings and use, but to keep the content the same so that repetition of the language features occurs. Table 9.1 provides a list of possibilities for varying the focus on the same content.

The activities in Column 2 of Table 9.1 all involve immediate repetition. Speeded listening involves listening to exactly the same text three times, but each time at a faster speed. Unexploded dictation involves making a written transcription of a spoken text by listening to it or parts of it over and over again. In the **Headlines** activity, each learner thinks of a funny or exciting thing that happened to them and writes a newspaper

Table 9.1 The Different Types of Repetition Activity

	Immediate repetition	Delayed repetition
Verbatim repetition	Speeded listening Unexploded dictation 4/3/2 Headlines The best recording Repeated reading Rewriting with less time	Relistening Retelling Re-reading Rewriting
Varied repetition	Pyramid procedure (think–pair–share) Linked skills Survey tasks Discuss and report Ask and answer Mind map and write Preteaching and listening Varying across outcomes	Varying across group size Recalling through a different skill (listening, speaking, reading and writing) Varying across genre or topic type Varying across dialogue and monologue Varying across the strands with deliberate attention and fluency development Varying across viewpoint (role play) Narrow listening or reading

headline to match. They write their headline in large letters on a piece of paper. Half of the class holds up their headline, while the other half walks around asking to hear their story. They may have to tell their story several times to different listeners. On another occasion, the other half become the story-tellers.

Notice how immediate repetition does not always have to be verbatim repetition. The **pyramid procedure** (Jordan, 1990; Nation, 2013b: 45–46) involves dealing with the same material individually, then in pairs, then in groups, and then with the class as a whole trying to reach agreement on the answer or solution. Many teachers know this as the **think–pair–share** technique. For example, with a problem-solving task, students should first be asked to think individually about the problem and to make notes on possible solutions. This is an important step for increasing the likelihood that all students will have an opinion to share. Teachers too often set a group work task without the individual thinking step. This increases the likelihood that weaker or less confident students will not participate well because of the pressure to think creatively and share ideas at the same time. Next, the students work in pairs, and then small groups, to reach an agreement. The final step involves whole-class work in which groups compare their proposed solutions and the teacher facilitates discussion of the solutions.

The **linked skills** activity involves dealing with the same material through three of the four skills of listening, speaking, reading, and writing—for example, read about something, talk about it, and then write about it.

In **survey tasks**, students work in groups to develop a set of survey questions on a topic they have been given or one they choose to investigate. Once the questions have been settled on, they can be handed to the teacher for feedback and language checking. Or, for lower-proficiency students, the teacher dictates the questions to the class or the class generates a set of questions together with the teacher's guidance. Students then circulate around the class and get answers to the questions or conduct the survey outside class in their school or community. Groups then pool the responses and prepare a report that they present orally or using the **poster carousel** technique.

Survey tasks have at least four strengths. First, almost any topic can provide the basis for a survey, and so they can easily fit with a course book. Second, they are an excellent example of a linked skills activity as they involve speaking, listening, reading, and writing, as well as presentation skills. Third, the survey provides many opportunities for learners to get repeated meaning-focused practice of the same language forms through designing the survey questions, conducting the survey (asking different people the same questions), and reporting their findings. Fourth, learners develop collaborative learning skills through working in groups to develop a survey and then combine and interpret their data.

Here is an example of a survey task adapted from Rossiter, Derwing, Manimtim, and Thompson (2010: 597) called **for or against?**. The teacher and students choose a topic related to the coursebook (e.g., Should the government ban the use of mobile phones by drivers? How can we reduce our environmental footprint?). With the teacher's guidance, students come up with a series of questions on the issue (including open-ended questions), along with openers ("Excuse me, ...") and closers ("Thanks for your time"). Students practise asking and answering the questions among themselves in class. For homework, they gather responses to the survey questions from six English speakers in the community. Results are tallied, reported, and analysed in the following class.

Delayed repetition, Column 3 of Table 9.1, can involve simply doing exactly the same task again at a later time. When retelling and rewriting, the learners may have less support than the first time to encourage retrieval.

In all of these activities, the goal is repetition of language features. Verbatim repetition involves exactly the same language features but requires some focus on speed or accuracy to keep the task interesting. Varied repetition enriches and strengthens knowledge of language features, but the teacher needs to be careful that repetition occurs and that the variation is not so great that the same items are not repeated.

Let us now look at an example of building repetition into a course. Your learners have each prepared a short talk on a topic of their choice. You now want them to have at least five opportunities to repeat this talk, making use of both verbatim and varied repetition, and both immediate and delayed repetition. How could you do this? Table 9.2 suggests a sequence of opportunities.

The example in Table 9.2 does not provide a lot of varied repetition, such as presenting in different genres or using different language skills. However, these could be easily added.

In a language course, time should be spent repeating the same activities and doing activities that recycle the same language and ideas content. Such repeated activities could make up around a third to a half of the total course time. The justification for this proposal is that repetition is essential for learning, and teachers thus must build repetition into their courses. The easiest way to do this is through repeating tasks and through recycling the same content and language in varied tasks. A useful goal would be to make sure that the same significant piece of content occurs five times in the course, involving two or three verbatim repetitions and two or three varied repetitions. Some of these five repetitions should be delayed repetitions.

Progress through a language course should not be about covering the material in the course book or syllabus. It should be about learning. The old material in a lesson is much more important than the new, because

Table 9.2 Presenting the Same Prepared Talk Five Times

Week 1	Week 2	Week 3	Week 4	Week 5 onwards
Present the talk in a pair or small group and get some feedback	Do the 4/3/2 activity	Work with a partner to prepare Ask and answer questions. Practice Ask and answer once	Quickly practice Ask and answer again	Present the talk to the class or a large group and answer questions about the talk
The feedback will provide a small amount of immediate varied repetition	This is a delayed verbatim repetition and also provides three immediate verbatim repetitions	This involves a varied delayed repetition with the question-making, and also involves a varied immediate repetition	A delayed verbatim repetition	A delayed verbatim repetition and an immediate varied repetition with the questions

that old material contains language features that are on the way to being learned, and further attention to them can bring them to the stage of being learned. The new material is just at the first step of being learned and so does not deserve a lot of time or attention. Learning is a cumulative process, with the later steps towards knowledge being most important because of the time already invested and the nearness of the goal.

Course Books and Autonomy

A well-designed language course should help learners learn how to learn. This should involve helping learners develop an understanding of the principles of learning and applying these principles to important learning activities such as extensive reading and extensive listening, deliberate vocabulary learning using flash cards and word part analysis, and the use of fluency development activities. These principles include balancing learning across the four strands, spending time on task, making use of repetition, including quality of processing, and focusing on the most useful language features. These principles and several others are described in Chapter 4 of Macalister and Nation (2021) and they are applied in the free book on Paul Nation's website called *What Do You Need to Know to Learn a Foreign Language?* Course books could easily include short descriptions of important learning principles and how to apply them. Most course books do not do this.

Course books provide a stable focus for a course, and movement through the course book is a clear marker of progress in learning the language. However, course books do not and cannot provide the quantity of material and the balance of opportunities for learning that are needed to learn a language. At best, course books can provide about half of what is needed. The teacher needs to make sure that the other half is provided. This involves substantial amounts of extensive listening and extensive reading. It involves the opportunity for fluency development across each of the four skills of listening, speaking, reading, and writing. This involves systematic deliberate learning of vocabulary and training in strategies that will help learners take control of their own learning.

Tasks

1. Look at a unit from a course book to see the opportunities for extensive listening and extensive reading.
2. Find two places on the internet that provide material that would be useful for extensive listening. Suggest how you could get learners to use this material.
3. Choose an activity from a unit in a course book and suggest ways to vary it in order to keep coming back to it at least five times, at different times.

Further Reading

Learning primarily depends on repetition and the quality of processing each repetition. Nation's (2018) "How vocabulary is learned" looks in detail at repetition and quality of processing. The article is available free from Paul Nation's website under Publications.

Chapter 15 of the book *What Should Every ESL Teacher Know?* is all about the linked skills activity. This activity involves dealing with the same material three times. It is a very useful activity. The book can be downloaded free in electronic form from the Compass Publishing website.

10 Language-focused Learning
Deliberate Teaching

This chapter looks at language-focused learning of vocabulary, grammar, and discourse with the aim of helping learners understand and produce spoken language.

Language-focused learning involves paying attention to features of the language not just for a particular message that they convey, but for their spoken or written form, their general meaning, the patterns that they fit into, or their correct use. For example, the teacher may explain the meaning of a word to learners and show the pattern it fits into, or the learners may work through exercises based on a rule, such as add *-ed* to make the past tense.

Surprisingly, the boundary between language-focused learning and meaning-focused instruction is not so easy to draw. Noticing an item is one of the steps in acquisition. This noticing is arguably attention to language—that is, the temporary decontextualisation of the item so that it is viewed as part of the language system rather than part of the message. In language-focused learning, the attention to the item as part of the system is likely to be teacher-directed (through explanation or through the design of an activity), obvious, and not brief. As Ellis (2003, 2018) shows, this attention to language can also be the focus of a communicative activity.

The Value and Limits of Language-focused Learning

There is now considerable evidence to show that language-focused learning can help second language learning. Reviews by Long (1988), Spada (1997), and Ellis (2006, 2016) indicate that language-focused learning can have the following effects:

1. A combination of language-focused learning and meaning-focused use leads to better results than either kind of learning alone.
2. Language-focused learning can speed up the rate of second language acquisition.

3. Language-focused learning may help learners to continue to improve their control of grammar rather than becoming stuck with certain errors.
4. Some language-focused learning can lead directly to acquisition, depending on the kinds of item focused on, especially vocabulary (Elgort, 2007, 2011).
5. Language-focused learning can indirectly provide meaning-focused input.

There are, however, limitations to the effect of language-focused learning. These limitations include the following:

1. Language-focused learning cannot change the order in which learners acquire certain complex, developmental features of the language, such as questions, negatives, and relative clauses.
2. Language-focused learning needs to be combined with the opportunity to use the same items in meaning-focused use.
3. Some grammatical items learned through language-focused learning may only be available to the learner in planned use until such time as they have been met extensively in meaning-focused input and used widely in meaning-focused output.

The most important finding, however, is that language-focused learning has an important role to play in second language acquisition. The purpose of this chapter is to show what this role is and how it is most effectively played.

Deliberate Vocabulary Learning

The best language-focused vocabulary instruction involves looking at a word as part of a system rather than as part of a message. This means paying attention to regular spelling and sound patterns in words, paying attention to the underlying concept of the senses of words (head of the school, head of a bed, head of a match, etc.), paying attention to word building devices, paying attention to the range and types of collocation of a word, and paying attention to the range of clues to the word's meaning provided by context.

It is also useful to study words isolated from context and as individual items. There is substantial research in this area and it shows how learners can take the first steps in quickly learning a large vocabulary (Nation, 2013a: Chapter 11), and that this learning results in implicit as well as explicit knowledge (Elgort, 2011).

Language-focused vocabulary learning has three main values. It speeds up vocabulary learning considerably. It contributes directly to implicit knowledge. It raises awareness of the systematic features of vocabulary. Let us look at each of these.

1. Larsen-Freeman and Long (1991) see one of the clearest findings from research on instructed second language acquisition as being that instruction can speed up the rate of learning. This finding is certainly true for second language vocabulary development. This research has focused on the initial learning of vocabulary and on the quantity of items learned (Nation, 2013a: 437–478). There is now a growing body of research on the effect of language-focused learning on the quality of vocabulary knowledge (Schmitt & Meara, 1997; Webb, 2005).
2. Research (Elgort, 2011) shows that language-focused vocabulary learning using word cards results in implicit knowledge. That is, as a result of deliberate learning, the vocabulary is subconsciously and fluently available for use and has entered into lexical relationships with other words. Knowledge of words learned this way is also explicitly available.
3. Just as the grammar of the language contains systematic features, so does the vocabulary. Language-focused attention to these features will speed up the development of explicit knowledge and will also make learners more aware of them when they are met in language use. This awareness will make them more likely to be noticed and thus more likely to be acquired.

The Requirements of Language-focused Vocabulary Instruction

Vocabulary instruction should focus on useful items. We have more frequency information about vocabulary than any other part of the language. What this information shows is that it is essential for learners to have good control over the relatively small number of high-frequency words. The most important 2000–3000 word families make up such a large proportion of both spoken and written use that it is difficult to use the language effectively without a good knowledge of them. These words can be found in the BNC/COCA lists on Paul Nation's website and the Academic Word List (Coxhead, 2000). However, to cope with unsimplified spoken language, a vocabulary size of around 6000 word families is needed (Adolphs & Schmitt, 2003; Nation, 2006).

For learners who have a good knowledge of the high-frequency words, the focus of instruction should be on learning and coping strategies, including using context clues for inferring meaning and using word parts and other mnemonic procedures for learning new low-frequency words. Learners need to take responsibility for using these strategies to increase their knowledge of low-frequency words.

Vocabulary instruction should involve thoughtful processing so that the words are remembered. Teachers should evaluate the procedures they use and the procedures their learners use to see their effectiveness. One way of doing this is to look at them from a "levels of processing" viewpoint (Baddeley, 1990: 160–173; Craik & Tulving, 1975) to see how thoughtful the learners have to be when they use a particular procedure. Evaluating a procedure from this point of view can involve asking questions such as these (see Webb & Nation, 2017: Chapter 5 for detailed analyses of a range of vocabulary learning activities):

- Are the learners paying attention to more than one aspect of the word? For example, meaning, form, use.
- Are the learners being original and creative in the way they look at the word?
- Are the learners relating the word to previous knowledge?

Vocabulary instruction should avoid grouping words that will interfere with each other. Research on the form and meaning relationships between words shows that near synonyms, opposites, free associates, and members of a lexical set such as names of fruit or items of clothing interfere with each other and make learning more difficult if they are learned together (Higa, 1963; Ishii, 2015; Nation, 2000; Tinkham, 1993, 1997; Waring, 1997). This means that, if *fat* and *thin* are both new items for a learner, and if they are learned at the same time, the learner will have difficulty in learning which is which and not mixing them up. Unfortunately most course designers are not aware of this research and deliberately group words in this way.

Vocabulary instruction should take account of the flexibility and creativity involved in normal vocabulary use by drawing attention to the systematic features of vocabulary. This means paying attention to affixes, the underlying meaning of words, and the way they collocate with other words.

Knowledge gained through deliberate learning should be enriched by opportunities to learn through meaning-focused input and meaning-focused output. Language-focused learning is a means to an end, and that end is not reached unless learners can easily find the words they need when they are using the language. It is, therefore, important to make sure that the words that are learned have plenty of opportunity to be used, and to be used fluently.

Techniques and Procedures for Vocabulary Learning

The following description of techniques and procedures has been arranged according to proficiency level—beginner, intermediate, and advanced.

Beginners

There are numerous possibilities for conveying the meaning of new vocabulary (see Nation, 1990a, especially Chapter 3; Nation, 2008). Both brief pre-teaching before meeting the words in context (Jenkins,

Stein, & Wysocki, 1984) and explanation in the context of listening to a story (Elley, 1989) have a substantial effect on learning compared with incidental learning without directly focused attention. This means that, before listening activities, it is worth drawing learners' attention to some of the vocabulary that will occur and the fact that it is worth learning. This can be done by listing words on the board and quickly discussing them, giving learners lists of words and meanings to work on at home, or doing a semantic mapping activity drawing on the learners' previous knowledge and introducing the target vocabulary into the map (Stahl & Vancil, 1986).

For adult beginners, it is useful to have a rapid expansion of vocabulary through direct vocabulary learning. An effective way of doing this for older learners is to make use of **vocabulary cards** or **flash card apps**. Vocabulary cards are small cards (about 4 cm × 3 cm) with the second language word on one side and the first language translation on the other. Particularly at the beginning level, it is useful to have a phrase containing the new word along with the word. Learners use these cards in their own time, looking at them frequently for a short time. It is good to change the order of the cards as they are looked at to avoid a serial effect in learning. The use of such cards should be combined with mnemonic techniques such as the **key word technique** or **word part analysis**, or simply creating a mental picture of the word or a situation where it is used. There are now flash card apps such as iKnow and Anki that apply good principles of learning (Nakata, 2011). The considerable amount of research on this rote learning procedure clearly shows its effectiveness (Nation, 2013a: Chapter 9; Nation, 2008).

Even at an early stage of language learning, it is worth looking at word building devices. The inflectional suffixes of English are a good start as they are all frequently used.

As the guessing from context strategy is so useful, it is worth practising it as early as possible. At this stage, many of the context clues will come from the situational context rather than the linguistic context. Use of a guided guessing procedure will add some depth of processing to the learning of new words.

At this level, direct teaching of vocabulary is useful. The techniques used can include the use of first language definitions, synonyms, pictures, or demonstration. Some items, particularly numbers, greetings, and polite phrases, should be practised to a high level of fluency. The teacher can suggest mnemonics for the words, but this should be regarded more as training in getting learners to create their own mnemonics, because research indicates that mnemonic tricks created by each learner result in better retention than those provided by others. Here are some examples for learning languages other than English.

- *Nana* (meaning "seven" in Japanese) is easy to learn because the shape of the number 7 is like the shape of a (ba)nana.

- *Khâw* (meaning "rice" in Thai) sounds like *cow* in English. The learner can think of an image of a cow eating rice, or a cow made of rice.
- *Kaiki* (meaning "all of it" in Finnish) sounds a little bit like *cake* in English, so think of an image of someone buying all the cakes in a shop.

Intermediate

An important focus at the intermediate level is expanding the uses that can be made of known words. This means drawing attention to the underlying meaning of a word by seeing its use in a variety of contexts. Exploring the meanings of words such as *head*, *fork*, or *agree* can be a useful activity. This type of activity can be done inductively, with the learners going in to the underlying meaning through the analysis of many examples, or deductively, by going out from a meaning to examples.

The guessing from context strategy should continue to be practised, with attention being paid mainly to clues in the linguistic context (see Nation, 1990a, 2008, for various ways of doing this).

Word parts should be used to help remember the meanings of new words. These should include affixes from levels 3 and 4 of Bauer and Nation (1993), which include -able, -er, -ish, -less, -ly, -ness, -th, -y, non-, un-, -al, -ation, -ess, -ful, -ism, -ist, -ity, -ize, -ment, -ous, in-, all with restricted uses.

Examples of the **key word technique** have been given above with *nana*, *khâw*, and *kaiki*. It is worth formalising the strategy at this stage. The key word strategy links the form of an unknown word to its meaning by using a key word, usually taken from the first language. Here is an example. Let us imagine a Spanish-speaking learner of English wants to learn the English word *car*. She then thinks of a Spanish word that sounds like *car*—for example, *caro* (which means "expensive"). The learner then has to think of the meanings "car" and "expensive" acting together in an image—for example, a very expensive car. The key word *caro* thus provides a form and meaning link for the meaning of car.

The key word procedure can be broken into these steps.

1. Look at the second language word and think of a first language word that sounds like it or sounds like its beginning. This first language word is the key word.
2. Think of the meaning of the second language word and the meaning of the first language word joined together in some way. This is where imagination is needed (Ellis & Beaton, 1993).
3. Make a mental picture of these two meanings joined together.

There are many techniques that can be used at this level to help learning vocabulary.

It's my word! (Mhone, 1988) or **word detectives** involves a learner reporting on a word that was learned out of class recently. The reporting can follow a pattern involving saying where the word was met, what it means, how it is used, and how it can easily be remembered.

Each week, the teacher can provide a time for revising the vocabulary worked on previously. One person in the class can be given the job of keeping a note of words to be revised as they occur. During the revision time, the words can be dictated in sentences to the learners. They can be put in true/false statements. They can be written on the whiteboard for the learners to pronounce or break into parts. They can be used in collocation activities where learners work in groups to put them into a variety of linguistic contexts.

The activities at the beginning and intermediate levels should focus on the essential general service vocabulary of English of approximately 2000 words.

Advanced

At the advanced level, learners who intend to study in English at secondary school or university need to focus on the academic vocabulary of English. This vocabulary can be found in the 570 word family Academic Word List (Coxhead, 2000). All learners at this level must refine the strategies they need for dealing with the large number of low-frequency words that they will meet. These strategies include, in order of importance, guessing unknown words from context, using word parts to remember the meanings of words, and using mnemonic techniques. At this level, there is little value in the direct teaching of vocabulary, although learners should be doing substantial amounts of direct learning using word cards or flash card apps. The main focus of teaching should be on strategy development.

Deliberate Grammar Learning

Grammar can be deliberately learned as a result of direct explanation and analysis, through doing grammar exercises, through consciousness-raising activities, and through feedback. Let us now look at each of these in turn.

Grammar-focused Description

This kind of language-focused learning results in learners being able to say what a grammatical feature means, how it is put together, or how it should be used. As the following techniques show, the instruction is teacher-produced description of rules or patterns, learner analysis of examples, or learner manipulation and joining of parts. Direct explanation of grammar points has certain advantages over more communicatively based problem-solving activities (Sheen, 1992). First, the direct teaching gets the point across quickly and allows more time for practice and meaning-focused use. Second, problem-solving group work that focuses on grammar may require vocabulary and constructions that the learners do not know. Discussing grammar is not easy. Sheen conducted a small-scale experiment comparing direct explanation with group problem-solving and found that, on his written test, there was no significant difference, but that there was a significant advantage for direct teaching on his oral test, possibly due to the extra time available for oral practice. Fotos (1993) also found a slight but non-significant advantage for teacher description.

Exploring Collocation Patterns

Some of the simplest explanations that could be of immediate value to learners involve the description of collocation possibilities. Here are some examples: *dismantle* is usually followed by the name of a structure with many parts, such as *dismantle the organisation, dismantle the machine*; *outdo* is usually followed by the name of a person, *outdo Jones*. Collocation patterns are like "local" rules and may be of more practical value to a learner than the more generally applied rules (Lewis, 1993; Meunier, 2020).

Learning Explicit Grammatical Rules

There are several exercise types that focus on explicit grammatical rules. They include transformation, ordering, constructing from rules, and classification. Let us look at each of these.

Eckman, Bell, and Nelson (1988) used **transformation exercises** to teach relative clauses. The learners were given a pair of sentences, such as *I saw a little boy. A woman was carrying him*, to transform into a single sentence. The set of combined sentences made up a story. Before doing the exercise, the learners were given a little explanation and teacher-led practice.

Consciousness Raising Activities

Ellis (1991: 232–241) distinguishes practice activities and consciousness-raising activities. Whereas practice activities focus on learning through repeated perception or production, **consciousness-raising** activities develop explicit understanding of how a grammatical construction works. The box has an example.

Read this description.
I am sitting in my bed looking out of the window. There's some wind today because the branches of the trees are moving. There's no sign of the sun, and there are some dark clouds moving quickly across the sky. There is a bird sitting on the branch of a tree.
Answer these questions about sentences beginning with *there*:

1. Find four examples of *there* in the description above.
2. Each sentence with *There* has three or four parts. Break each example into four parts. Can you think of a name for each part?
3. How can we decide if we should use *There is* or *There are*?
4. Make four sentences beginning with *There* about the picture in Figure 10.1.

Figure 10.1 Consciousness-raising Activity Focusing on Formal *There*

The goal of consciousness-raising activities is to help learners notice language items when they appear in meaning-focused input and thus increase the chances that they will be learned through being noticed and processed more deeply. Consciousness-raising activities therefore have limited, delayed aims. They need not result in deliberate production, but develop an awareness of the form, function, and meaning of particular items at the level of explicit knowledge. This awareness need not involve the understanding of grammatical terminology. Success in a consciousness-raising activity would be measured by the learner consciously noticing the same item in meaning-focused input and thinking something like, "I have seen that before".

Consciousness-raising activities can involve the following:

- Having to underline or note examples of an item in a text
- Being given examples and having to construct a rule
- Having to classify examples into categories such as countable/uncountable or active/passive
- Correcting errors based on a given rule
- Using a rule to construct a sentence
- Recognising instances of a rule in operation.

Language-focused Correction

Tomasello and Herron (1989) suggest that some activities should be designed so that learners make errors and then get immediate feedback to make them aware of the gaps in their knowledge. Their deliberate encouragement of errors through incorrect analogy is called the "garden path" technique. The expression "to lead someone down the garden path" means to deliberately trick someone. It is important to note that it is not the error that is important in the garden path technique, but the noticing that comes from it. Here is a typical garden path activity:

Teacher: Here is a sentence using these words, *think* and *problem*. *I thought about the problem.* Now you make one using these words, *talk* and *problem*.

Learner: We talked about the problem.

Teacher: Good. *argue* and *result*.

Learner: We argued about the result.

Teacher: Good. *discuss* and *advantages*.

Learner: We discussed about the advantages.

Teacher: No. With *discuss* we do not use *about*.

Tomasello and Herron (1989) found that learners who made an error and were immediately corrected learned more than learners who simply had the correct form explained to them. "Students learn best when they produce a hypothesis and receive feedback, because this creates maximal conditions under which they may cognitively compare their own system to that of mature systems. Such comparisons are clearly important in L1 acquisition" (p. 392). Tomasello and Herron argue that, because the activity was done as a group rather than an individual activity, there were no negative motivational effects. The learners involved could see that many others were making the same error, and that their errors were deliberately caused by the teacher. Strong and Boers (2018), however, found negative effects from focusing on error.

There are two major factors to consider when deciding what to do about errors. The first is the cause of the error, and the second is the effect of correction. Error correction as a means of consciousness-raising has several advantages (Ellis, 1990: 193–194). First, it can be a striking way of noticing, particularly if the error interfered with communication of a message. Second, it pushes the learner to notice a gap, exemplified by the difference between the error and the correction. Third, it assists the learning of accurate, explicit rules that can be used to produce output that may become input for implicit knowledge. However, there is evidence from collocation learning that making errors makes learning more difficult, and thus it is better to use activities that avoid error (Elgort, 2017; Strong & Boers, 2018).

Ellis (2005, 2006) describes useful principles for guiding language-focused grammar learning. These include the following: grammar teaching should focus on form, meaning, and use; there should be separate grammar lessons as well as incidental attention to grammar; and corrective feedback is important for learning grammar.

Corrective Feedback

Correcting errors is best done if there is some understanding of why the error occurred. This involves error analysis. Error analysis is the study of errors to see what processes gave rise to them. Useful surveys of error analysis can be found in Richards (1974), Dušková (1969), and Lennon (1991). Table 10.1 lists some of the causes along with examples.

Many errors have more than one cause. For example, interference from the first language is encouraged if the learner has to perform beyond their normal level of competence. Then, the first language becomes the main resource to fall back on. Errors resulting from the over-use of second language patterns are more likely to occur where the first language patterns provide little support. From a teaching point of view, it is thus useful to regard errors as at least partly a result of the conditions under which speaking occurred. Table 10.2 looks at four task-based sources of error and suggests how a factor in the design of the task could be considered partly responsible for an error the learner makes while doing the task. General solutions are also suggested. The errors the learners make could show first

Table 10.1 Causes and Examples of Second Language Errors

Cause	Example error	Explanation
Interference from the first language	There are too many difference. When I was young I was very sick. But now that I am a virgin I can take care of myself.	The first language does not mark singular and plural. *Virgin* and *adolescent* are the same word in the first language.
Interference from the second language	One factor which aids second language learning to occur.	The use of *aid* is modelled on the use of *help*.
Reduction to increase efficiency	Big square on top of small square.	The learner was under time pressure to complete a task and so left out unnecessary items.
Accidental error	I said … told him not to do it.	Self-correction indicates that the learner knows what to say.

language, second language, efficiency, or accidental influences. It should not be assumed that every error should be corrected or prevented. One of the major contributions of error analysis is the demonstration that some errors are signs of developing competence and will largely disappear when full competence in that particular area is reached.

Table 10.2 shows that teachers can play a part in the control of errors.

Inevitably, however, errors will occur. This is especially true in teaching approaches that emphasize *using* the language communicatively as a way to learn it. In task-based language teaching, for example, errors are a natural part of performing a task that is a little challenging. Some errors are naturally addressed when learners negotiate for meaning (see Chapter 7). Other errors can become the focus of instruction in the post-task phase. Skehan (2014) is a short and readable discussion that is freely available online on how to use the post-task phase effectively. Both during the task and in the post-task phase, the teacher can also provide corrective feedback, which we discuss next.

The Effect of Correction

In English, we use the phrase "make a mistake". This phrase has two parts, "make" and "a mistake". If a teacher places most emphasis on "making" or creative language use, then that teacher will have to be prepared to tolerate mistakes. If a teacher places most emphasis on "mistakes" and their avoidance, then that teacher will have to reduce the amount of "making"

Table 10.2 Task-based Sources of Error and Possible Design Solutions

Source of error	Solution
The learners were not sufficiently prepared for the task, or the control of the task was not sufficient	Check the language, ideas, skill, and text aspects of the task to make sure that at least three of the four aspects are well within the learners' previous experience Use input-based tasks before tasks that require output, and use the post-task phase to give explicit attention to important language forms Provide planning time Repeat the task or use similar tasks
The other learners in the group did not provide support or feedback	Change the group work activity so that each learner has a particular support job to do, and so that the activity has a procedure to make it better organised
The task was not guided enough; the contribution that the learner had to make was too great	Redesign the task so that guidance is provided in the area in which the error occurred
The learner's self-monitoring and coping strategies were not sufficient	Review the strategies that the learner has for monitoring and checking language production Allow more time for the post-task phase in which learners are guided to reflect on their task performance, to identify gaps in their language knowledge or strategy use, and to plan ways to fill the gaps

that the learners do. Reducing the amount of making means getting the learners to take fewer risks in their language use and to do mainly guided activities. Similarly, continually correcting learners when they make mistakes may have the effect of reducing the amount of "making" that they do. That is, the continual correction will discourage the learners from speaking or from saying things that might contain an error.

There is another aspect to the effect of correction. Will the correction be successful in bringing about a change in the learners' spoken production? Correcting errors is a part of remedial work.

George (1972) describes the following steps for carrying out remedial work:

1. The mistakes that the learners make should be found and listed.
2. From that list, the teacher should choose a limited number of mistakes or types of mistake for remedial work. This choice should depend on the following points:

(a) The amount of time that can usually be given for such work. Remedial work often takes time that might be more useful for teaching new material.
(b) The possibility of the remedial work being successful. Often, in spite of a great deal of effort over a long time, the learners still make the same mistakes, such as agreement between subject and verb, the use of plural forms, and so on. If teachers have tried unsuccessfully for a long time to correct these mistakes, it is unlikely that extra remedial work will be successful.
(c) The feelings of the learners. If the learners are not really worried by the mistakes or they see no value in correcting them, remedial work will probably be unsuccessful. The learners should be able to see that it is possible to make great improvement and that they are really learning something useful. Remedial work should not be just a reminder of the learners' past failures. Many learners, however, welcome remedial work and, particularly where English is taught as a second language, see English classes as a way of getting the informed correction that they do not get outside class.
(d) The frequency of mistakes. Some mistakes are found very often in the learners' speech. Others are rarely found.
(e) The effect of the mistakes on understanding. Some mistakes are found frequently in a learner's work, but they do not make it difficult for anyone to understand what the learner is trying to say. Mistakes with *a* and *the*, plurals, agreement, and some pronunciation mistakes are like this. Other mistakes, such as the use of stress, vocabulary, and certain sentence patterns, make it very difficult for someone to understand what the learner is trying to say.
(f) The feelings of the listeners or readers about the learners' mistakes. Some mistakes are easily accepted by the speakers of a certain language, whereas others might make a listener feel that the speaker who makes the mistake is "uneducated".

3. The teacher should carefully study each mistake chosen, try to find the reasons why the learners make the mistake, and look at ways for reteaching or correcting, using new techniques and procedures and a new way of looking at and explaining the problem. Using new techniques is very important because there is no value in using techniques that have already been unsuccessful in dealing with a particular problem.
4. The teacher should decide whether written activities should be used to support spoken work.

5. The teacher should see that there is a large number of repeated opportunities for the learners to give their attention to the features that the teacher has chosen to correct.

Johnson (1988) suggests that learners need the following four things in order to get rid of a mistake:

1. The desire or need to get rid of the mistake.
2. An internal representation of what the correct form is like.
3. The ability to know that a mistake has been made.
4. An opportunity to practise the correct form in real conditions.

There are considerable overlaps between George's and Johnson's suggestions.

Correction Procedures

Sheen (2004) points out that "teachers' provision of corrective feedback is often arbitrary, idiosyncratic, ambiguous and unsystematic" (p. 265). If teachers want to be more effective at providing corrective feedback, a first step is to become familiar with the range of feedback options available to them. Here is a list of possible corrective feedback procedures with a brief explanation of how each one might work, based on Hendrickson (1978):

1. The teacher interrupts and corrects the error, thus providing immediate feedback.
2. The teacher says "What?" each time the error occurs, as if the error made understanding difficult. Research reported by Ellis (1992) indicates that this meaning-focused type of correction is more effective than language-focused correction. This may be because the learners attach greater importance to the meaning of messages than their form.
3. The teacher repeats the learner's utterance as if confirming what the learner said, but with the error corrected as well. This is called a recast and is supposed to be like the type of natural modelling that is done by caregivers in their interactions with children learning their first language.
4. The teacher makes a written note about the error that is later given to the learners. This type of correction does not interrupt the speaking and may encourage future monitoring.
5. The teacher devotes some lesson time to pointing out errors that the learners have made, explains how to correct them, and encourages them to monitor for these errors in future speaking activities. The

learners may be reminded to monitor just before the activities. This type of correction relies on awareness and monitoring.
6. The learners practise using correct forms in their "careful" style of speaking. Supporters of a variable competence theory of learning (Ellis, 1986) argue that learning that becomes stable in one style may then be transferred to other less careful styles.
7. The learners do group work that requires accurate performance, such as the split information activity in Figure 7.1 in Chapter 7. This encourages peer correction.

A second step, perhaps in the form of a small action research project, is for teachers to observe and reflect on their corrective feedback practices. This includes gathering evidence on how effective these practices are, identifying gaps in their practice, experimenting with new approaches, and again gathering evidence on effectiveness of these new approaches. Evidence can include observing how learners respond to different kinds of feedback, asking learners to share their preferences and experiences, observing uptake of corrections, and drawing on learners' feedback logs. Here is what Ricky, an EFL teacher in Japan, said about his corrective feedback practices:

> I found that when I prompt my learners to correct an error in their speech they can quite often do so, especially for errors related to language items which they have already learnt about but not yet fully mastered. In such cases, the learners are able to reflect on why I have given them corrective feedback and more easily notice and fill the gap in their communication. For example, if my learner is familiar with the use of English articles "a" and "the" but has difficulty using them correctly in their speech, they may say "I went to the cafe in Tokyo", but if I repeat their phrase with emphasis on "the", the learner is drawn to realize that this is the wrong use of "the" in this context in which the listener does not know of this café and so is able to self-correct "the" to "a". But prompting isn't always effective, especially if the learner doesn't know how to fix the error. In such cases, I have found recasts or explicit correction are much more helpful since they push the learner to take up the new language forms without completely distracting from the message they are trying to communicate.

Notice how Ricky distinguishes between different types of feedback and the reasons for using them. Let us now look more closely at the different options for giving feedback as presented in Table 10.3. In the table, we illustrate the different feedback options using the example of "*She has car*". This sentence may make sense, but it is not grammatically correct. Notice that, at the broadest level, the

Table 10.3 Examples of Corrective Feedback

Type of corrective feedback	Definition	Example
Reformulation		
Conversational recast	The teacher reformulates part or all of the wrong word or phrase in order to confirm understanding. The recast is often a confirmation check	"*Oh, she has a car?*" (checking that it was in fact a car that the learner mentioned)
Didactic recast	The teacher recasts even though meaning is clear. Emphasis is put on the corrected form	"*Oh, she has a car.*" (emphasis on "a")
Explicit correction	The teacher alerts the learner to the error and then provides the correct form	"*No, you should say, 'She has a car'.*"
Explicit correction + explanation	As above, with an explanation of the nature of the error	"*She has a car. Remember to use an article with countable nouns.*"
Prompt		
Repetition	The teacher repeats the utterance and emphasises where the error is	"*She has car???*"
Clarification request	The teacher indicates that there is an error and that meaning is unclear, and then asks the learner to reformulate it	"*Sorry? What does she have?*"
Elicitation	The teacher prompts the learner to correct the error by pausing at the point where the error occurred so that the learner can complete it with the correct form	"*She has …?*"
Metalinguistic feedback	The teacher provides technical linguistic information about an error without explicitly giving the correct answer	"*You need an indefinite article.*"

(adapted from Lyster & Ranta, 1997; Lyster, Saito, & Sato, 2013)

teacher has the choice of either *reformulating* the error (i.e., correcting it) or *prompting* the learner to do the correction. A second choice concerns how implicit and explicit the teacher wishes the feedback to be. In the table, the options presented for both reformulations and prompts move from implicit to explicit. So, for example, for reformulations, a conversational recast is very implicit, but explicit correction + explanation is very explicit.

Overall, research indicates that more explicit types of feedback are more effective than more implicit forms of feedback. But, as Lyster, Saito, and Sato (2013) point out, "[t]he most effective teachers are likely to be those who are willing and able to orchestrate, in accordance with their students' language abilities and content familiarity, a wide range of CF [corrective feedback] types that fit the instructional context" (p. 30). Ellis and Shintani (2013) add the caution that over-correction, including not being selective in which errors are corrected, is counter-productive, and that uptake and learning are more durable when the learner and not the teacher corrects the error—that is, when different forms of prompts are used.

It is also possible that feedback procedures that seem new to the learners will be more effective. There are several reasons for this. First, there is little sense in using procedures that have already been unsuccessful for those learners. They will just remind them of past failures. Second, a new correction procedure allows the learner to account for a previous lack of success, as in, "If this way of correcting had been used before, I wouldn't have continued to make the error". Third, a variety of procedures will create more interest in correction.

Finally, some researchers and writers on language teaching suggest that teachers should not correct their learners' spoken language because it causes embarrassment, anxiety, and loss of confidence. These, in turn, reduce learners' willingness to use the language creatively, to try new constructions, and to take risks. There is, however, a role for correction, particularly if it is directed towards errors that will benefit from attention, and if it is done in a way that the learners find acceptable. Teachers need to think through their approaches to corrective feedback and should discuss these with their learners. At certain stages in their learning, learners may want correction and may feel that they are missing out if they do not get it. In fact, as discussed by Lyster, Saito, and Sato (2013), research suggests that some learners may wish to receive more feedback than teachers feel comfortable providing. Vásquez and Harvey (2010) describe how a group of practising teachers enrolled in a university course on second language acquisition were guided to reflect on their approach to feedback. In doing so, these teachers became less preoccupied with the affective impact of feedback and more confident in using feedback to guide learning.

Corrective feedback is part of the cycle of teaching and assessing learning, and so we return to the topic in Chapter 12.

Paying Deliberate Attention to Discourse Features

In Chapter 8, we looked at the Q → SA + EI strategy that suggests a question (Q) should be followed by a short answer (SA) plus extra information (+ EI). This is a strategy that can be used to keep the conversation going.

How long have you been here? (Q)
Three months (SA), and I found it quite difficult at first (+ EI)

Alternatively, using Q → SA it is possible to kill a conversation:

Have you been here long? (Q)
Yes. (SA)

Learners can be given training in providing extra information. The extra information can be a feeling, a factual piece of information, or a question. The Q → SA + EI strategy is a particularly powerful one if used well because it can be used to continue or stop a conversation, to steer a conversation away from an unwanted topic to a wanted or familiar topic, and to take control of a conversation by turning the extra information into a long turn. The strategy is particularly useful in interviews where the person being interviewed can direct the interview by the kind of extra information they provide (Nation, 1980).

Other useful discourse features that could be given deliberate attention include appeals for help with language, how to take a long turn (see Chapter 7), how to bid for a turn in a conversation, how to be vague and imprecise (Brown, 1979), how to encourage others to continue speaking, and how to turn to different topics.

Stenstrom (1990: 144) has a useful and suggestive list of items that are used in spoken language from the London–Lund corpus.

Apologies:	pardon, sorry, excuse me, I'm sorry, I beg your pardon
Smooth-overs:	don't worry, never mind
Hedges:	kind of, sort of, sort of thing
Expletives:	damn, gosh, hell, fuck off, good heavens, the hell, for goodness sake, good heavens above, bloody hell
Greetings:	hi, hello, good evening, good morning, Happy New Year, how are you, how do you do
Initiators:	anyway, however, now
Negative:	No
Orders:	give over, go on, shut up

Politeness markers:	please
Question tags:	is it, isn't it
Responses:	ah, fine, good, uhuh, OK, quite, really, right, sure, all right, fair enough, I'm sure, I see, that's good, that's it, that's right, that's true, very good
Softeners:	I mean, mind you, you know, you see, as you know, do you see
Thanks:	thanks, thank you
Well:	Well
Exemplifiers:	Say
Positive:	mhm, yeah, yes, yup

In Appendix D, we provide a sample unit from Riddiford and Newton (2010) that shows how these kinds of feature are addressed in a course for helping new migrants in New Zealand communicate effectively in the professional workplace.

Fitting Language-focused Learning into a Course

Typically, too much time has been given to language-focused learning in courses, and it has dominated rather than served the learning goals. There are several reasons for this, but the main one probably is that teachers and course designers consider that a language course should systematically cover the important grammatical features of the language. This is a reasonable and praiseworthy principle, as long as it is put into practice in a way that takes into account what we know about second language acquisition and what we learn from corpus linguistics:

1. The limitations placed on language-focused learning by a learner's developmental readiness to acquire certain structures need to be considered, so that time is not wasted on items that the learners are not ready to learn.
2. Where teaching is directed to structures that the learners are ready to learn, the information must be accurate, simple, and accessible.
3. Teachers and course designers need to be aware that the effect of much language-focused grammar learning will be to add to explicit knowledge, often simply by raising consciousness about items. If this is to contribute to implicit knowledge, further substantial meaning-focused activity is needed.

4. Task-based language teaching advocates such as Willis and Willis (2009) and Long (2015) argue strongly on the basis of research that grammar-focused instruction should not take place prior to a communicative task. They argue that, when grammar is pre-taught, it reduces the following meaningful task to a structure practice activity in the minds of the learners, rather than the genuinely communicative experience that was intended. Instead, it is argued, attention to grammar should come from the learners as they seek to find the language they need to express their meanings during the task. Attention to grammar can also be a major focus of post-task activities and instruction, such as when learners write about the solution they agreed on in a problem-solving task or review new structures and words they met in the task.
5. Unfamiliar items tend to be introduced at a rate that is much faster than most learners can manage. This is partly a result of not making sure that items introduced in language-focused learning also appear in meaning-focused use and in fluency development activities. Repetition of various kinds is essential for learning.
6. Many language items that appear in beginners' courses may not be important enough to spend time on. They could be more usefully replaced with items that have a wider range and higher frequency of use (Biber, Johansson, Leech, Conrad, & Finegan, 1999).
7. Putting grammatical constructions in contrast when teaching them can make learning more difficult by encouraging interference between the constructions. It is better to focus on one construction and leave contrast for later when the contrasted constructions are being established. For example, contrasting active and passive—"three follows two, two is followed by three"—can result in great confusion.

As a rough rule, language-focused learning should not make up more than about 25 per cent of the whole range of contact that learners have with the language. If there is a lot of opportunity for meaning-focused use outside the classroom, then much of the classroom time could be on language-focused learning. If learners' only contact with the language is within the classroom, then less than a quarter of this time should be given to language-focused learning.

The range of language-focused activities could include the following:

1. The study of new items, including sounds, vocabulary, grammatical constructions, pragmatics, discourse. This could involve formal presentation by the teacher, individualised exercises, or group activities. For explicit knowledge, this would have both consciousness-raising and monitored production goals. Some of this study would also add directly to implicit knowledge.
2. Familiarisation with and practice of previously met items. This may involve activities such as substitution table practice and completion,

transformation, identification, or distinguishing activities. These would have the learning goals of adding to implicit knowledge or monitored production.
3. In the post-task phase of a lesson, studying the language features of recordings of model task performances by proficient speakers of the target language. Willis and Willis (2009) suggest that teachers can make these recordings with friends and colleagues and use them, along with transcripts of the recordings, for careful language study after learners have performed a task. The advantage of this approach is that, having performed the task, the learners will have noticed gaps in their performance and be highly tuned in to language in the input to fill these gaps.
4. Formal feedback on performance. This could involve the regular use of feedback activities such as dictation, and monitored exercises and talks.

Here are some examples of the language-focused learning in existing programmes.

In a beginners' programme in a country where there was no substantial opportunity to use the language, the class involved regular teaching of vocabulary, set phrases (greetings, politeness formulas), and the explanation of useful patterns. These items were also practised in repetition, pattern practice, and dialogue activities. The course lacked opportunities for feedback and correction. This language-focused learning occupied about 25 per cent of the class time.

In a pre-university course in a country where English was the main language outside the classroom, learners were encouraged to use small cards to learn academic vocabulary. There was a regular class time to be tested on these each week, mainly as an encouragement to learning. There was also systematic study of word parts as a means of vocabulary expansion. Learners would do two dictations each week and gave talks on which there was written feedback. These activities occupied about 10 per cent of class time.

Tasks

1. Explain how the use of vocabulary cards or flash card apps applies the following principles of vocabulary learning:

Repetition is necessary for learning
Learners should do retrieval (recall) when trying to learn a word form or meaning
Repetitions should be spaced rather than massed.

2. Add six activities to the following four strands chart for listening and speaking:

1. Meaning-focused input	Conversation and group work
2. Meaning-focused output	Problem-solving speaking
3. Language-focused learning	Strategy training Listening with questions
4. Fluency development	Quicklistens

3. Look carefully at the range of feedback types in Table 10.3 and Figure 10.1. Which do you find yourself using the most? Why? Which don't you use? Why not?

Further Reading

Read Nakata (2011) on criteria for evaluating a flash card app.

There is an interesting lecture on communicative grammar for multilevel English language learners at www.youtube.com/watch?v=ArxrGKIkM3c

11 Developing Fluency

The Nature of Fluency

In this book, fluency is used with the same meaning given to it by Schmidt (1992), described below, except that it is not restricted to "the planning and delivery of speech", but is also extended to the comprehension of speech. Fluency has the following characteristics in all of the four skills of listening, speaking, reading, and writing:

1. Fluent language use does not require a great deal of attention and effort from the learner.
2. Fluent language use involves "the processing of language in real time" (Schmidt, 1992: 358). That is, learners demonstrate fluency when they take part in meaning-focused activity and do it with speed and ease without holding up the flow of talk. There are observable signs that can be used to measure changes in fluency (Arevart & Nation, 1991; Lennon, 1990). These include speech rate (as measured in words or syllables per minute; Griffiths, 1991a, 1991b), number of filled pauses such as *um*, *ah*, *er*, and number of unfilled pauses.
3. If we consider the four goals of language, ideas, skill, text (LIST), fluency is a skill. Although it depends on quality of knowledge of the language, and its development involves the addition to and restructuring of knowledge, in essence it involves making the best possible use of what is already known.

The four characteristics of activities designed to develop fluency are (1) the use of easy, familiar material, (2) some pressure to go faster, (3) plenty of practice, and (4) a focus on communication. It is worth remembering that fluency in speaking in the first language is partly a reflection of personal characteristics, and this personal style can carry over to the second or foreign language (de Jong & Mora, 2019).

Fluency and Accuracy

A useful distinction can be made between fluency, accuracy, and complexity (Skehan, 1998). Fluency is typically measured by speed of access or production and by the number of hesitations; accuracy by the amount of error; and complexity by the presence of more complicated constructions, such as subordinate clauses.

Schmidt's (1992) comprehensive review of the psychological mechanisms underlying second language fluency shows that it is not possible to account for developments in fluency simply through an increase in speed of processing. Substantial increases in fluency also involve changes in the nature of the knowledge of language. Anderson's (1989) ACT* theory of skill development includes joining sequences into larger units, broadening the use of some rules, narrowing the scope of others, and strengthening those that are most effective. Cheng (1985: 367) sees restructuring as the essential feature underlying skilled performance. Restructuring involves changing the integration and organisation of knowledge components so that "the procedure involving the old components [is] replaced by a more effective procedure involving the new components". Even theories that see repeated practice as the major determinant of development see fluency as being related to a change in knowledge.

One of the main ways in which restructuring occurs is through single words being combined into "chunks", which can include collocations and formulaic sequences. From a psycholinguistic point of view, a formulaic sequence is a word string that has become proceduralised in a speaker's mind. It functions for that speaker as a prefabricated unit. As such, its use reduces the processing demand of constructing an utterance.

From a corpus-linguistics point of view, a formulaic sequence is a word string that has become standardised in a given linguistic community. Using it helps communication run smoothly among members of that community —that is, it facilitates fluency in the production and reception of messages and it marks community membership. Consider the following (made-up) dialogue that is common in New Zealand social interaction from the perspective of formulaic sequences:

A: How's it going?
B: Pretty good. You?
A: Not so bad thanks.
B: See you later.

Formulaic language seems to be the knowledge component that drives fluency. In that sense, fluency is much more based on item-learning (lexis, including multiword units such as formulaic sequences) than on system-learning (i.e., grammar rules). Once learned, these sequences are then available to the learner in pre-packaged form and so can be accessed quickly and do not require as much conscious effort as having to construct an utterance word by word. Common collocations include "boys and girls", "make decisions", "think about it". Examples of formulaic sequences that are particularly common and useful for speaking include, "all that kind of thing", "things like that", "quite a bit", "I was wondering if you wouldn't mind". Wood (2009) argues that "chunks" or formulaic sequences drive fluency. However, there are many thousands of chunks in language, and acquisition of L2 chunk knowledge has been found to be a very slow process.

Wood (2009) describes a fluency workshop that consists of a series of linked tasks in which memorising and using formulaic sequences is emphasised. Learners first listen to recordings of people telling personal stories, such as of a childhood memory, and do activities related to the content. They then listen again while studying transcripts, with their attention drawn to formulaic sequences. They then shadow the recording with a transcript (eight times!) and do a dictogloss activity. Next, in a **mingle jigsaw** activity, each learner is given a slip of paper with a formulaic sequence from the transcript they have studied. Each learner has to memorise their chunk and then mingle and share it (without the slip of paper) with others, as well as listen to the others telling theirs. They do this until they have heard and recorded all the formulaic sequences. Finally, using the **donut arrangement** (see page 148), learners take turns talking to a partner spontaneously for 2 minutes on a topic they have been given related to the original story. When both have spoken, the inner circle of the donut moves around so each learner is facing a new partner and does the same thing again, but with a different topic. Wood's account of a case study learner participating in these workshops over 6 weeks shows that the learner made substantial fluency gains and used more and more complex formulaic sequences by the end of the 6 weeks.

Other ways to help students with chunk learning include:

- Paired-associates learning—put the target word in a couple of frequent chunks
- Introduce chunks whenever explaining new words
- Extensive reading
- Fluency development activities
- Reading activities based on chunks
- Shadowing
- Dictogloss
- Analysing transcripts of recordings with a focus on lexico-grammatical patterns (e.g., learners highlight all the phrases in a description of the layout of a house that refer to location).

Developing Fluency

Gatbonton and Segalowitz (2005: 327) eloquently describe the dilemma that communicative language teachers face in seeking to provide fluency practice:

> Although one component of fluency is automatic, smooth, and rapid language use, there are no provisions in current CLT [communicative language teaching] methodologies to promote language use to a high level of mastery through repetitive practice. In fact, focused practice continues to be seen as inimical to the inherently open and unpredictable nature of communicative activities. Thus, when teachers believe that learning has reached the point where reinforcement of new forms through practice is necessary, they tend to revert to non-communicative means for attaining this end [such as pattern practice].

We can address this dilemma by ensuring that fluency activities meet the following four conditions:

1. *The learners take part in activities where all the language items are within their previous experience.* This means that the learners work with largely familiar topics and types of discourse, making use of known vocabulary and structures. These kinds of activity are called "experience" tasks because the knowledge required to do the activity is already well within learners' experience. Having the opportunity to plan what to say can also result in making the task easier.
2. *There is support and encouragement for the learner to perform at a higher than normal level.* This means that, in an activity with a fluency development goal, learners should be speaking and comprehending faster, hesitating less, and using larger planned chunks than they do in their normal use of language. A fluency development activity provides some deliberate push to the higher level of performance, often by using time pressure.
3. *There is plenty of opportunity for repeated practice.* Fluency improvement occurs as a result of repeated, sustained practice.
4. *The activity is meaning-focused.* The learners' interest is on the communication of a message and is subject to the "real-time" pressures and demands of normal meaning-focused communication (Brumfit, 1984: 56–57).

There need to be substantial opportunities for both receptive and productive language use where the goal is fluency. There must be plenty of sustained opportunities either inside or outside the classroom to take part in meaning-focused experience tasks. If the items that have been learned are not readily available for fluent use, then the learning has been for little purpose.

Designing Fluency Activities

How can we design fluency activities that make use of the four conditions mentioned above? Fluency activities depend on several design requirements and features to achieve their goal. These can appear in a variety of techniques over the whole range of language skills. By looking at these requirements and features, we can judge whether an activity will develop fluency in an efficient way, and we can devise other activities that will. Let us look first at a well-researched activity. The **4/3/2** technique (originally 5/4/3) was devised by Keith Maurice (1983). In this technique, learners work in pairs, with one acting as the speaker and the other as listener. The speaker talks for 4 minutes on a topic while their partner listens. Then the pairs change, with each speaker giving the same information to a new partner in 3 minutes, followed by a further change and a 2-minute talk. So, the speaker speaks three times, each time with a different listener. Each listener listens to three different speakers.

From the point of view of fluency, this activity has these important features. First, the demands of the activity are limited to a much smaller set than would occur in most uncontrolled learning activities. This can be achieved through the teacher's control, as is the case in most receptive fluency activities such as reading graded readers or listening to stories, or it can be done by choice, planning, or repetition on the part of the learner. In the 4/3/2 activity, the speaker chooses the ideas and language items and plans the way of organising the talk. The 4- and 3-minute deliveries allow the speaker to bring these aspects well under control, so that fluency can become the learning goal of the activity. Second, with each repetition of the talk, the learner's attention is still focused on the message, because each time a new person is listening. Third, the learner is helped to reach a high level of performance by the challenge of having decreasing time to convey the same message and by having the opportunity to repeat. Fourth, the user is encouraged to process a large quantity of language. In 4/3/2, this is done by allowing the speaker to perform without interruption and by having the speaker make three deliveries of the talk.

Easy Tasks

Experience tasks for the development of fluency involve making sure that the language, ideas, and discourse requirements of the activity are all within the learners' experience so that the learners are able to develop the skill aspect (in this case, fluency) of the activity. In listening tasks, this is usually done by using simple texts or through the teacher controlling the level of language they use when speaking with the class. However, it can also be achieved by using learner control. This is done for listening activities by getting learners to provide input for other learners, such as when learners present short talks to the class. In speaking activities, allowing learners to provide their own topics and to speak based on their own writing, for example, provides learner control, which makes the activity an experience task and thus suitable for the development of fluency. Planning what to say can also have a marked effect on fluency and may have a stronger effect than content familiarity (Bui & Huang, 2018).

Time Pressure

One way of encouraging learners to reach a higher than usual level of performance is by limiting the time in which they can do something. This is used in 4/3/2 by decreasing the time for each repetition. In split information activities such as **same or different** or **find the difference**, it is done by putting a time limit on each set of five items and getting learners to change partners after the set time. Learners may also keep a regular record of how long it takes them to perform a task and then try to reduce the time it takes them. This could be done with learners recording a description of an object or reading aloud.

Quantity of Practice

Most fluency tasks involve a focused practice time that is relatively short, often around 5–10 minutes, but they occur regularly—for example, two or three times a week. Speed reading is a good example of this. This practice continues for several weeks. Successful language learners often attribute their success in part to watching the same movies or TV series repeatedly so that the language becomes very familiar to them.

Message Focus

Having a clear outcome to an activity encourages a meaning focus because the learners use language to achieve the outcome. Commonly used outcomes in spoken activities include completion; distinguishing, matching, classifying; ranking, ordering, choosing; problem-solving; listing implications, causes, and uses; data gathering; and providing directions. Some activities, such as 4/3/2, do not have a demonstrable outcome but are meaning-focused because the speaker has a strong sense of speaking to an audience, even though it may only be an audience of one person.

A justification for a message focus is found in the transfer-appropriate processing (TAP) model of memory (Goldstein, 2015). From a TAP perspective, the way we process information determines what we will remember or get better at. For fluency development, this means that, to become fluent with the kind of processing required in a target task, this same kind of processing needs to be practised in classroom activities that prepare learners to perform that task fluently. In other words, learners need opportunities to *practise the performance*. This, of course, is what experienced teachers have always known. The use of role plays and scenarios in communicative language learning is a good example of this principle being put into practice. In contrast, if learners are preparing for an exam in which they have to write a short essay, lots of reading or grammar study will only get them part of the way there. Thus, the TAP model provides one explanation for why form-focused drills are not adequate preparation for communicative performance.

Planning and Preparation

Another way of reaching a higher than usual level of performance is to work on the quality of the performance. This can be done through having an opportunity for planning and preparation. Crookes (1989) investigated learners who were given 10 minutes to plan what words, phrases, and ideas they would use in their explanation of how to build a Lego model or complete a map. He found that, compared with learners who were not given time to plan, the learners who planned produced longer utterances and more grammatically complex speech.

Planning and preparation can be done individually, with the help of guide sheets, or in groups. Before doing a same or different split information activity, all the learners who are A get together and work on what they will say. Similarly, all the learners who are B get together and plan and practise. After this has been done, the As pair up with the Bs to do the activity. This is an example of the jigsaw arrangement (Aronson, 2002).

There are numerous ways of designing a planning and preparation element for listening and speaking activities. Here are some brief suggestions of things to do before the fluency activity begins:

- Brainstorming the topic
- Pre-reading on the topic
- Observation of others doing the activity
- Repeated opportunities to do the activity
- Preparing and practising in the first language
- Prediction activities.

The purpose of the preparation is to make the quality of the subsequent listening or speaking reach a higher level than it would without the preparation.

Repetition

Repetition of an activity is a sure way of developing fluency with the particular items and sequences used in the activity. It is necessary to change the audience when designing repetition into meaning-focused speaking activities so that the speaker does not feel that they have to change the spoken message to try to retain the interest of a listener who has already heard the message. The success of repetition activities largely depends on the repetitions involving substantially the same message. In the 4/3/2 activity, the work is done in pairs, and the listener in each pair is replaced by a different listener for each repetition.

In listening activities, the purpose of listening may need to change in order to keep the learner interested in the repeated message.

Figure 11.1 illustrates repeated listening within a metacognitive listening cycle, as proposed by Vandergrift and Tafaghodtari (2010). The metacognitive dimension of this cycle is seen in the way that each repeated listen is managed metacognitively to achieve a purpose.

Fitting Fluency into a Course

Many of the techniques described in Chapter 3 on learning language through listening, such as **listen and draw** and **information transfer**, are easily adapted to meet the conditions for developing fluency. It is likely that the two goals of learning new language items and the development of fluency can be reached in the same activities, provided the conditions for both kinds of learning occur.

Only a relatively small amount of knowledge is needed for successful language use. It is important that this knowledge is available for use,

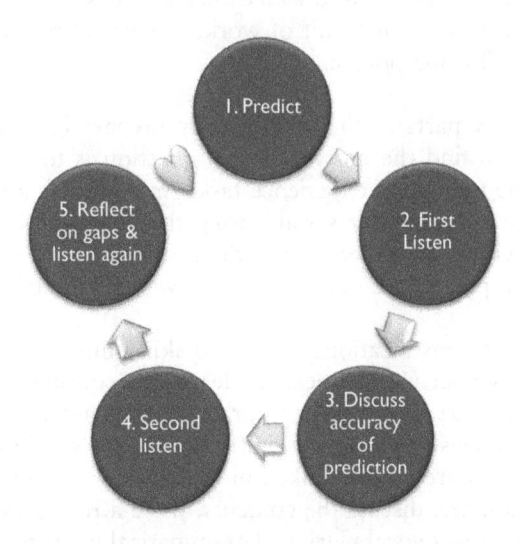

Figure 11.1 The Cycle of Repeated Listening

and, therefore, a part of class time should be given to fluency activities. Where the second language is not used outside the classroom, the principle of the four strands suggests about a quarter of class time is given to these activities. Brumfit (1985: 12) suggests it should be even more: "Right from the beginning of the course, about a third of the total time could be spent on this sort of fluency activity, and the proportion will inevitably increase as time goes on". When learners have access to online resources for fluency practice and effective teacher support and guidance to use these resources, more of this fluency practice can be scheduled outside classroom hours.

If fluency activities are included in each lesson and make use of new language items taught in that lesson, then these items should occur at a low density in the fluency material. In listening material, this means that 99 per cent of the running words should be familiar to the learners. A second alternative is to include fluency activities in each lesson that make use of items learned several days or weeks before. A third alternative is periodically to give large blocks of time to fluency activities. This suggestion corresponds to Brumfit's (1985) "syllabus with holes in it". These holes or gaps are times when no new material is presented, and there are fluency-directed activities.

Many fluency techniques involve the linking of skills. For example, reading is followed by listening, discussion is followed by listening, writing is followed by speaking. The reason for linking skills in this way is so that the earlier activities can provide preparation and support for the later activity. The preparation and support then allow a high level of performance to be reached in the later activity—much higher than there would have been if the later activity had not been linked with earlier activities.

If fluency is the goal of a unit of work, it is useful to look at the unit to check the following points:

1. Do the early parts of the unit usefully prepare for the later parts? One way to find the answer to this question is to regard the final part of the unit as an experience task. As fluency is a skill goal, the earlier parts of the unit should bring the language, ideas, and text features within the experience of the learners.
2. Is the final part of the unit a fluency development activity?

There are other justifications for linked skill units besides the fluency goal. These include: (1) the need to learn prerequisite items or skills before doing a task; (2) the wish to practise some aspect of language or language use intensively; (3) the cultural logic of the linked activities (i.e., the activities are usually linked in the world outside the classroom, such as read a letter, discuss the contents, write a reply); (4) the need to get learners to repeat vocabulary and grammatical items to help learning; and (5) practicality (it is easier for the teacher to make material that follows on from previous work; it is also easier for the learners to understand). When making a linked skills unit, it is worth considering what the justifications for the linking are. This then allows the teacher to see if the linking is being done in the most effective way.

Developing Fluency in Listening and Speaking

We can distinguish three approaches to fluency development that can all usefully be part of a language course.

The first approach relies primarily on repetition and could be called "the well-beaten path approach" to fluency. This involves gaining repeated practice on the same material so that it can be performed fluently. The second approach to fluency relies on making many connections and associations with a known item. Rather than following one well-beaten path, the learner can choose from many paths. This could be called "the richness approach" to fluency. This involves using the known item in a wide variety of contexts and situations. Most of the suggested techniques in this chapter follow this approach. The third approach to fluency is the aim and result of the previous two approaches. This could be called "the well-ordered system approach". Fluency occurs because the learner gains better control of the system of the language and can use a variety of efficient, well-connected, and well-practised paths to the wanted item.

Techniques for Developing Fluency in Listening

All the techniques described here set up the four conditions for the development of fluency discussed earlier in the chapter:

1. They place very limited demands on the learners in that they rely heavily on language items, topics, and experiences with which the learners are already familiar. This familiarity may come from having met or produced the material themselves in a different medium, or through drawing on knowledge gained through the first language. The demands of the task may also be limited through the use of controlled input and through the use of supporting material, such as the use of pictures and written texts to support the listening input.
2. The techniques encourage learners to reach a high level of performance through the use of meaning-focused repetition, increasing speed of input, and the opportunity for prediction and the use of previous background knowledge.
3. The activities involve plenty of practice opportunities.
4. The techniques involve meaning-focused activity. They involve listening to interesting stories, puzzle and quiz activities, and activities with clear communication outcomes.

In listening and reading activities, a distinction is sometimes made between activities where the learner brings a lot of topic-related background knowledge to the task (top–down processing) and activities where the learner relies primarily on the language of the text to understand (bottom–up processing; Richards, 1990). Most comprehension activities are a combination of these two approaches, but usually one is predominant. Fluency tasks should be largely top–down processing because these are the ones that allow learners to perform at speed without having to puzzle over language forms.

Top–down processing is encouraged by getting learners to listen when the topic is very familiar to them, when the organisation and other genre conventions are familiar to them, when their attention is strongly focused on the message, and when there is not a concern for linguistic detail.

Bottom–up processing occurs when the main source of information is the text itself, and the listener cannot draw on preparation and previous experience to assist in comprehension. Top–down and bottom–up processing tasks usually have different learning goals and set up conditions for different kinds of learning.

The following techniques are roughly graded from those most suitable for beginners to those most suitable for advanced learners:

In the **name it!** activity, the teacher says some sentences that describe something, for example:

"We use it to clean our teeth."

The learners answer by saying or writing the name of the thing that is described, or by choosing it from a group of pictures, or by choosing its name from a group of words on a slide or whiteboard. The learners can have a list of multiple-choice answers in front of them. They listen to the sentence and then choose the answer. The items that are described are all things that the learners are familiar with through everyday experience.

Listening to questions is an activity where the teacher asks the learners questions, and they answer them. The questions can be based on a picture, a reading passage, or general knowledge. When asking questions, the teacher should ask the question and then select a learner to answer it. In this way, everyone in the class tries to think of the answer in case the teacher chooses them. One way to do this is to hand out numbered cards at the beginning of the class. The teacher can then select a student randomly by calling out a number. Each number that is called is then written on the whiteboard to keep track of who has and hasn't answered a question. In many cultures, pointing at people is considered rude, and so the numbering approach avoids this problem. It also adds a small game element to classroom interaction, especially if it is the students who get to choose the next number.

As well as questions, true/false sentences can be used. Each sentence has a number. The teacher says:

"Number one: A bicycle has three wheels."
The learners write 1F. The teacher says:
"Number two. I am a teacher."
The learners write 2T. (F means false, T means true.)

Questions can easily become a game, with different teams trying to beat the others.

A variation of this technique is to put the answer to each question, either a single word, a short phrase, or a sentence, in a list on the whiteboard, but the answers are in a different order from the teacher's questions. The learners must listen to the teacher's question, choose the correct answer, and write it. So, for example, the teacher says:

"What colour is my shirt?"

The learners look at this list, which is on the whiteboard, and choose the answer:

at home   white   a book   paper   at six o'clock

Blown-up books are a useful way of using listening to introduce learners to reading and getting them excited about reading. These very large books have pages that are about eight times the size of ordinary pages and they contain plenty of pictures. As they are so large, they can be shown to the whole class while the teacher reads them aloud, and all the learners can see the words and pictures. Increasingly, these books are presented on PowerPoint slides rather than as physical books.

The teacher reads the story to the learners while they look at the words and pictures. The same story will be read several times over several weeks, and the learners will soon be able to say parts of the sentences that they recall from previous readings. This technique is also useful for listening fluency, as the teacher can read the story a little faster each time.

The **listening to pictures** technique (McComish, 1982) is a way of providing quantity of input (see page 30). Because of the support that the pictures provide and because of the opportunities for repetition using the same picture, this is also a useful fluency technique.

Listening to stories is particularly suitable for young learners who read well but whose listening skills are poor. The teacher chooses an interesting story, possibly a graded reader, and each day reads a chapter aloud to the learners. The learners just listen to the story and enjoy it. While reading the story, the teacher sits next to the whiteboard and writes any words that the learners might not recognise in their spoken form. Any words the learners have not met before may also be written, but the story should be chosen so that there are very few of these. During the reading of the first chapters, the teacher may go fairly slowly and repeat some sentences. As the learners become more familiar with the story, the speed increases, and the repetitions decrease. Learner interest in this activity is very high, and the daily story is usually looked forward to with the same excitement people have in television serials. If the pauses in telling the story are a little bit longer than usual, this allows learners to consider what has just been heard and to anticipate what may come next. It allows learners to listen to language at normal speed without becoming lost. See the Extensive Reading Foundation website for good books (https://erfoundation.org/).

In **listen again**, the teacher retells a story that the learners have already heard before, but uses different words from the previous telling. The learners are told that one of the events in the story will be different from the previous telling. They listen and note the difference.

In a **visit and listen** activity, the teacher and the learners visit a place outside the school, such as a zoo, a factory, a special school, or a fire station. They take notes during the visit, and, when they return to the school, the teacher talks to them about the visit. This is a kind of linked skills activity.

Quicklistens (Chang & Millett, 2016; Millett, 2008, 2014) involve listening to an easy extended text, such as a recording of a graded reader, over several days. After several minutes of listening, there are some easy questions for the learners to answer. The easy text and the continuing story provide support for faster listening. Sonia Millett's section on the LALS resources page at https://www.wgtn.ac.nz/lals/resources contains several sets of questions for Quicklistens.

Listening while reading involves the learners listening to a text and looking at a copy of the text while they listen. Before listening to the passage, the learners can have time to read it or read something containing much the same ideas or vocabulary. When learners have access to a transcript of a listening passage or an audio version of a book they are reading, a range of options open up for developing listening fluency. Here are seven of them:

> Read, then listen (a) without reading along or (b) while reading along
> Listen, then read (a) without listening or (b) while listening again
> Listen, then read, then listen again (a) without reading along or (b) while reading along
> Listen and read along

Each option has advantages and disadvantages, so it is useful for the teacher to provide practice for these different options in class and to get learners to think about what they like and don't like about each option and why.

Listening in a controlled vocabulary can be done using **peer talks**. Learners prepare talks to deliver to the whole class or to a small group. These talks help improve listening skills because the level of the language used is usually well suited to the listeners. For adult learners, the topics can focus on the speaker's job or special skills. For younger learners, the topics may be based on an article in the newspaper, an interesting event, or a story that the learner has just read. Farid (1978) suggests allowing learners to question the speaker after the talk and then to question each other on their understanding of the talk.

Recorded **interviews** can be an interesting source of listening material. Learners can be given responsibility for interviewing more proficient speakers. This has two good effects. First, it puts the learner in control of the types of question to ask and the amount of information given, and, second, it makes the interviews more accessible for other learners because the person being interviewed will have adjusted their speaking to the learner they were talking to. The interviewer can also include lots of clarification requests and understanding checks that will help the listeners. While listening, the learners can fill in an information transfer chart or complete statements.

In a **predicting** activity, the learners are given some information about a talk and have to predict what will occur in the talk. After they have made their predictions, they listen to the talk and see if their predictions were correct. The information that they are given can include a set of incomplete statements, a table of statistics, the title of the talk, or the introductory section of the talk (Watts, 1986). This is a kind of linked skills activity because discussion (the predicting) is followed by listening.

Techniques for Developing Fluency in Speaking

The following speaking fluency activities make use of repetition and rehearsal and are discrete activities. It is also possible for theme-based work over several days to develop into fluency development opportunities.

The **4/3/2** technique has already been described. It combines the features of focus on the message, quantity of production (the speakers speak for a total of 9 minutes), learner control over the topic and language used, repetition, and time pressure to reach a high rate of production through the decreasing amount of time available for each delivery. There is now a considerable amount of research on the 4/3/2 technique (Boers, 2014, 2017; de Jong & Perfetti, 2011; Thai & Boers, 2016).

The best recording is a useful fluency activity. The learner records themselves talking about a previous experience or describing a picture or set of pictures. The learner listens to the recording, noting any points where improvement could be made. Then, the learner re-records the talk.

This continues until the learner is happy with the recording. The learner then uploads the recording to a shared online class folder, such as in Google Docs, where other students can listen to it and where the teacher can provide feedback. This technique can involve planning and encourages repetition through the setting of a quality-based goal.

The **ask and answer** technique (Simcock, 1993) is a follow-up to reading. The learners read a text to a high level of comprehension and then they work in pairs, with one learner questioning the other about the text from a list of teacher-prepared questions. The answers to these questions provide a summary of the ideas in the text. The goal of the activity is for learners to perform the asking and answering in front of the class at a high level of fluency, and so each pair practises asking and answering several times before doing their class presentation.

Rehearsed talks involve learners using the pyramid procedure of preparing a talk individually, rehearsing it with a partner, practising it in a small group, and then presenting it to the whole class.

Activities described in other chapters of this book can be used to develop spoken fluency if the four conditions of limited demands, meaning focus, a high level of performance, and quality of opportunity are met. These activities include **ranking, information transfer, split information** activities, and **interviews**. Repeating an activity that was previously done with a language learning goal is a useful way of developing fluency. A gap of about 1 or 2 weeks is probably sufficient for enough memory of the previous activity to remain.

Monitoring Fluency Tasks

Examining the Context of the Material

When using experience tasks for language teaching, it is useful to have a way of checking to see what parts of the task are within the learners' experience and what part of the task is being focused on as the learning goal. In Chapter 1, we looked at four sets of goals—Language item goals, Idea or content goals, Skill goals, and Text or discourse goals. The mnemonic LIST can be used to remember these goals. A useful rule to follow is that any experience task should have only one of these goals, and the other three should already be within the learners' experience. So, if the teacher wants the learners to master the ideas or content of a text, then the language items (vocabulary, grammar, language functions) should all be within the learners' experience.

When checking an experience task, it is useful to ask these two questions:

1. What is the learning goal of the task?
2. Are the three other aspects of the task kept within the learners' experience?

Table 11.1 Fluency Checklists

A checklist for examining fluency material
1. What keeps the learners interested in the message and involved in the activity?
2. How is the activity made easy for the learners to do?
3. What encouragement is there for the learners to perform at a faster than usual level?

A checklist for observing a listening fluency activity
1. Are the learners interested in the message?
2. Are the learners easily able to understand the message?
3. Is the message coming to the learners at a rate that stretches the fluency of the learners?

A checklist for observing a speaking fluency activity
1. Are the learners interested in the activity and its outcome?
2. Are they easily able to find things to talk about?
3. Are they speaking without a lot of hesitation?
4. Are they speaking at a fast rate?

So, if the task has a skills goal, such as fluency, then the language, ideas, and organisation of the text should already be within the learners' knowledge.

Examining the Teaching Material

The checklists in Table 11.1 can be used to look at material and activities to develop fluency. They focus on the conditions needed for fluency development.

Fluency activities can also be monitored to see if learners are increasing the fluency with which they deal with tasks. Lennon (1990) found that, over a period of several months, the measures that showed a change were speech rate and filled pauses. Wood (2009) found that improved fluency involved increased use of formulaic sequences and use of longer sequences. It would be necessary to make careful transcripts of recorded spoken production to measure such changes, but teachers may be able to make more subjective judgements that are of value.

Fluency is often a neglected strand of a course, probably because the teacher feels that new material needs to appear in each lesson. Fluency development activities are a very useful bridge between knowing and using.

Tasks

1. Here is an analysis of Quicklistens. Do a similar analysis of 4/3/2.

	Quicklistens	4/3/2
1. Easy	An easy text is chosen for the listening input	
2. Push to go faster	The speed of the input can be increased using a speed control app	
3. Quantity of practice	The learners listen to the whole story over several days	
4. Message focus	There are comprehension questions to check understanding	

2. Design a linked skills activity with fluency of listening as the goal of the third task in the series. Chapter 15 of Nation (2013c) deals with linked skills activities. This book is available free from the Compass Publishing website.

Listening

3. Repeated activities are one way of developing fluency. Suggest two ways in which you could get learners to repeat the same dialogue and still find it interesting.

Further Reading

Look at the technique videos at https://tinyurl.com/Language-Teaching-Techniques for some of the activities described in this chapter.

Thai and Boers (2016) look at the 4/3/2 activity and examine claims from previous research.

Gatbonton and Segalowitz (2005) provide an excellent discussion of fluency. They outline and illustrate a classroom approach to developing fluency that they call ACCESS—Automatization in Communicative Contexts of Essential Speech Segments.

12 Assessing Progress

Monitoring Progress

Careful observation of learners while they are involved in listening and speaking activities can provide useful information about their progress, which in turn guides teaching decisions. In his influential book *Visible Learning for Teachers* (2012), John Hattie emphasises the importance of assessment for learning. Here are two principles drawn from the book:

- *"Mind frame 1: Educators believe that their fundamental task is to evaluate the effect of their teaching on students' learning"* (p. 160). Teachers believe that the "best" teaching does not mean employing the top teaching methods; rather, it involves altering instruction "on the fly" based on feedback about the effects they are having on students.
- *"Mind frame 4: Educators see assessment as feedback about their impact"* (p. 163). Of course, assessment is about the student, but teachers need to begin to see classroom assessment as feedback for the teacher as well—Who did you teach well and who not so well? What did you teach well and not so well?

Here are some suggestions for setting up an information gathering system on student learning:

1. The teacher gets learners to do regular self-assessment of their progress, as well as gathering evaluative feedback from them regarding the course. There are good reasons for involving a class in coming up with their own self-assessment criteria regarding their participation in speaking activities. This activity raises awareness of shared values and goals and, in so doing, builds classroom community. Self-assessment also builds metacognitive learning skills and autonomy. Crabbe (2007) refers to learners thinking about learning as an opportunity to build "learning understanding", which he defines as:

Consciously attending to the process of one's own language learning in order to establish better metacognitive control over that learning. This would include a detailed representation of the overall task of language learning, an analysis of the specific difficulties encountered in performance and an awareness of strategies to overcome the difficulties.

(p. 119)

2. Where possible, get learners to keep a record of their performance on regular classroom activities. For example, learners could develop a list of items that caused problems in the dictation and see if the errors associated with these items or structures decrease.
3. The teacher uses simple observation checklists when learners are performing listening and speaking activities. Many of them have been described at the end of chapters in this book. This is not a very reliable means of assessment but could alert teachers to issues to address.
4. The teacher crosses items off a syllabus list when satisfied that the learners are able to cope with that part of the syllabus. Appendix C was adapted from van Ek and Alexander (1980) to be the basis of a home tutoring course for beginners. Appendix A is for a very short course in survival language.
5. The learners build up a sequenced portfolio of completed activities and feedback. This can show improvement during the course, and the record of feedback is a useful revision tool.
6. The teacher does regular testing.

The Purposes for Testing

We have looked at monitoring learners' progress, but testing has a wide range of aims, including testing for placement, testing for diagnosis, testing for achievement, and testing for proficiency.

Placement Testing

If learners enter a programme where there are classes at various levels that they could join, there may be a need for a placement test that will quickly allow learners to be placed in the right class. Placement testing is quite tricky for several reasons. First, there is the pressure to make a quick decision. When learners begin a course, they do not want to wait several days before they know what class they are in. Second, there is the problem of making an accurate judgement. Once learners are placed at a certain level, they develop relationships with those in the class and are reluctant to move to another class. It is difficult to know from someone's score on a test what they will be like in 2 or 3 weeks' time. For some learners, their score may represent the result of rich and helpful opportunities to learn English. For others, it may represent what they were able to achieve in rather poor learning conditions. After 2 or 3 weeks in a well-run course, there could be a big difference between the learners. Third, placement tests need to involve some assessment of overall language proficiency as well as measures of the particular language skills that are central to the goals and nature of the course. In the 1970s, there was a strong interest in "integrative tests" that tried to measure underlying language proficiency. The main types of test used for this were the cloze test and dictation (Oller, 1979). It was considered that these tapped the kind of grammar knowledge that was needed for all kinds of uses of the language. Because cloze and dictation tests are easy to make and reasonably easy to score, they are still often used in placement tests.

Now that vocabulary tests are more readily available, in particular the updated Vocabulary Levels Test (Webb, Sasao, & Ballance, 2017) and the new Vocabulary Levels Test (McLean & Kramer, 2015), it makes sense to include a test of relevant vocabulary levels in a placement test battery.

Where there are large numbers of learners to be tested, a test of speaking is not usually included in a placement test. If the number of learners is small, and the course gives emphasis to spoken language, an interview test using questions of increasing difficulty may be a major part of placement testing.

Diagnostic Testing

A good teaching programme takes account of the needs of individual learners. When individual learners are not making good progress, it is important to work out the reasons for this. Diagnostic testing involves finding out a learner's strengths and weaknesses, investigating their attitudes and motivation, and revealing other obstacles to their progress. Most diagnostic testing can be rather informal and can include talking with the learner, getting them to perform certain language skills such as reading aloud, engaging in conversation with the teacher, doing part of a cloze test or dictation, and translating or explaining the meaning of certain words. In addition, the teacher can gather information from their regular classwork. In some cases, the learner may be required to sit a more formal test such as the updated Vocabulary Levels Test or the Picture Vocabulary Size Test, or a substantial test of reading or writing. Tests of productive language, speaking or writing, may use a global assessment where a single grade is given to a learner's production, or may use a more analytical form of assessment where scores are given for different aspects of the skill. For speaking, each learner could be assessed on fluency, intelligibility, accuracy of language, richness and appropriateness of language, and overall impression. Each of the five factors could receive a score out of 5, making a possible total perfect score of 25. The assessment is done while the learner engages in a simulation or role play with the tester. The scores on such an analytical approach to testing could be used for diagnosis. Diagnosis implies treatment, and so the results of diagnosis need to be used to plan ongoing teaching and learning.

Achievement Testing

Achievement testing is often contrasted with proficiency testing, although occasionally, in a well-thought-out course, they could be the same thing. Achievement testing looks at what has been studied or practised during the course and sees how well the material in the course has been learned. Achievement tests include short weekly tests, mid-term and end-of-term tests, and final tests. Small achievement tests can have the purposes of testing learning to award grades, of encouraging learning by giving the learners something to study for, and of giving feedback to the teacher and learners (i.e., assessment *for* learning). In a later section of this chapter, we look at a wide range of tests for doing this for listening and speaking. Achievement testing can be related to stated performance objectives (Brown, 1995).

The difficulty of an achievement test will depend partly on the amount of time between the teaching and learning and the testing, and between the similarity of the teaching and testing.

Proficiency Testing

Proficiency testing uses tests that are not based on a particular course but on a set of standards or an analysis of features of the language or language use. Well-known proficiency tests of overall language knowledge include IELTS (International English Language Testing System), TOEFL (Test of English as a Foreign Language), and TOEIC (Test of English for International Communication). Such tests award scores that have meaning beyond any particular language course. They provide a way of comparing learners from different countries and learning programmes. The scoring of such international tests is largely computerised, although this provides a considerable challenge for the productive skills of speaking and writing. In a listening and speaking programme, it is a good idea to try to include some internal proficiency testing. Including such testing forces course designers to consider the goals and activities of the course, making sure that they are aiming at learning that is useful outside the course. Such tests also allow comparison between different deliveries of the course over several years, even when the course itself changes over that time.

Proficiency tests can be language-focused, such as vocabulary tests or grammar tests, or can be skill- or use-focused, such as listening or speaking tests. Different focuses provide different kinds of information that can be used for diagnosis, course evaluation, or learner assessment, Let us now look at what makes a good test, and then at a range of ways of testing listening and speaking.

Testing Listening and Speaking

Like any tests, satisfactory tests of listening and speaking have to fulfil three criteria—reliability, validity, and practicality. Usually, some compromise has to be made between the criteria because what is most reliable might not be the most valid, and what is most valid might not be practical. Over the past decade or so, some testing scholars have adopted a new way of framing test qualities called argument-based validity (Kane, 2013), but the three criteria are still widely used in planning assessment.

Reliability

A reliable test is one the results of which are not greatly affected by a change in the conditions under which it is given and marked. For example, if a test is given on different days by different people, it should still give the same results. If the same answer paper is marked by different people, the score should be the same.

There are ways of checking statistically to see if a test is reliable. They all share similar features, but they look at different aspects of reliability. One way of checking is called test/retest. In this procedure, the same test is given to the same people twice, usually with a gap of a week or more between the first test and the retest. A reliable test should give very similar results on the two occasions, but the practice effect is likely to result in higher scores on the second test. Another way of checking is called split halves. In this procedure, the test is given to a group of learners, and then, when the test is being marked, the items in the test are randomly split into two groups. For example, if the test had 50 items, all the odd-numbered items would be put into one group, and all the even-numbered items would be in the other. The scores for the two groups of items are compared. For a reliable test, the scores for the two groups of items would be similar. A third way of checking is to make two equivalent forms of the same test. The two forms should be as similar to each other as possible, without being exactly the same. When the same learners are tested with the two forms of the test, the scores for the two forms should be similar. What is common about all of these ways of checking reliability is that they are trying to see if the test does the same job on all occasions that it is used. If performance on the test keeps changing when the same learners sit it again, it cannot be measuring what it is supposed to be measuring. A reliable test is not necessarily a valid test, but an unreliable test cannot be valid.

There are several features of listening and speaking tests that affect their reliability, and teachers can use these to guide their making and use of tests.

1. A listening test will be more reliable if the learners listen to a recording rather than the teacher reading aloud. The recording ensures that, whenever the test is used, the speed of speaking and the accent will be the same. This assumes that the quality of the playback and the room in which the recording is played provide consistent conditions. Note that recording the listening input could make the test less valid.
2. A test is more reliable if it has several points of assessment. This means, for example, that a listening test consisting of fifty separate multiple choice or true/false items is likely to be more reliable than a test involving twelve questions based on a listening text. A test of speaking is more reliable if the speaker is assessed on several speaking tasks and on several subskills of speaking rather than on one.
3. A test is more reliable if it can be marked in relation to a set of correct answers or if the marking is based on clearly understood criteria. Sometimes, it is necessary to give markers some training if several markers are involved. Marking a dictation or scoring a role play, for example, requires a good understanding of the marking criteria plus some marking practice and discussion. Sometimes, it is necessary to have two markers for scoring interviews or role plays (as well as making a recording for later reassessment if the two markers significantly disagree).
4. A test will be more reliable if the learners are all familiar with the format of the test. It is worth giving a little practice in answering a particular type of test before it is used for testing.

Validity

A test is valid if it measures what it is supposed to measure and when it is used for the purpose for which it is designed. This last part of the definition of validity is important, because a test may be valid when it is used for a particular purpose but not valid when it is used for another purpose. For example, a pronunciation test may be valid as a test of pronunciation but not valid as a test of spoken communicative ability. For a clear discussion of authenticity and validity, see Leung and Lewkowicz (2006).

There are several kinds of validity (e.g., authenticity, interactiveness, and impact—see Bachman and Palmer (1996)), but, because we are concerned with measuring progress and diagnosis, the two kinds that most concern us are face validity and content validity (Davies, 1990: 24).

Face validity is a very informal judgement. It simply means that the people sitting the test, the people giving the test, and others affected by it such as parents, employers, and government officials see the test as fair and reliable. A reliable test that may have good content and predictive value may be so different from what the public expect or consider relevant that its poor face validity is enough to stop it being used. Good face validity is not a guarantee of reliability or other kinds of validity.

Content validity involves considering whether the content of the test reflects the content of the skill, language, or course being tested. For example, in order to decide if a test of academic listening skill has content validity, we would need to decide what the components of the academic listening skill are and how this skill is used. We might decide that academic listening involves note-taking, dealing with academic vocabulary, and seeing the organisation of the formal spoken discourse. Typically, the listener has had some opportunity to read on the topic or it is one of a series of related lectures. Lectures are typically delivered at a certain speed (data on speech rates can be found in Tauroza and Allison (1990)). The next step is to see how well the test includes these components, and to see if it includes components that are not part of normal academic listening. If the content of the test matches well with the content of the skill, the test has high content validity. If the test does not cover the components of the skill well, or includes other components that are not part of the skill, or requires the learner to process the components in an unusual way, then it has low content validity. For another example, it is interesting to consider the content validity of dictation as a test of listening skill. What components of listening are not included in dictation? What are the components of dictation that are not typically part of the listening skill? Is the process of listening to a dictation like ordinary listening?

Kellerman (1990) stresses the importance of being able to see the speaker while listening, especially under conditions of difficulty as in listening to a foreign language. Video can thus add an aspect of validity to a test that an audio recording does not. There continues to be wide debate on the boundaries of validity among assessment scholars.

Practicality

Tests have to be used in the real world where there are limitations of time, money, facilities and equipment, and willing helpers. There is no point in designing a 100-item listening test that is too long to fit into the

40 minutes that are available for testing. Similarly, a speaking test that requires two or more testers to spend 20 minutes with every learner individually will be very expensive to run and will not be practicable if there is not money available.

Practicality can be looked at from several aspects: (1) economy of time, money, and labour; (2) ease of administration and scoring; and (3) ease of interpretation. Practicality can only be accurately determined in relation to a given situation, but, generally, a practical test is short (notice that this may conflict with reliability), does not require lots of paper and equipment, does not require many people to administer it, is easy to understand, is easy to mark, has scores or results that are easy to interpret, and can be used over and over again without upsetting its validity. It is not easy to meet all these requirements and still have a reliable and valid test. Most tests are a compromise between the various criteria. When making the compromise, it is important that validity is not lost.

In a well-reported large-scale project, Walker (1990) demonstrated how it is possible, with limited resources, to test the speaking proficiency of enormous numbers of learners. Learners had sat a written test in previous years, but now the written test was to be replaced with a spoken test to encourage more focus on speaking in the course leading up to it. So, all the learners were tested by an individual interview on a graded reader they had read (about 5 minutes) and by general conversation on a topic such as holidays, accommodation, or language study (2 minutes), totalling 7 minutes. The time available to each learner was calculated by estimating the total staff time used for the old written test and then allocating the same time to the oral test. In the case of Walker's language department, this turned out to be 2 full working days for the entire teaching staff of thirty. This ensured that, in terms of time and staff effort, the oral testing of about 1000 learners was practical. Reliability was controlled by (1) using an interview format that was the same for everybody, with clearly described types of information to cover and well explained criteria on a five-point scale for judging; (2) systematically training all the testers; (3) monitoring the testers during the testing; and (4) checking statistically that all the testers were consistent in relation to each other in assigning grades.

Although the concepts of reliability, validity, and practicality continue to be valuable, their role in assessment for formative purposes—that is, assessment *for* learning—has been debated.

The Effect of a Test on Teaching

One further criterion for a test is the influence of the form and the content of the test on the classroom (this is sometimes called the "washback" effect). For example, many schools do not test learners' oral proficiency in English. As a result, much classroom time is spent on the skills such as reading and listening that are tested, and very little time is spent on practising speaking because it is not in the test. Here is another example. If the listening test is made up of true/false statements, this could have the effect of very little work being done on listening beyond the sentence level. A good test sets a good model for what should happen in the classroom.

Listening Tests

This section and the following one contain descriptions of a wide variety of listening and speaking test procedures. While looking at the test procedures, it is worth considering the reliability, validity, and practicality criteria that have been looked at above.

Dictation

The teacher reads aloud a text of approximately 150 words, phrase by phrase. The learners write each phrase as they hear it. This kind of test has been used as a test of general language proficiency (Oller, 1979).

Partial Dictation

The learners have an incomplete written text in front of them. As they listen to a spoken version of the text, they fill in the missing parts in the written text.

Text with Questions

The learners have a list of multiple-choice questions in front of them while they listen to a text being read or a recorded dialogue. As they listen, they answer the questions.

Responding to Statements

The learners listen to statements or questions and respond to them by choosing from multiple-choice items of words or pictures, by indicating true or false, or by giving a short answer.

Three Choice True/False

Instead of responding to statements with just true or false, three categories of response are allowed: true, false, or opinion (Emery, 1980), or true, false, not stated.

Recorded Cloze

The learners listen to a recording where every fifteenth word has been replaced by a "bleep" sound and with pauses at the end of each sentence. As they listen, the learners write down the missing words (Templeton, 1977).

Information Transfer

The learners listen to a description or dialogue and label a diagram or fill in a chart or table while they listen. Palmer (1982) describes a wide range of possibilities for information transfer.

Rating Scales and Lists

Based on learners' performance on a task or based on teachers' knowledge of their learners, teachers indicate on a scale where they consider their learners are in terms of listening proficiency. The Australian Second Language Proficiency Ratings, for example, use a nine-point scale ranging from zero proficiency to native-like proficiency. The third point on the scale, *elementary proficiency*, is described as "Able to comprehend readily only utterances which are thoroughly familiar or are predictable within the areas of immediate survival needs". The sixth point on the listening scale, *minimum social proficiency*, is described as "Able to understand in routine social situations and limited work situations" (Ingram, 1981, 1984). Rating scales may also be used for self-assessment. Learners look at the items in a list, preferably of functions such as "I can use the telephone", "I can follow a lecture", and indicate what they can do. Nunn (2000) provides very useful examples of rating scales for measuring learners' performance in small-group interaction. These scales are useful both for testing and for diagnostic analysis of learners' conversation skills.

The Common European Framework of Reference for Languages (CEFR) offers a useful source of information on assessing listening and speaking (as well as the other skills). It includes a readily available, comprehensive set of scales of language proficiency that are widely used worldwide (although, in the USA, the American Council on the Teaching of Foreign Languages Proficiency Guidelines are more commonly used, and, in Canada, the Canadian Language Benchmarks are used). The CEFR framework provides detailed descriptors of second language proficiency on a six-level scale, from A1 (basic user) to C2 (proficient user). The scale (including various subscales) and the assessment tools available online for CEFR users are useful both for testing and for diagnostic analysis of students' communicative proficiency. Also available online, without cost, is a CEFR self-assessment grid that has been developed to help students identify what they "can do" based on these scales.

The Pearson Global Scale of English Learning Objectives is a well-developed scale in which learning objectives are listed for each of the four language skills according to the CEFR levels (www.english.com/gse). A scale is available for adult learners and another for academic English. Here is an example from the academic English scale at the beginner end of the scale.

Academic English (Below A1: Listening)

CSE10-21

a. Can recognise simple informal greetings
b. Can understand the letters of the alphabet
c. Can understand cardinal numbers from 1–20
d. Can recognise a few familiar everyday words, if delivered slowly and clearly
e. Can recognise the letters of the English alphabet when pronounced
f. Can recognise simple formal greetings
g. Can understand very basic common classroom instructions
h. Can understand the time of day when expressed in full hours
i. Can understand cardinal numbers from 21–100
j. Can understand ordinal numbers from 1–100
k. Can understand simple language related to prices and quantities
l. Can understand basic personal details if given carefully and slowly
m. Can understand basic questions about personal details if addressed slowly and clearly.

Speaking Tests

The two main aspects of direct procedures for testing speaking are: (1) the way in which the person being tested is encouraged to speak (this can include being interviewed, having to describe something for someone to draw, being involved in a discussion, etc.); and (2) the way in which the speaker's performance is assessed (this can include rating scales, communicative result, and assigning marks for the parts of an outcome). Owing to the practical problems in measuring the speaking proficiency of large groups of people, there has been a continuing interest in more practicable indirect group measures.

Interviews and Scales

Each learner is interviewed individually. The interviewer does not need to follow a set series of questions, but it is best to keep at least part of each interview as similar as possible. The interviewees are scored on rating scales from one to five for each of fluency, intelligibility, grammatical correctness, richness of language, and overall impression (see Henning, 1983). As van Moere (2006) has shown, it is not easy to get good agreement between raters.

Group Oral Exam

The learners are divided into groups of four or five people. They are given a card with a topic and a few questions to think about. After a few moments' thought, the group discusses the topic. Two observers grade each learner using a set of scales (Folland & Robertson, 1976; Hilsdon, 1991; Reves, 1982). Instead of discussions, role plays, partly scripted dialogues, or partly improvised plays can be used to get the learners to speak (Hayward, 1983).

Dycoms (Split Information)

The learners are divided into two equal groups. All the people in Group A have a sheet with fifty items on it, as in Figure 12.1. Those in group B have a slightly different sheet (Figure 12.2; Nation, 1977).

Some of Group B's items are exactly the same as the items on Group A's sheet. Some are slightly different. The class forms pairs, with someone from group A and someone from group B in each pair. The learners in each pair describe their items to each other and decide if they are the same or different. They must not show their pictures to each other. They write S next to the items that they decide are the same, and D next to the items that are different. After comparing five items, they change partners and do another five. This continues until they have had ten partners, thus completing the fifty items. Each learner's paper is collected and marked. Their score out of 50 is a measure of their skill in communicating with ten different people (Byers, 1973). In tests where candidates are paired, who someone is paired with can affect the outcome of the assessment (Norton, 2005).

Describe and Draw

The learner is given a picture that they have to describe so that their partner, the examiner, can draw it. Marks are given for describing each part of the picture correctly, with specific marks assigned for each part (Brown, Anderson, Shillcock, & Yule, 1984; Politzer & McGroarty, 1983). In the test, the examiner need not draw the item being described, but can just assign the points for each part described successfully.

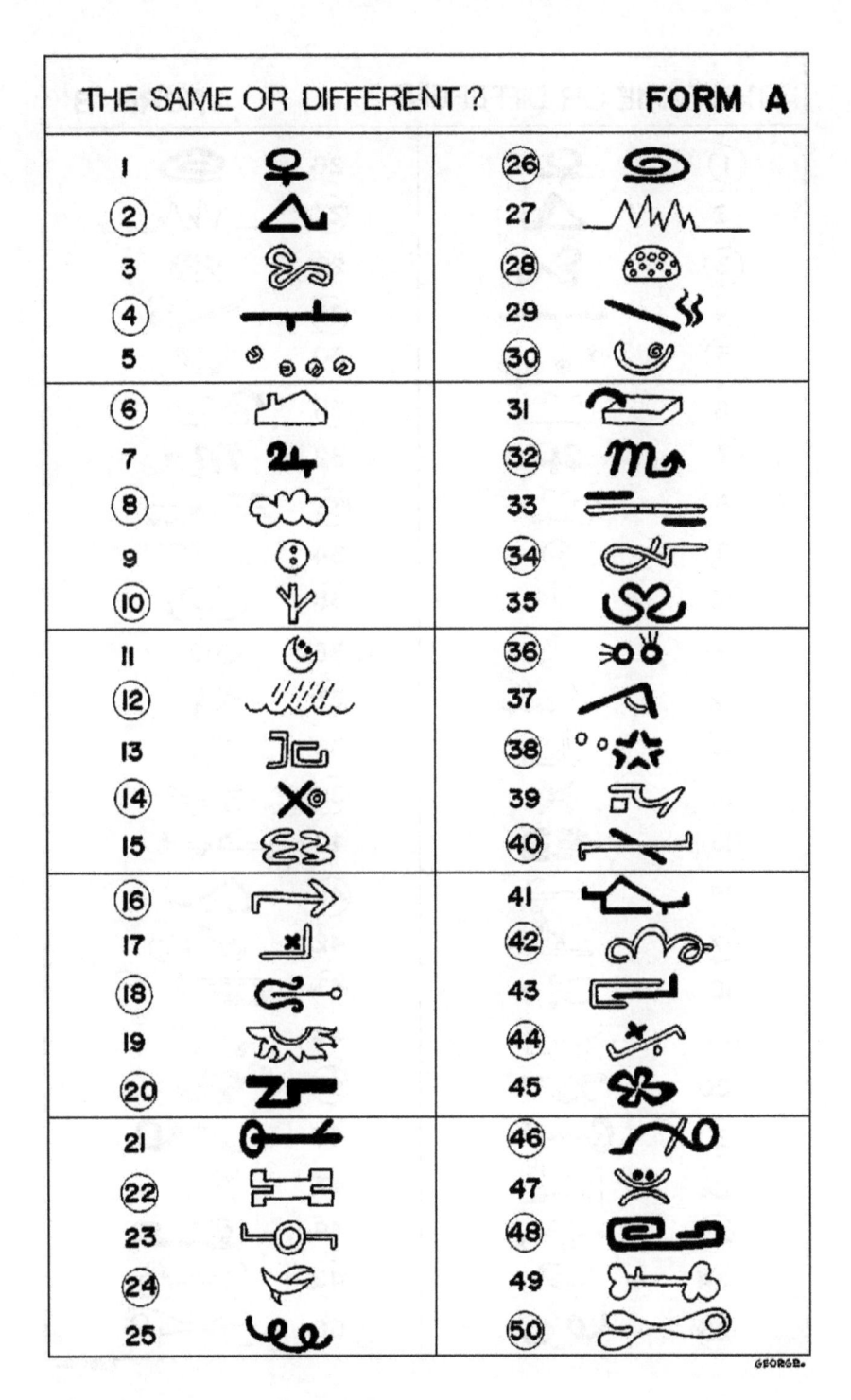

Figure 12.1 Split Information Sheet A

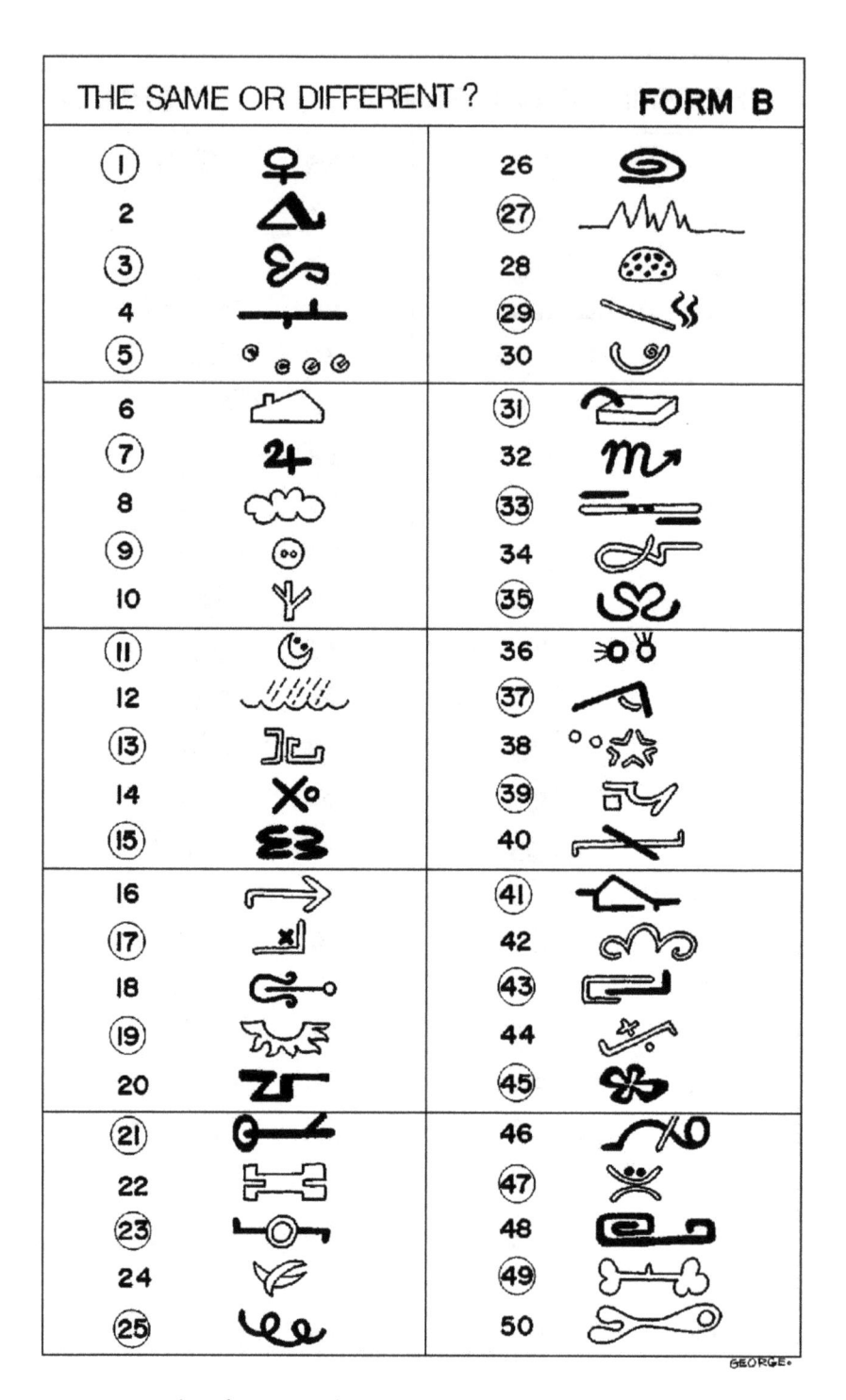

Figure 12.2 Split Information Sheet B

Conversational Cloze

This test does not involve any listening or speaking by learners. The learners are given a transcript of a conversation. Every seventh word is omitted from the transcript. The learners have to write in the missing words (Brown, 1983; Hughes, 1981). Brown (1983) found a high correlation of .84 between conversational cloze and oral interview tests. Other researchers have found similar correlations between cloze tests based on non-conversational texts and oral interviews. There are problems in using indirect measures such as cloze in place of measures involving direct performance of the skill being measured. These include lack of diagnostic information, poor face validity, problems in interpreting scores, and the washback effect.

Multiple-choice Speaking Tests

The learners are given a scenario and written multiple-choice items to choose from. They do not speak during the test. Here is an example from Politzer and McGroarty (1983: 190):

> The students are taking a test and the teacher wants them to know that they can use their books. What are two ways that he could say this?
>
> A. Whose books are those?
> B. You may use your books for this test.
> C. Don't you know how to open your books?
> D. This is an open-book test.

Discourse Completion Test

Discourse completion tests (DCTs) have been widely used to assess pragmatic competence—that is, the ability to communicate appropriately in context. There has been support for them to be used in language testing (Labben, 2016; Roever & McNamara, 2006). A DCT is like a role play. It begins with a description of a situation and, sometimes, with the beginning of a piece of communication. The learner reads this and decides how to respond. The response can be written or spoken. If it is spoken, the DCT usually requires a second person to play a role, but it can also be done non-interactively, as a recording. Here are some examples of DCTs:

Example 1: Request

You want your neighbour to help you move a heavy piece of furniture. Phone him and ask for his help.
You: _____
Neighbour: No problem. I'll be right over.

Example 2: Refusal

A neighbour wants to invite you to a meal. Unfortunately, you find it difficult to eat the food he cooks. Find a way of saying no.
Neighbour: I have some friends coming around on Thursday for a meal. I'd love you to come too.
You: _____

Example 3: Apology

You had arranged to phone your friend in the morning but you forgot. Phone your friend to say sorry.
Friend: I was expecting you to call me this morning. What happened?
You: _____

Imitation

Learners listen to recorded sentences of different lengths and repeat them. Usually, a large number of sentences are used. Henning (1983) used ninety in his test. The sentences are judged as being correct or incorrect. A correct sentence is one that is repeated without any errors.

Role Plays

The learners are given a card that describes a situation. For example,

> You want to join an English course, but you want to find out several things about the course before you make your final decision. Some of the things you want to know are the cost, the hours, the size of the groups. You are rather worried about being put in a large group where you will not get much individual attention.

The examiner also has a role to play.

> You are the course director. The course costs £150. There is an average of 14 people in a class. Classes are held from 9am to 3pm each weekday, with an hour for lunch. You want to make sure that anyone who does the course attends regularly.

After the role play, the examiner scores the learner's performance on a set of scales. This procedure is particularly useful for testing English for specific purposes, as the role plays can be suited to the jobs of the learners.

A Speaking Assessment Case Study: Assessing Spoken Presentation Skills

A programme of academic seminars given by students in an EAP course at Victoria University of Wellington[1] illustrates how assessment can be integrated into an instructional package so as to provide assessment both *of* and *for* learning. The goal of the programme is for students to present a 10-minute seminar on a topic of their choosing for summative assessment purposes. This is a high-stakes assessment as the grade a student receives on their presentation contributes to their overall grade, which is used to gain access to mainstream university programmes. To prepare students for this assessment, the following steps are involved:

1. Teachers provide instruction and models on how to prepare an academic seminar. A seminar booklet is provided for this purpose. Course learning objectives (CLOs) that focus on qualities such as awareness of genre features, critical thinking, and fluency are presented and discussed.
2. Students engage in a cycle of 5-minute seminars to prepare for the final 10-minute seminar. For these short seminars, the class is divided into small groups of listeners, with each group given responsibility to provide feedback in relation to one of the objectives. These CLOs are circulated among the groups so that, over the seminar practice cycle, each group has the opportunity to give feedback on the full range of objectives. The teacher also provides comments on each CLO.
3. Each speaker watches a video of their presentation and completes a self-evaluation form that they hand to the teacher for further comment.

We can see how assessment *for* learning in this instructional cycle provides students with rich opportunities to develop their formal presentation skills. In the process, the seminar programme reflects the following three aspects of assessment for learning identified by Chappius and Stiggins (2002):

1. Student-involved assessment
2. Effective teacher feedback
3. The skills of self-assessment.

The choice of a format for testing speaking will depend on a range of factors, including the proficiency level of the learners, their experience of various kinds of speaking activity, the reasons for testing, and how well the format satisfies the requirements of reliability, validity, and practicality.

Reasons for Testing

Learners are tested for a purpose, and, when evaluating tests, we need to consider the reasons why we are testing. There are two major reasons for testing—to find out what learners have gained from a particular course (achievement testing) and to see where learners are in their knowledge of the language (proficiency testing).

An achievement test draws its content from the material that the learners have studied. Some teachers use weekly achievement tests to get and give feedback on what has been taught and studied, and to motivate learners to study. Short-term achievement tests tend to have only a small number of items and thus may be unreliable. Teachers may try to increase the reliability of the test by signalling to learners what will be in the test so that each learner has a chance to prepare for the test. Usually, short-term achievement tests use very familiar formats.

Long-term achievement tests are likely to be used near the end of a course, and a long course may have a mid-term achievement test.

The major potential weakness of achievement tests is that poor curriculum design could result in the learners being tested on material that is not very useful for them, but it is in the test because it was in the course material.

A proficiency test draws its content from what is important to be able to know and use the language. Tests such as IELTS, TOEFL, and TOEIC are proficiency tests. Tests of vocabulary size and grammatical knowledge are also proficiency tests that focus on one aspect of knowing a language. When people design a proficiency test, they build on some idea of what knowledge is needed to know and use a language. These ideas can change, and the TOEFL of 40 years ago is rather different from the TOEFL of today.

Proficiency tests may be used as placement tests to put learners in the appropriate group at the beginning of a course, as selection tests to decide if learners have enough knowledge of the language to do academic study or to do a particular job such as practise as a doctor, and as ways of evaluating and comparing language learning programmes.

When teachers help learners prepare for a proficiency test, they tend to treat it as if it is an achievement test. That is, they look at previous versions of the test to see what questions were asked and try to create a programme that will focus on the test. Such programmes can be successful in getting learners very familiar with the test format and with strategies that help in dealing with a timed test.

If a proficiency test is well designed, it can be a very useful way of evaluating learning and course design. In an ideal world, there would be little difference between proficiency tests and achievement tests, because courses would cover what is really important for using the language, and tests would test what is really important for using the language.

When planning a language programme, it is good to have a well-thought-out system of achievement tests so that the learners are motivated to study, can see progress during the course, and get feedback on their work. Some kind of proficiency test is useful as an entry test to the course so that learners can be put into the level of class that will suit their needs. It is also worth considering whether a proficiency test should be included at the end of a course to guide learners on their future needs, and to see if the course is really doing what it is supposed to be doing.

Feedback as Part of Assessment

It is all too easy to think of giving feedback as providing information about what is wrong. But it is much more than this. As Boud and Molloy (2013) argue, feedback is not an act that occurs at a single point in time, but is a learning process "whereby learners obtain information about their work in order to appreciate the similarities and differences between the appropriate standards for any given work, and the qualities of the work itself, in order to generate improved work" (p. 6).

We can see two other points about feedback in this quote. First, for an activity to be considered as feedback, it must involve a feedback loop whereby the feedback is understood and results in some kind of impact on learning (Boud, 2015). Second, feedback is a responsive process involving two-way interactions in which the learner is an "active agent" (Boud, 2015: 4) who seeks and chooses how to use information obtained through feedback. A further implication is that teachers need to work with learners to develop in them (a) an appropriate disposition towards the feedback process and (b) the skills to manage the feedback process and make effective use of it. These skills involve knowing what the appropriate standards are, being able to analyse one's work in comparison with these standards, and knowing how to close the gap between the two (Sadler, 1989, as cited in Boud, 2015: 6). We can see here a strong connection between effective feedback processes and helping learners to become good managers of their learning.

We conclude the chapter with a broad view of how effective feedback practices are viewed from an *assessment for learning* perspective. Below are six principles for engaging in feedback from the general education literature. Notice how important the learner's active role in feedback is in these principles:

1. The assessment is prospective: students are told about their strengths and are told what **areas for improvement** need attention.
2. Information is communicated clearly and made intelligible to students in terms of what they have learned, clarifying **what good performance is** and also fostering **a close link** between teaching, learning, and assessment.

3. Students are provided with opportunities to act on feedback and to improve their performance—that is, **to close the gap**.
4. Students play **an active role** in managing their own learning—for example, engaging in peer/self-assessment and/or a dialogue with the teacher.
5. Students enhance their **motivation and self-esteem** as a result.
6. Feedback is used to improve **teaching**.

(Black & William, 1998; Boud, 2015; Nicol & Macfarlane-Dick, 2006)

Tasks

1. Work in groups of three. One person is the learner being examined. One is an examiner who participates in the role play. The other is an examiner who does not participate but just scores the test performance. At the end, the two examiners compare their scores. Here is the role play. The learner does not know what is on the examiner's role play card.

Learner	*Examiner*
You are at a shop. You need to buy a card to use when travelling on buses around town. You want to spend $20 so that you can have $20 worth of travel.	The customer wants to buy a bus card. Find out how much money they want to put on the card. Explain that the card itself costs $5 and extra money needs to be added to pay for the travel. If the customer is a student, they can get a special card that allows them cheaper travel.

2. Evaluate the use of dictation as a listening test. Give a score out of 5 for each of reliability, validity, and practicality.
3. Make a chronological plan of testing and assessment for a listening and speaking course. Indicate the purpose of each test, and the format and type of the test.

Further Reading

Ockey and Wagner (2018) have a rich range of suggestions for assessing listening.

Hughes (2011) has a useful section on assessing speaking. The second edition (2011) of this book can be downloaded free from the internet.

Henning (2012) is a reprint of an article published in 1982. It gives very practical advice based on sound testing principles. It is freely available on the English Teaching Forum website (https://americanenglish.state.gov/forum).

Note

1 My thanks to Jill Musgrave, an ex-teacher in the Victoria University of Wellington English Proficiency Programme, for sharing this material.

Conclusion

This book and its companion book, *Teaching ESL/EFL Reading and Writing*, are based on the idea that a well-balanced language course should consist of four strands. These are the strands of meaning-focused input, meaning-focused output, language-focused learning, and fluency development. Each of these strands provides different kinds of opportunity for learning and requires different conditions for the learning to occur. The meaning-focused input and the meaning-focused output strands have the conditions that the learners should be largely familiar with the language used in the strand, and it should only contain a small amount of new material. This small amount of unknown language thus has an opportunity to be learned because it is in a largely familiar, supportive context. The language-focused learning strand involves deliberate learning. Learning in this strand is usually very efficient, because learners are focused on what they should be learning and are aware of what they should be learning. The fluency development strand provides the opportunity to become really good at using what is already known. This strand requires that all of the material being worked with is familiar to the learners. In a well-balanced course, each of these four strands has roughly the same amount of time.

Another way of looking at a course is to take a curriculum design approach. This typically involves looking at: (1) the situation in which the course occurs; (2) the needs of the learners; (3) the principles on which the course is based; (4) the goals of the course; (5) the content of the course; (6) the way in which the course is presented, that is, the activities that are used in the course and the format of the coursebook; (7) the monitoring and assessment used in the course; and, finally, (8) the evaluation of the course (Macalister & Nation, 2020). This book has largely focused on the way in which the course is presented, although some attention has been given to the principles that lie behind a course, the content of the course, and monitoring and assessment. Because this book is focused on the presentation of a course, a large number of teaching techniques have been described and justified. These techniques, however, have to be seen as providing opportunities for learning to take place or, to put it another way, as opportunities for putting principles into practice.

It is, therefore, important for teachers to develop the skill of looking at an activity while it is being used to see what signs there are that learning is occurring. An activity can involve the learners, keep them busy and interested, and yet have little learning value. Throughout this book, we have looked at the conditions needed for the various strands. Meaning-focused input and output require a focus on the message, interest in the message, only a small amount of unfamiliar language features, a supportive context, and a friendly, non-threatening learning environment. Language-focused learning requires deliberate attention to language features with the opportunity for repetition and thoughtful processing. Fluency development activities require very easy material, no unfamiliar language items, pressure to go faster, quantity of practice, and a focus on the message. When looking at activities, teachers need to note whether the learners are truly engaged with the material, but teachers also need to note whether the conditions needed for a particular strand are likely to be present or not. If they are not, then adjustments need to be made to bring them in.

This book has tried to provide a practical, principled introduction to the teaching of listening and speaking. Whenever possible, it has based its suggestions and principles on research. This kind of book is one source of information for improving teaching and learning. Another important source is thoughtful and informed observation and reflection by teachers. We wish you well in that aspect of your development as a teacher.

Appendix A
The Survival Syllabus

This appendix contains a language syllabus containing approximately 120 items. It represents an easily achievable short-term goal for people wishing to visit a foreign country for a month or more. The syllabus is the result of needs analyses involving interviews with learners, analysis of guide books, and personal experience. In addition, the items in the syllabus have been checked for frequency, coverage, and combinability, and so it is made up of very useful words, phrases, and sentences.

The syllabus is divided into eight categories: greetings and being polite, buying and bargaining, reading signs, getting to places, finding accommodation, ordering food, talking about yourself, and controlling and learning language. This list is intended for travellers making a short visit to another country. The full article is Nation and Crabbe (1991). You can find the article under Publications on Paul Nation's website.

The syllabus has been divided into eight sections on the basis of information revealed during the interviews. The sections have been ranked and numbered according to the number of interviewees indicating that they used items in the sections divided by the number of items. So, the section Greetings and Being Polite was the most useful one. Items that occur in more than one section are indicated by numbers in brackets. So, *I want* … in Section 2 also occurs in Sections 5, 6, and 9. The slash (/) indicates alternatives. So, when asking about items in a shop in Section 2, you can use *Do you have* …? or *Is there* …?

A.1 Greetings and Being Polite

Hello/Good morning, etc. + reply [there are many cultural variants of these, including *Where are you going? Have you eaten?*]
How are you? + reply; e.g., Fine, thank you.

Goodbye
Thank you + reply; e.g., It's nothing, You're welcome.
Please

Excuse me [sorry]
It doesn't matter

Delicious (6)

Can I take your photo?

A.2 Buying and Bargaining

I want ... (4, 6)
Do you have ...?/Is there ...?
Yes (8)
No (8)
This (one), That (one) [to use when pointing at goods]
There isn't any

How much (cost)? (5, 6)
A cheaper one (5)

Numbers (5, 7; these need to be learned to a high degree of fluency)
Units of money (5, 6)
Units of weight and size
How much (quantity)?
Half
All of it
(One) more
(One) less

Excuse me [to get attention] (4)

Too expensive
Can you lower the price? + reply (Some countries do not use bargaining. In others, it is essential.)
Names of important things to buy (These can include stamps, a newspaper, a map.)

A.3 Reading Signs

Gents
Ladies

Entrance/in
Exit/out
Closed

A.4 Getting to Places

Excuse me (to get attention) (2)
Can you help me?
Where is ...? (5)
Where is ... street?
What is the name of this place/street/station/town?

Toilet
Bank
Department store
Restaurant
Airport
Train station
Underground
Bus station
Hospital
Doctor
Police
Post office
Telephone
Market
I want ... (2, 5, 6)

How far?/Is it near?
How long (to get to ...)?

Left
Right
Straight ahead
Slow down (directions for a taxi)
Stop here
Wait

Ticket

When

A.5 Finding Accommodation

Where is ... (4)
Hotel

How much (cost)? (2, 6)
A cheaper one (2)

I want ... (2, 4, 6)
Leave at what time?
Numbers (2, 7)
Today
Tomorrow

A.6 Ordering Food

How much (cost)? (2, 5)
The bill, please

I want ... (2, 5, 9)

Names of a few dishes and drinks
A few cooking terms
Delicious (1)

A.7 Talking about Yourself and Talking to Children

I am (name)
Where do you come from?
I am (a New Zealander)/I come from (New Zealand)
What do you do?
I am a (teacher)/tourist
You speak (Chinese)!
A little/very little
What is your name? (Especially for talking to children.)
How old are you? + reply
Numbers (2, 5)
I have been here ... days/weeks/months
I am sick

A.8 Controlling and Learning Language

Do you understand?
I (don't) understand
Do you speak English? (7)
Yes (2)
No (2)

Repeat
Please speak slowly
I speak only a little (Thai)

What do you call this in (Japanese)?

Appendix B
Topic Types

Johns and Davies (1983) described twelve topic types. Some are much more common than others. The following list is adapted from Johns and Davies and lists the most important topic types and their parts. The topic type hypothesis says that texts that are on different topics but are all of the same topic type will contain the same general kinds of information.

The Most Useful Topic Types and Their Parts

Characteristics

What are the features of the thing described?
What is the proof that some of these features exist?
What general category does this thing fit into?
What other information is there about this thing?

Physical Structure

What are the parts?
Where are the parts located?
What are they like?
What do they do?

Instruction

What are the steps involved?
What materials and equipment are needed?
What do we need to be careful about at some steps?
What is the result of the steps?
What does this result show?

Process

What are the stages involved in the development?
What material is involved at each stage?
Where and when does each stage occur?
How long does each stage last?
What acts at each stage to bring about change?
What is the thing like at each stage?
What happens at each stage?

State/Situation

Who are the people, and so on, involved?
What time and place are involved?
What is the background leading up to the happening?
What happened?
What are the effects of this happening?

Principle

What is the law or principle involved?
Under what conditions does the principle apply?
What are some examples of the principle in action?
How can we check to see that the principle is in action?
How can we apply the principle?

Theory

What is the hypothesis?
What led to this hypothesis?
How is it tested?
What are the results of testing?
What is the significance of the results?

Appendix C
Topics for Listening and Speaking

Giving Information about Yourself and Your Family/Asking Others for Similar Information

name   origin
address   job
phone   age

partner and family
length of residence

Meeting People

greetings
talking about the weather
inviting for a meal, etc.
telling the time and day
saying what you like
saying you are sorry
joining a club

Going Shopping

finding goods
asking for a quantity
understanding prices

Using Important Services

post office
bank
public telephone

police
garage

Asking How to Get to Places/Telling Others Directions

directions
distance and time
using public transport

Taking Care of Your Health

contacting a doctor
reporting illness
describing previous illness and medical conditions
calling emergency services

Describing Your Home, Town, and Country/Asking Others for Similar Information

house\flat
furniture
features of the town
features of your country

Describing Your Job/Asking Others about Their Job

job
place
working conditions
travelling to work

Finding Out How to Get a Job

kind of job
where to look
what to do

Finding Food and Drink

getting attention
using a menu
ordering a meal
offering food
praising the food

finding a toilet
giving thanks

Taking Part in Sport and Entertainment

saying when you are free
buying tickets
say what you like and do not like doing

Special Needs

Learners should add necessary words and phrases.

Appendix D
Sample Unit from Riddiford and Newton (2010)

Unit 6 Making Complaints and Criticising

Part A: Mistakes Creeping into Our Work

The Context

Sara is the manager of a team within a government department. Rebecca, Ella, Simon and Mary are all members of the team. The team has worked together for about one year. Sara has noticed an increasing number of writing errors in documents produced by the team.

1. **Thinking about context**
   Working with a partner, use the context information and complete the table.

Sara and the team	High	Medium	Low
Status difference		√	
Level of familiarity			
Level of difficulty (how hard is it to make the complaint?)			

2. **Thinking about communication**
   Here is one way that Sara could raise the problem:

   Look, I'm very unhappy with the quality of your writing. It's full of mistakes and I'm really embarrassed by it. It gives us all a bad name. You need to do something about it or else there might be consequences.

256 *Appendix D*

What is wrong with this approach? Find at least three problems with this communication.

(i) _____

(ii) _____

(iii) _____

3. **Role-play**
   The first part of the conversation between Sara and the team is provided below. Work with a partner to role-play the conversation. When you have role-played, write down your conversation.
   The conversation:

   SARA: ... which leads me on to one other item which I haven't got on the agenda, um, is it all right if I ...?
   REBECCA: Yep, yeah, sure
   SARA: ... um, and that's the, the issue of writing [deep breath].

4. **Comparison and analysis**

   a. <u>Comparing the conversation</u>
      Compare your conversation with the original conversation between Sara and her team (see p. 54). What differences do you notice?
   b. <u>Analyzing the conversation</u>
      Underline words or phrases that Sarah and her team use to make the conversation go smoothly. See p. 59 for a range of phrases. Note:

      - The phrases they use to agree and acknowledge each other's comments.
      - The way Sara phrased the complaint.
      - The words or phrases used to soften the force of the complaint.
      - Whether Sara and her team are trying to be co-operative. How can you tell?
      - Whether humour is used. Why or why not?
        Listen to the way the complaint is expressed. Listen in particular to:

- The volume of Sara's voice (loud or soft).
- The stress pattern of the complaint. Which words are stressed?
- The use of pauses.
- The use of any sighs or inhaling and exhaling (noticeable breathing in and out).
- The intonation pattern of the complaint. Is it a falling, rising or mixed falling and rising pattern?

c. Evaluating the conversation
   Rate Sara's communication using the scales below (circle a number in each scale). Discuss the evidence you used to make your rating.

(i) How **polite** was Sara?

Polite			Impolite
1	2	3	4

(ii) How **direct** was Sara?

Direct			Indirect
1	2	3	4

(iii) Overall, how **effective** was Sara's communication style? Effective communication involves achieving your purpose efficiently while also maintaining good relationships.

Very effective			Not at all effective
1	2	3	4

d. Focus on turn-taking
   Read the conversation again and focus on the steps taken in the dialogue.

   - How does the dialogue begin? Brainstorm some other useful openers.
   - Where in the conversation does the complaint come?
   - How is the complaint responded to? What other responses would be appropriate?

e. Cross-cultural comparison
   Compare this communication style with the style used in your country. Are there any differences or similarities?

f. Work with a partner to identify some ways to communicate effectively based on your analysis of Sara's communication.

Can you think of situations when it is appropriate to be more direct and not use these softening words or phrases?

5. **E-mail and telephone communication**
   a. Imagine that this communication takes place via e-mail. Write Sara's initial e-mail to her team. How might a team member reply?
   b. Write what Sara would say to a team member if she telephoned him/her about this matter.
   c. What changes, if any, have you made to the communication in *a* and *b* compared to the face-to-face version?

The original conversation between Sara and the team

1 2	Sara	... Which leads me on to one other item which I haven't got on the agenda, um, is it all right if I ...?
3	Rebecca	Yep, yeah, sure
4 5 6 7 8 9 10 11	Sara	... Um, and that's the, the issue of writing [deep breath]. Um when, um whenever you – well, we're drafting, well, I've noticed a couple of mistakes creeping into our work. That's stuff that ... that even I've looked at. I notice them because the letters go through – all the letters that go out of the ministry go through what's called the day file. They also go through ... each manager as well as our own staff. But suddenly sometimes as I'm re-reading, I spot a spelling mistake that I didn't see the first time or a grammatical mistake.
12	Simon/ Rebecca	... mm, yeah
13 14 15 16 17 18 19 20	Sara	I really ask for all of you to make sure that you take it to one other person, okay?, At least to look at before you, before you post it. Even when you send it to me to look at, it must also be checked by others. Of course when you're doing a big chunk of work then that's normal for us, we'll always, we always do that checking. But even with just simple letters make sure that they're looked at. It's so easy to overlook just a simple mistake and the less mistakes we send out the better.
21	Simon	Yeah,
22 23 24	Rebecca	I'd, I'd like to take that a bit further too 'cos, um, if we're going to use other languages in the letter, I think we should make sure that they're checked as well.
25	Simon	Mm

References

Abbott, G. (1986). A new look at phonological "redundancy". *ELT Journal, 40*(4), 299–305.
Acton, W. (1984). Changing fossilized pronunciation. *TESOL Quarterly, 18*(1), 71–85.
Adolphs, S., & Schmitt, N. (2003). Lexical coverage of spoken discourse. *Applied Linguistics, 24*(4), 425–438.
Alexander, R. (2020). *A dialogic teaching companion*. Routledge, New York.
Allen, R. L. (1972). The use of rapid drills in the teaching of English to speakers of other languages. *TESOL Quarterly, 6*(1), 13–32.
Ammar, A., & Hassan, R. M. (2018). Talking it through: Collaborative dialogue and second language learning. *Language Learning, 68*(1), 46–82.
Anderson, A., & Lynch, T. (1988). *Listening*. Oxford University Press, Oxford.
Anderson, J. (2019). Deconstructing jigsaw activities. *Modern English Teacher, 28*(2), 35–37.
Anderson, J. R. (1989). Practice, working memory, and the ACT* theory of skill acquisition: A comment on Carlson, Sullivan, and Schneider. *Journal of Experimental Psychology: Learning Memory, and Cognition, 15*, 527–530.
Arevart, S., & Nation, I. S. P. (1991). Fluency improvement in a second language. *RELC Journal, 22*(1), 84–94.
Arnold, J., Dörnyei, Z., & Pugliese, C. (2015). *The principled communicative approach*. Helbling Languages, London.
Aronson, E. (2002). Building empathy, compassion, and achievement in the jigsaw classroom. In J. M. Aronson (Ed.) *Improving academic achievement* (pp. 209–225). Elsevier, Oxford.
Asher, J. J., Kosudo, J. A., & De La Torre, R. (1974). Learning a second language through commands: The second field test. *Modern Language Journal, 58*, 1–2, 24–32.
Aston, G. (1986). Trouble-shooting in interaction with learners: The more the merrier? *Applied Linguistics, 7*(2), 128–143.
Atkins, P. W. B., & Baddeley, A. (1998). Working memory and distributed vocabulary learning. *Applied Psycholinguistics, 19*, 537–552.
Aufderhaar, C. (2004). Learner views of using authentic audio to aid pronunciation: "You can just grab some feelings". *TESOL Quarterly, 38*(4), 735–746.
Bachman, L. F., & Palmer, A. S. (1996). *Language testing in practice: Designing and developing useful language tests* (Vol. 1). Oxford University Press, Oxford.

Baddeley, A. (1990). *Human memory*. Lawrence Erlbaum, Hillsdale, MI.

Baddeley, A., Gathercole, S., & Papagno, C. (1998). The phonological loop as a language learning device. *Psychological Review, 105*(1), 158–173.

Badger, R. (1986). Grids. *English Teaching Forum, 24*(4), 36–38.

Barcroft, J. (2015). *Lexical input processing and vocabulary learning*. John Benjamins, Amsterdam.

Barnett, J. E., Di Vesta, F. J., & Rogoszinski, J. T. (1981). What is learned in note-taking? *Journal of Educational Psychology, 73*(2), 181–192.

Bauer, L., & Nation, I. S. P. (1993). Word families. *International Journal of Lexicography, 6*(4), 253–279.

Biber, D. (1989). A typology of English texts. *Linguistics, 27*, 3–43.

Biber, D., Johansson, S., Leech, G., Conrad, S., & Finegan, E. (1999). *Longman grammar of spoken and written English*. Longman, Harlow.

Bismoko, J., & Nation, I. S. P. (1974). English reading speed and the mother-tongue or national language. *RELC Journal, 5*(1), 86–89.

Black, P., & William, D. (1998). Assessment and classroom learning. *Assessment in Education, 5*(1), 71–74.

Boers, F. (2014). A reappraisal of the 4/3/2 activity. *RELC Journal, 45*(3), 221–235.

Boers, F. (2017). Repeating a monologue under increasing time pressure: A replication of Thai and Boers (2016). *The TESOLANZ Journal, 25*, 1–10.

Boers, F., Eyckmans, J., Kappel, J., Stengers, H., & Demecheleer, M. (2006). Formulaic sequences and perceived oral proficiency: Putting the lexical approach to the test. *Language Teaching Research, 10*(3), 245–261.

Boers, F., Warren, P., Grimshaw, G., & Siyanova-Chanturia, A. (2017). On the benefits of multimodal annotations for vocabulary uptake from reading. *Computer Assisted Language Learning, 30*(7), 709–725.

Boud, D. (2015). Feedback: Ensuring that it leads to enhanced learning. *Clinical Teacher, 12*(1), 3–7.

Boud, D., & Molloy, E. (Eds.). (2013). *Feedback in higher and professional education: Understanding it and doing it well*. Routledge, New York.

Breitkreuz, H. (1972). Picture stories in language teaching. *ELT Journal, 26*(2), 145–149.

Briere, E. J. (1967). Phonological testing reconsidered. *Language Learning, 17*(3 & 4), 163–171.

Briere, E. J. (1968). *A psycholinguistic study of phonological interference*. Mouton de Gruyter, The Hague.

Brown, A. (1989). Models, standards, targets/goals and norms in pronunciation teaching. *World Englishes, 8*(2), 193–200.

Brown, D. (1983). Conversational cloze tests and conversational ability. *ELT Journal, 37*(2), 158–161.

Brown, D., & Barnard, H. (1975). Dictation as a learning experience. *RELC Journal, 6*(2), 42–62.

Brown, G. (1978). Understanding spoken language. *TESOL Quarterly, 12*(3), 271–283.

Brown, G. (1981). Teaching the spoken language. *Studia Linguistica, 35*(1–2), 166–182.

Brown, G. (1986). Investigating listening comprehension in context. *Applied Linguistics, 7*(3), 284–302.

Brown, G., Anderson, A., Shillcock, R. and Yule, G. (1984). *Teaching Talk*. Cambridge University Press, Cambridge.

Brown, H. D. (1993). Requiem for methods. *Journal of Intensive English Studies*, 7, 1–12.

Brown, J. (1979). Vocabulary: Learning to be imprecise. *Modern English Teacher*, 7(1), 25–27.

Brown, J. D. (1995). *The elements of language curriculum*. Newbury House, New York.

Brown, R., Waring, R., & Donkaewbua, S. (2008). Incidental vocabulary acquisition from reading, reading-while-listening, and listening to stories. *Reading in a Foreign Language*, 20(2), 136–163.

Brumfit, C. J. (1984). *Communicative methodology in language teaching: The roles of fluency and accuracy*. Cambridge University Press, Cambridge.

Brumfit, C. J. (1985). Accuracy and fluency: A fundamental distinction for communicative teaching methodology. In C. J. Brumfit (Ed.), *Language and literature teaching: From practice to principle* (pp. 3–32). Pergamon Press, Oxford.

Buckeridge, D. (1988). "Ask 'n' move"—A role play for elementary students. *Modern English Teacher*, 15(2), 24–26.

Bui, G., & Huang, Z. (2018). L2 fluency as influenced by content familiarity and planning: Peformance, measurement and pedagogy. *Language Teaching Research*, 22(1), 94–114.

Bui, T. (2019). *The implementation of task-based language teaching in EFL primary school classrooms: A case study in Vietnam*. (PhD thesis), Victoria University of Wellington, Wellington.

Burton, D. (1986). The odd man out. *Modern English Teacher*, 13(4), 43–44.

Buzan, T. (1974). *Use your head*. BBC, London.

Byers, B. H. (1973). Testing proficiency in interpersonal communication. *RELC Journal*, 4(2), 39–47.

Bygate, M. (1988). Units of oral expression and language learning in small group interaction. *Applied Linguistics*, 9(1), 59–82.

Cabrera, M., & Martinez, P. (2001). The effects of repetition, comprehension checks, and gestures on primary school children in an EFL situation. *ELT Journal*, 55(3), 281–288.

Cárdenas-Claros, M. (2015). Design considerations of help options in computer-based L2 listening materials informed by participatory design. *Computer Assisted Language Learning*, 28(5), 429–449.

Cárdenas-Claros, M., & Gruba, P. (2012). Listeners' interactions with help options in CALL. *Computer Assisted Language Learning*, 27(3), 228–245.

Cárdenas-Claros, M. S., & Campos-Ibaceta, A. (2017). L2 listeners' use of transcripts: From reasons to practice. *ELT Journal*, 72(2), 151–161.

Carr, E. B. (1967). Teaching the *th* sounds of English. *TESOL Quarterly*, 1(1), 7–14.

Cauldwell, R. (2013). *Phonology for listening: Teaching the stream of speech*. Speech in Action, Birmingham.

Celce-Murcia, M., Brinton, D. M., & Goodwin, J. M. (2010). *Teaching pronunciation: A course book and reference guide*. Cambridge University Press, Cambridge.

Chang, A. C.-S., & Millett, S. (2014). The effect of extensive listening on developing L2 listening fluency: Some hard evidence. *ELT Journal*, 68(1), 31–39.

Chang, A. C.-S., & Millett, S. (2016). Developing L2 listening fluency through extended listening-focused activities. *RELC Journal*, *47*(3), 349–362.

Chang, A. C.-S., Millett, S., & Renandya, W. (2019). Developing L2 listening fluency through supported extensive listening practice. *RELC Journal*, *50*(3), 422–438.

Chappuis, S., & Stiggins, R. J. (2002). Classroom assessment for learning. *Educational Leadership*, *60*(1), 40–44. Retrieved from http://hssdnewteachers.pbworks.com/w/file/fetch/50394085/Classroom.Assessment.for.Learning.Chappuis.pdf

Cheng, P. W. (1985). Restructuring versus automaticity: Alternative accounts of skill acquisition. *Psychological Review*, *92*, 414–423.

Chung, M., & Nation, I. S. P. (2006). The effect of a speed reading course. *English Teaching*, *61*(4), 181–204.

Clare, A. (2016). Creativity in ELT: Ideas for developing creative thinking. In D. Xerri & O. Vassallo (Eds.), *Creativity in English language teaching* (pp. 45–56). ELT Council, Malta.

Clarke, D. F. (1991). The negotiated syllabus: What is it and how is it likely to work? *Applied Linguistics*, *12*(1), 13–28.

Clennell, C. (1999). Promoting pragmatic awareness and spoken discourse skills with EAP classes. *ELT Journal*, *53*(2), 83–91.

Coe, N. (1972). What use are songs in FL teaching? *IRAL*, *10*(4), 357–360.

Cole, P. (1972). Some techniques for communication practice. *English Teaching Forum*, *10*(1), 2–5, 20.

Coughlan, P., & Duff, P. (1994). Same task, different activities: Analysis of SLA from an activity theory perspective. In J. Lantolf & G. Appel (Eds.), *Vygotskian approaches to second language research* (pp. 173–194). Ablex, Norwood, NJ.

Couper, G. (2011). What makes pronunciation teaching work? Testing for the effect of two variables: Socially constructed metalanguage and critical listening. *Language Awareness*, *20*(3), 159–182.

Cowen, R. (2019). Listening logs. *Modern English Teacher*, *28*(3), 61–63.

Coxhead, A. (2000). A new academic word list. *TESOL Quarterly*, *34*(2), 213–238.

Crabbe, D. (2007). Learning opportunities: Adding learning value to tasks. *ELT Journal*, *61*(2), 117–125.

Craik, F. I. M., & Lockhart, R. S. (1972). Levels of processing: A framework for memory research. *Journal of Verbal Learning and Verbal Behavior*, *11*, 671–684.

Craik, F. I. M., & Tulving, E. (1975). Depth of processing and the retention of words in episodic memory. *Journal of Experimental Psychology*, *104*, 268–284.

Cramer, S. (1975). Increasing reading speed in English or in the national language. *RELC Journal*, *6*(2), 19–23.

Crookes, G. (1989). Planning and interlanguage variation. *SSLA*, *11*, 367–384.

Cross, J. (2014). Promoting autonomous listening to podcasts: A case study. *Language Teaching Research*, *18*(1), 8–32.

Cunningham, A. E., & Stanovich, K. E. (1991). Tracking the unique effects of print exposure in children: Associations with vocabulary, general knowledge, and spelling. *Journal of Educational Psychology*, *83*(2), 264–274.

Danan, M. (2016). Enhancing listening with captions and transcripts: Exploring learner differences. *Applied Language Learning, 26*(2), 1–24.
Dauer, R. M. (1983). Stress-timing and syllable-timing reanalysed. *Journal of Phonetics, 11*, 51–62.
Davies, A. (1990). *Principles of language testing*. Basil Blackwell, Oxford.
Day, R. (1981). Silence and the ESL child. *TESOL Quarterly, 15*(1), 35–39.
de Guerrero, M. C. M., & Commander, M. (2013). Shadow-reading: Affordances for imitation in the language classroom. *Language Teaching Research, 17*(4), 433–453.
de Jong, N., & Mora, C. (2019). Does having good articulatory skills lead to more fluent speech in first and second languages? *Studies in Second Language Acquisition, 41*, 227–239.
de Jong, N., & Perfetti, C. (2011). Fluency training in the ESL classroom: An experimental study of fluency development and proceduralization. *Language Learning, 61*(2), 533–568.
Denham, P. A. (1974). Design and three-item paradigms. *ELT Journal, 28*(2), 138–145.
Derwing, T., & Munro, M. (2005). Second language accent and pronunciation teaching: A research-based approach. *TESOL Quarterly, 39*(3), 379–398.
Derwing, T. M., & Munro, M. J. (2015). *Pronunciation fundamentals: Evidence-based perspectives for L2 teaching and research* (Vol. 42). John Benjamins, Amsterdam.
Deyes, A. F. (1973). Language games for advanced students. *ELT Journal, 27*(2), 160–165.
Dickerson, W. B. (1990). Morphology via orthography: A visual approach to oral decisions. *Applied Linguistics, 11*(3), 238–252.
Dobbyn, M. (1976). An objective test of pronunciation for large classes. *ELT Journal, 30*(3), 242–244.
Dunn, A. (1993). Dictogloss—When the words get in the way. *TESOL in Context, 8*(2), 21–23.
Duppenthaler, P. (1988). Hints. *English Teaching Forum, 26*(3), 46.
Dupuy, B. (1999). Narrow listening: An alternative way to develop listening comprehension in the foreign language classroom. *System, 24*(1), 97–100.
Dušková, L. (1969). On sources of errors in foreign language learning. *IRAL, 7*, 11–36.
Eckman, F. R., Bell, L., & Nelson, D. (1988). On the generalisation of relative clause instruction in the acquisition of English as a second language. *Applied Linguistics, 9*(1), 1–20.
Elgort, I. (2007). The role of intentional decontextualised learning in second language vocabulary acquisition: Evidence from primed lexical decision tasks with advanced bilinguals. PhD thesis, Victoria University of Wellington, New Zealand.
Elgort, I. (2011). Deliberate learning and vocabulary acquisition in a second language. *Language Learning, 61*(2), 367–413.
Elgort, I. (2017). Incorrect inferences and contextual word learning in English as a second language. *Journal of the European Applied Linguitics Association, 1*(1), 1–11.

Elkins, R. J., Kalivoda, T. B., & Morain, G. (1972). Fusion of the four skills: A technique for facilitating communicative exchange. *Modern Language Journal*, 56(7), 426–429.

Elley, W. B. (1989). Vocabulary acquisition from listening to stories. *Reading Research Quarterly*, 24(2), 174–187.

Elley, W. B., & Mangubhai, F. (1981). *The impact of a book flood in Fiji primary schools*. NZCER, Wellington.

Ellis, N. C., & Beaton, A. (1993). Psycholinguistic determinants of foreign language vocabulary learning. *Language Learning*, 43(4), 559–617.

Ellis, R. (1986). *Understanding second language acquisition*. Oxford University Press, Oxford.

Ellis, R. (1990). *Instructed second language acquisition*. Basil Blackwell, Oxford.

Ellis, R. (1991). The interaction hypothesis: A critical evaluation. In E. Sadtono (Ed.),, *Language Acquisition and the Second/Foreign Language Classroom*, RELC Anthology Series, 28, 179–211.

Ellis, R. (1992). Learning to communicate in the classroom: A study of two language learners' requests. *SSLA*, 14(1), 1–23.

Ellis, R. (2003). *Task-based language learning and teaching*. Oxford University Press, Oxford.

Ellis, R. (2005). Principles of instructed language learning. *System*, 33, 209–224.

Ellis, R. (2006). Current issues in the teaching of grammar: an SLA perspective. *TESOL Quarterly*, 40(1), 83–107.

Ellis, R. (2009). The differential effects of three types of planning on fluency, complexity and accuracy in L2 oral production. *Applied Linguistics*, 30(4), 474–509.

Ellis, R. (2016). Focus on form: A critical review. *Language Teaching Research*, 20(3), 405–428.

Ellis, R. (2018). *Reflections on task-based language teaching*. Multilingual Matters, Bristol.

Ellis, R. (2019). Towards a modular language curriculum for using tasks. *Language Teaching Research*, 23(4), 454–475. doi:10.1177/1362168818765315.

Ellis, R., & Shintani, N. (2013). *Exploring language pedagogy through second language acquisition research*. New York, Routledge, New York.

Emery, P. (1980). Evaluating spoken English: A new approach to the testing of listening comprehension. *ELT Journal*, 34(2), 96–98.

Esling, J. H., & Wong, R. F. (1983). Voice quality settings and the teaching of pronunciation. *TESOL Quarterly*, 17(1), 89–95.

Farid, A. (1978). Developing the listening and speaking skills: A suggested procedure. *ELT Journal*, 33(1), 27–30.

Feng, Y., & Webb, S. (2019). Learning vocabulary through reading, listening, and viewing. *SSLA*, 1–25.

Fernández Dobao, A. (2014). Vocabulary learning in collaborative tasks: A comparison of pair and small group work. *Language Teaching Research*, 18(4), 497–520.

Field, J. (2000). "Not waving but drowning": A reply to Tony Ridgway. *ELT Journal*, 54(2), 186–195.

Field, J. (2003). Promoting perception: Lexical segmentation in L2 listening. *ELT Journal*, 57(4), 325–334.

Flege, J. E. (1981). The phonological basis of foreign accent: A hypothesis. *TESOL Quarterly*, 15(4), 443–455.

Flege, J. E. (1987). A critical period for learning to pronounce foreign languages. *Applied Linguistics*, 8(2), 162–177.

Flege, J. E., & Port, R. (1981). Cross-language phonetic interference: Arabic to English. *Language and Speech*, 24, 125–146.

Flenley, T. (1982). Making realistic listening material. *Modern English Teacher*, 10(2), 14–15.

Fletcher, J. D., & Tobias, S. (2005). The multimedia principle. In R. Mayer (Ed.), *The Cambridge handbook of multimedia learning* (pp. 117–133). Cambridge University Press, Cambridge.

Folland, D., & Robertson, D. (1976). Towards objectivity in group oral testing. *ELT Journal*, 30(2), 156–167.

Folse, K. (1991). Could you repeat that? An innovative way of getting students to speak up. *TESL Reporter*, 24(2), 23–25.

Foster, P., & Ohta, A. S. (2005). Negotiation for meaning and peer assistance in second language classrooms. *Applied Linguistics*, 26(3), 402–430.

Fotos, S. (2002). Structure-based interactive tasks. In E. Hinkel & S. Fotos (Eds.), *New perspectives on grammar teaching in second language classrooms* (pp. 181–198). Lawrence Erlbaum, Mahwah, NJ.

Fotos, S., & Ellis, R. (1991). Communicating about grammar: A task-based approach. *TESOL Quarterly*, 25(4), 605–628.

Fotos, S. F. (1993). Conscious raising and noticing through focus on form: Grammar task performance versus formal instruction. *Applied Linguistics*, 14(4), 385–407.

Fowles, J. (1970). Ho! Ho! Ho! Cartoons in the language classroom. *TESOL Quarterly*, 4(2), 155–159.

Franken, M. (1987). Self-questioning scales for improving academic writing. *Guidelines*, 9(1), 1–8.

Gary, J. D., & Gary, N. G. (1981). Caution: Talking may be dangerous for your linguistic health. *IRAL*, 19(1), 1–13.

Gass, S. (1997). *Input, interaction and the second language learner*. Lawrence Erlbaum, Mahwah, NJ.

Gass, S., Winke, P., Isbell, D. R., & Ahn, J. (2019). How captions help people learn languages: A working-memory, eye-tracking study. *Language Learning & Technology*, 23(2), 84–104.

Gatbonton, E., & Segalowitz, N. (2005). Rethinking communicative language teaching: A focus on access to fluency. *Canadian Modern Language Review*, 61(3), 325–353.

George, H. V. (1965). The substitution table. *ELT Journal*, 20(1), 46–48.

George, H. V. (1972). *Common errors in language learning*. Newbury House, Rowley, MA.

George, H. V. (1990). Listening skills. *Guidelines*, 12(1), 14–25.

George, H. V., & Neo, B. C. (1974). A theory of stress. *RELC Journal*, 5(1), 50–63.

Gerhiser, A., & Wrenn, D. (2007). Second language pronunciation assessment handout packet. *GA TESOL*. Retrieved from http://teachingpronunciation.pbworks.com/f/Pronunciation+assessment+packet+.pdf

Gibson, R. E. (1975). The strip story: A catalyst for communication. *TESOL Quarterly*, 9(2), 149–154.

Gilbert, J. B. (2001). Six pronunciation priorities for the beginning student. *The CATESOL Journal*, 13(1), 173–182.

Givon, T., Yang, L., & Gernsbacher, M. A. (1990). The processing of second language vocabulary: From attended to automated word-recognition. In H. Burmeister & P. L. Rounds (Eds.), *Variability in second language acquisition* (Vol. 1, pp. 345–362). Department of Linguistics, University of Oregon.

Goh, C. (2000). A cognitive perspective on language learners' listening comprehension problems. *System*, 28(1), 55–75.

Goldstein, E. B. (2015). *Cognitive psychology: Connecting mind, research and everyday experience*. Cengage Learning, Stamford, CT.

Gower, R. (1981). Structured conversations. *Modern English Teacher*, 9(1), 27–29, (2), 141–150.

Green, K. (1975). Values clarification theory in ESL and bilingual education. *TESOL Quarterly*, 9(2), 155–164.

Gregg, K. R. (1984). Krashen's monitor and Occam's razor. *Applied Linguistics*, 5, 79–100.

Grgurović, M., & Hegelheimer, V. (2007). Help options and multimedia listening: Students' use of subtitles and the transcript. *Language Learning and Technology*, 11(1), 45–66.

Griffin, G. F., & Harley, T. A. (1996). List learning of second language vocabulary. *Applied Psycholinguistics*, 17, 443–460.

Griffiths, R. (1991a). Language classroom speech rates: A descriptive study. *TESOL Quarterly*, 25(1), 189–194.

Griffiths, R. (1991b). Pausological research in an L2 context: A rationale, and review of selected studies. *Applied Linguistics*, 12(4), 345–364.

Guiora, A. Z., Beit-Hallami, B., Brannon, R. C. L., Dull, C. Y., & Scovel, T. (1972a). The effects of experimentally induced changes in ego states on pronunciation ability in a second language: An exploratory study. *Comprehensive Psychiatry*, 13, 421–428.

Guiora, A. Z., Brannon, R. C. L., & Dull, C. Y. (1972b). Empathy and second language learning. *Language Learning*, 22(1), 111–130.

Gurrey, P. (1955). *Teaching English as a foreign language*. Longman, London.

Hall, R. W. (1971). Ann and Abby: The agony column on the air. *TESOL Quarterly*, 5(3), 247–249.

Halverson, J. (1967). Stress, pitch, and juncture. *ELT Journal*, 21(3), 210–217.

Hamada, Y. (2016). Shadowing: Who benefits and how? A booming EFL teaching technique for listening comprehension. *Language Teaching Research*, 20(1), 35–52.

Hamada, Y. (2019). Shadowing: What is it? How to use it. Where will it go? *RELC Journal*, 50(3), 386–393.

Hammerly, H. (1982). Contrastive phonology and error analysis. *IRAL*, 20(1), 17–32.

Hamp-Lyons, L. (1983). Survey of materials for teaching advanced listening and notetaking. *TESOL Quarterly*, 17(1), 109–122.

Harris, D. P. (1970). Report on an experimental group administered memory span test. *TESOL Quarterly*, 4(3), 203–213.

Hattie, J. (2012). *Visible learning for teachers: Maximizing impact on learning.* Routledge, New York.

Hayward, T. (1983). Passive assessor tests: An alternative to interviews for assessing communicative performance in spoken English. *World Language English*, 3(1), 39–43.

Hendrickson, J. M. (1978). Error correction in foreign language teaching: Recent theory, research and practice. *Modern Language Journal*, 62(8), 387–398.

Henning, G. (1983). Oral proficiency testing: Comparative validities of interview, imitation, and completion methods. *Language Learning*, 33(3), 315–332.

Henning, G. (2012). Twenty common testing mistakes for EFL teachers to avoid. *English Teaching Forum*, 50(3), 33–36, 40.

Henning, W. A. (1966). Discrimination training and self-evaluation in the teaching of pronunciation. *IRAL*, 4(1), 7–17.

Herman, P. A., Anderson, R. C., Pearson, P. D., & Nagy, W. E. (1987). Incidental acquisition of word meaning from expositions with varied text features. *Reading Research Quarterly*, 22(3), 263–284.

Higa, M. (1963). Interference effects of interlist word relationships in verbal learning. *Journal of Verbal Learning and Verbal Behavior*, 2, 170–175.

Hill, L. A. (1969). Delayed copying. *ELT Journal*, 23(3), 238–239.

Hilsdon, J. (1991). The group oral exam: Advantages and limitations. In J. C. Alderson & B. North (Eds.), *Language testing in the 1990s: The communicative legacy* (pp. 189–197). Macmillan, London.

Hirvela, A. (1987). Extended story-telling. *Modern English Teacher*, 14(3), 18–21.

Hole, J. (1983). Pronunciation testing—What did you say? *ELT Journal*, 37(2), 127–128.

Holmes, J., & Brown, D. F. (1976). Developing sociolinguistic competence in a second language. *TESOL Quarterly*, 10(4), 423–431.

Hsu, W. (2019). Voice of America news as voluminous reading material for mid-frequency vocabulary learning. *RELC Journal*, 50(3), 408–421.

Hu, M., & Nation, I. S. P. (2000). Unknown vocabulary density and reading comprehension. *Reading in a Foreign Language*, 13(1), 403–430.

Hughes, A. (1981). Conversational cloze as a measure of oral ability. *ELT Journal*, 35(2), 161–167.

Hughes, G. S. (1985). Positioning: Drama and communication. *English Teaching Forum*, 23(3), 40–41.

Hughes, R. (2011). *Teaching and researching speaking* (2nd ed.). Longman & Pearson, Harlow.

Hughes, R., & Reed, B. S. (2016). *Teaching and researching speaking.* Taylor & Francis, Boston, MA.

Ilson, R. (1962). The dicto-comp: A specialized technique for controlling speech and writing in language learning. *Language Learning*, 12(4), 299–301.

Ingram, D. (1981). The Australian second language proficiency ratings. In J. A. S. Read (Ed.), *Directions in language teaching* (pp. 108–136). RELC Anthology Series 3, RELC.

Ingram, D. (1984). *Australian second language proficiency ratings.* Department of Immigration and Ethnic Affairs, Canberra.

Ishii, T. (2015). Semantic connection or visual connection: Investigating the true source of confusion. *Language Teaching Research*, 19(6), 712–722.

Izumi, S. (2002). Output, input enhancement, and the noticing hypothesis: An experimental study on ESL relativization. *SSLA, 24*, 541–577.

Jenkins, J. (2002). A sociolinguistically based, empirically researched pronunciation syllabus for English as an international language. *Applied Linguistics, 23*(1), 83–103.

Jenkins, J. R., Stein, M. L., & Wysocki, K. (1984). Learning vocabulary through reading. *American Educational Research Journal, 21*(4), 767–787.

Joe, A. (1998). What effects do text-based tasks promoting generation have on incidental vocabulary acquisition? *Applied Linguistics, 19*, 357–377.

Joe, A., Nation, P., & Newton, J. (1996). Vocabulary learning and speaking activities. *English Teaching Forum, 34*(1), 2–7.

Johns, T., & Davies, F. (1983). Text as a vehicle for information: The classroom use of written texts in teaching reading in a foreign language. *Reading in a Foreign Language, 1*(1), 1–19.

Johnson, K. (1988). Mistake correction. *ELT Journal, 42*(2), 89–96.

Jones, D. (1960). *An outline of English phonetics* (9th ed.). Heffer, Cambridge.

Jones, R. E. (2001). A consciousness-raising approach to the teaching of conversational storytelling skills. *ELT Journal, 55*(2), 155–163.

Jordan, R. R. (1990). Pyramid discussions. *ELT Journal, 44*(1), 46–54.

Kane, M. (2013). The argument-based approach to validation. *School Psychology Review, 42*(4), 448–457.

Kellerman, S. (1990). Lip service: The contribution of the visual modality to speech perception and its relevance to the teaching and testing of foreign language listening comprehension. *Applied Linguistics, 11*(3), 272–280.

Kim, Y., & McDonough, K. (2008). The effect of interlocutor proficiency on the collaborative dialogue between Korean as a second language learners. *Language Teaching Research, 12*, 211–234.

Kissling, E. M. (2015). Phonetics instruction improves learners' perception of L2 sounds. *Language Teaching Research, 19*(3), 254–275.

Krashen, S. D. (1981). The "fundamental pedagogical principle" in second language teaching. *Studia Linguistica, 35*(1–2), 50–70.

Krashen, S. D. (1985). *The input hypothesis: Issues and implications*. Longman, London.

Kuhn, M., & Stahl, S. (2003). Fluency: A review of developmental and remedial practices. *Journal of Educational Psychology, 95*(1), 3–21.

Kung, F., & Wang, X. (2019). Exploring EFL learners' accent preferences for effective ELF communication. *RELC Journal, 50*(3), 394–407.

Labben, A. (2016). Reconsidering the development of the discourse completion test in interlanguage pragmatics. *Pragmatics, 26*(1), 69–91.

Lado, R. (1965). Memory span as a factor in second language learning. *IRAL, 3*(2), 123–129.

Larsen-Freeman, D., & Long, M. H. (1991). *An introduction to second language acquisition research*. Longman, London.

Leeman, J. (2007). Feedback in L2 learning: Responding to errors during practice. In R. DeKeyser (Ed.), *Practice in a second language* (pp. 111–137). Cambridge University Press, Cambridge.

Leeser, M. J. (2004). Learner proficiency and focus on form during collaborative dialogue. *Language Teaching Research, 8*, 55–81.

Lennon, P. (1990). Investigating fluency in EFL: A quantitative approach. *Language Learning*, *40*(3), 387–417.

Lennon, P. (1991). Error: Some problems of definition, identification, and distinction. *Applied Linguistics*, *12*(2), 180–196.

Leonard, K. R. (2019). Examining the relationship between decoding and comprehension in L2 listening. *System*, *87*, 1–12.

Leung, C., & Lewkowicz, J. (2006). Expanding horizons and unresolved conundrums: Language testing and assessment. *TESOL Quarterly*, *40*(1), 211–234.

Levine, D. R., & Adelman, M. B. (1982). *Beyond language: Cross-cultural communication*. Prentice Hall RegentsEnglewood Cliffs, NJ.

Levis, J. (2005). Changing contexts and shifting paradigms in pronunciation teaching. *TESOL Quarterly*, *39*(3), 369–377.

Lewis, M. (1993). *The lexical approach*. Language Teaching Publications, Hove.

Li, S., Ellis, R., & Zhu, Y. (2016). Task-based versus task-supported language instruction: An experimental study. *Annual Review of Applied Linguistics*, *36*, 205–229.

Lilja, N., & Piirainen-Marsh, A. (2019). Connecting the language classroom and *the Wild*: Re-enactments of language use experience. *Applied Linguistics*, *40*(4), 594–623.

Lindgren, E., & Muñoz, C. (2013). The influence of exposure, parents, and linguistic distance on young European learners' foreign language comprehension. *International Journal of Multilingualism*, *10*, 105–129.

Lindstromberg, S., Eyckmans, J., & Connabeer, R. (2016). A modified dictogloss for helping learners remember L2 academic English formulaic sequences for use in later writing. *English for Specific Purposes*, *41*, 12–21.

Locke, J. L. (1970). The value of repetition in articulation learning. *IRAL*, *8*(2), 147–154.

Long, M. (1988). Instructed interlanguage development. In L. Beebe (Ed.), *Issues in second language acquisition* (pp. 115–141). Newbury House, New York.

Long, M. H. (1996). The role of the linguistic environment in second language acquisition. In W. C. Ritchie & T. K. Bhatia (Eds.), *Handbook of language acquisition* (Vol. 2: Second language acquisition, pp. 413–468). Academic Press, New York.

Long, M. H. (2009). Methodological principles for language teaching. In M. H. Long & C. Doughty (Eds.), *The handbook of language teaching* (pp. 373–394). Wiley-Blackwell, Malden, MA.

Long, M. H. (2015). *Second language acquisition and task-based language teaching*. John Wiley, West Sussex.

Lynch, T. (2001). Seeing what they meant: Transcribing as a route to noticing. *ELT Journal*, *55*(2), 124–132.

Lynch, T., & Mendelsohn, D. (2002). Listening. In N. Schmitt (Ed.), *An introduction to applied linguistics* (pp. 193–210). Arnold, London.

Lyster, R., & Ranta, L. (1997). Corrective feedback and learner uptake. Negotiation of form in communicative classrooms. *Studies in Second Language Acquisition*, *19*, 37–66.

Lyster, R., Saito, K., & Sato, M. (2013). Oral corrective feedback in second language classrooms. *Language Teaching*, *46*(1), 1–40.

Macalister, J., & Nation, I. S. P. (2021). *Language curriculum design* (2nd ed.). Routledge, New York.

Mackey, A. (1999). Input, interaction, and second language development. *SSLA*, *21*, 557–587.

Major, R. C. (1987). Foreign accent: Recent research and theory. *IRAL*, *25*(3), 185–202.

Martinez, R., & Schmitt, N. (2012). A phrasal expressions list. *Applied Linguistics*, *33*(3), 299–320.

Maurice, K. (1983). The fluency workshop. *TESOL Newsletter*, *17*(4), 29.

Mayo, M. (2002). The effectiveness of two form-focused tasks in advanced EFL pedagogy. *International Journal of Applied Linguistics*, *12*(2), 156–175.

McCarthy, M., & Carter, R. (2003). What constitutes a basic spoken vocabulary? *Research notes: Cambridge University Press*. Retrieved from www.CambridgeESOL.org/researchnotes/, August 5–7.

McComish, J. (1982). Listening to pictures. *Modern English Teacher*, *10*(2), 4–8.

McKay, H., & Tom, A. (1999). *Teaching adult second language learners*. Cambridge University Press, Cambridge.

McLarty, R. (2019). Of course we want coursebooks. *Modern English Teacher*, *28*(2), 4–7.

McLean, S., & Kramer, B. (2015). The creation of a new Vocabulary Levels Test. *Shiken*, *19*(2), 1–11.

Mennim, P. (2003). Rehearsed oral L2 output and reactive focus on form. *ELT Journal*, *57*(2), 130–138.

Messer, S. (1967). Implicit phonology in children. *Journal of Verbal Learning and Verbal Behavior*, *6*, 609–613.

Meunier, F. (2020). Resources for learning multiword items. In S. Webb (Ed.), *The Routledge handbook of vocabulary studies* (pp. 336–350). Routledge, New York.

Mhone, Y. W. (1988). It's my word, teacher! *English Teaching Forum*, *26*(2), 48–51.

Millett, S. (2008). A daily fluency programme. *Modern English Teacher*, *17*(2), 21–28.

Millett, S. (2014). Quicklistens: Using what they already know. *Modern English Teacher*, *23*(4), 64–65.

Mohsen, M. A. (2015). The use of help options in multimedia listening environments to aid language learning: A review. *British Journal of Educational Technology*, *47*(6), 1232–1242.

Montero Perez, M., Peters, E., & Desmet, P. (2018). Vocabulary learning through viewing video: The effect of two enhancement techniques. *Computer Assisted Language Learning*, *31*(1–2), 1–26.

Montero Perez, M., van den Noortgate, W., & Desmet, P. (2013). Captioned video for L2 listening and vocabulary learning: A meta-analysis. *System*, *41*(3), 720–739.

Munro, M. J., & Derwing, T. M. (2006). The functional load principle in ESL pronunciation instruction: An exploratory study. *System*, *34*(4), 520–531.

Murphy, J. M. (2013). Intelligible, comprehensible, non-native models in ESL/EFL pronunciation teaching. *System*, *42*, 258–269.

Nakahama, Y., Tyler, A., & van Lier, L. (2001). Negotiation of meaning in conversational and information gap activities: A comparative discourse analysis. *TESOL Quarterly*, *35*, 377–405.

Nakata, T. (2011). Computer-assisted second language vocabulary learning in a paired-associate paradigm: A critical investigation of flashcard software. *Computer Assisted Language Learning*, 24(1), 17–38.

Nassaji, H. (2016). Interactional feedback in second language teaching and learning: A synthesis and analysis of current research. *Applied Linguistics*, 20(4), 535–562.

Nassaji, H. (2017). Grammar acquisition. In S. Loewen & M. Sato (Eds.), *The Routledge handbook of instructed second language acquisition* (pp. 205–223). Routledge, New York.

Nation, I. S. P. (1975). Motivation, repetition and language teaching techniques. *ELT Journal*, 29(2), 115–120.

Nation, I. S. P. (1977). The combining arrangement: Some techniques. *Modern Language Journal*, 61(3), 89–94.

Nation, I. S. P. (1978). "What is it?" A multipurpose language teaching technique. *English Teaching Forum*, 16(3), 20–23, 32.

Nation, I. S. P. (1980). Graded interviews for communicative practice. *English Teaching Forum*, 18(4), 26–29.

Nation, I. S. P. (1988). Using techniques well: Information transfer. *Guidelines*, 10(1), 17–23.

Nation, I. S. P. (1989a). Improving speaking fluency. *System*, 17(3), 377–384.

Nation, I. S. P. (1989b). Group work and language learning. *English Teaching Forum*, 27(2), 20–24.

Nation, I. S. P. (1990a). *Teaching and learning vocabulary*. Newbury House, New York.

Nation, I. S. P. (1990b). A system of tasks for language learning. In S. Anivan (Ed.), *Language teaching methodology for the nineties* (pp. 51–63). RELC Anthology Series No 24. RELC, Singapore.

Nation, I. S. P. (1992). Controlling the teacher. *Practical English Teaching*, 13(1), 50–51.

Nation, I. S. P. (2000). Learning vocabulary in lexical sets: Dangers & guidelines. *TESOL Journal*, 9(2), 6–10.

Nation, I. S. P. (2006). How large a vocabulary is needed for reading & listening? *Canadian Modern Language Review*, 63(1), 59–82.

Nation, I. S. P. (2007). Vocabulary learning through experience tasks. *Language Forum*, 33(2), 33–43.

Nation, I. S. P. (2008). *Teaching vocabulary: Strategies & techniques*. Heinle Cengage Learning, Boston, MA.

Nation, I. S. P. (2013a). *Learning vocabulary in another language* (2nd ed.). Cambridge University Press, Cambridge.

Nation, I. S. P. (2013b). *What should every EFL teacher know?* Compass Publishing, Seoul.

Nation, I. S. P. (2013c). *What should every ESL teacher know?* Compass Publishing, Seoul.

Nation, I. S. P. (2018). How vocabulary is learned. *Indonesian Journal of English Language Teaching*, 12(1), 1–12.

Nation, I. S. P. (2019). *Fast track*. Seed Learning, Sache, TX.

Nation, I. S. P. & Crabbe, D. (1991). A survival language learning syllabus for foreign travel. *System*, 19(3), 191–201.

Nation, I. S. P., & Macalister, J. (2021). *Teaching ESL/EFL reading and writing* (2nd ed.). Routledge, New York.

Nation, I. S. P., & Waring, R. (2020). *Teaching extensive reading in another language*. Routledge, New York.

Nation, I. S. P., & Yamamoto, A. (2012). Applying the four strands to language learning. *International Journal of Innovation in English Language Teaching and Research*, 1(2), 167–181.

Nation, P., & Wang, K. (1999). Graded readers and vocabulary. *Reading in a Foreign Language*, 12(2), 355–380.

Newmark, L. (1981). Participatory observation: How to succeed in language learning. In H. Winitz (Ed.), *The comprehension approach to foreign language instruction* (pp. 34–48). Newbury House, Rowley, MA.

Newton, J. (1995). Task-based interaction and incidental vocabulary learning: A case study. *Second Language Research*, 11(2), 159–177.

Newton, J. (2013). Incidental vocabulary learning in classroom communication tasks. *Language Teaching Research*, 17(2), 164–187.

Newton, J. (2016). Teaching language skills. In G. Hall (Ed.), *The Routledge handbook of English language teaching* (pp. 428–440). Routledge, New York.

Newton, J. (2017). Comprehending misunderstanding. *ELT Journal*, 71(2), 237–244.

Newton, J., & Bui, T. (2017). Teaching with tasks in primary school EFL classrooms in Vietnam. In M. Ahmadian & M. D. P. García Mayo (Eds.), *Current trends in task-based language teaching and learning* (pp. 259–278). Mouton de Gruyter, Boston, MA.

Newton, J., & Kennedy, G. (1996). Effects of communication tasks on the marking of grammatical relations by second language learners. *System*, 24(3), 159–177.

Newton, J., & Nguyen, B. T. T. (2019). Task repetition and the public performance of speaking tasks in EFL classes at a Vietnamese high school. *Language Teaching for Young Learners*, 1(1), 34–56.

Newton, J. M., Ferris, D. R., Goh, C. C., Grabe, W., Stoller, F. L., & Vandergrift, L. (2018). *Teaching English to second language learners in academic contexts: Reading, writing, listening, and speaking*. Routledge, New York.

Nguyen, B. T. T., & Newton, J. (2019). Learner proficiency and EFL learning through task rehearsal and performance. *Language Teaching Research*, XX, Pages 1–28.

Nguyen, B. T. T., & Newton, J. (2020). Vietnamese EFL learners' use of the third-person singular–s in oral communicative tasks. Unpublished manuscript.

Nicol, D. J., & Macfarlane-Dick, D. (2006). Formative assessment and self-regulated learning: A model and seven principles of good feedback practice. *Studies in Higher Education*, 31(2), 199–218.

Nielson, K. B. (2014). Can planning time compensate for individual differences in working memory capacity? *Language Teaching Research*, 18(3), 272–293.

Nord, J. R. (1980). Developing listening fluency before speaking: An alternative paradigm. *System*, 8(1), 1–22.

Norton, J. (2005). The paired format in the Cambridge Speaking Tests. *ELT Journal*, 59(4), 287–297.

Nunan, D. (1998). Approaches to teaching listening in the language classroom. In *Proceedings of the 1997 Korea TESOL Conference*. KOTESOL, Taejon, Korea.

Retrieved November 15, 2007 from www.kotesol.org/publications/proceedings/1997/nunan_david.pdf (html version).

Nunn, R. (2000). Designing rating scales for small-group interaction. *ELT Journal*, 54(2), 169–178.

Ockey, G. J., & Wagner, E. (Eds.). (2018). *Assessing L2 listening*. John Benjamins, Amsterdam.

Ohta, A. (2005). Interlanguage pragmatics in the zone of proximal development. *System*, 33(3), 503–517.

Oller, J. (1979). *Language tests at school*. Longman, London.

Oller, J. W., & Streiff, V. (1975). Dictation: A test of grammar-based expectancies. *ELT Journal*, 30(1), 25–36.

Ortega, L. (1999). Planning and focus on form in L2 oral performance. *SSLA*, 21(1), 109–148.

Palmer, D. M. (1982). Information transfer for listening and reading. *English Teaching Forum*, 20(1), 29–33.

Palmer, H. (1925). Conversation. In R. C. Smith (Ed.), 1999. *The writings of Harold E. Palmer: An overview* (pp. 185–191). Hon-no-Tomosha, Tokyo.

Pan, Y., Tsai, T., Huang, Y., & Liu, D. (2018). Effects of expanded vocabulary support on L2 listening comprehension. *Language Teaching Research*, 22(2), 189–207.

Papagno, C., Valentine, T., & Baddeley, A. (1991). Phonological short-term memory and foreign-language vocabulary learning. *Journal of Memory and Language*, 30, 331–347.

Patkowski, M. (1990). Age and accent in a second language: A reply to James Emil Flege. *Applied Linguistics*, 11, 73–89.

Pavia, N., Webb, S., & Faez, F. (2019). Incidental vocabulary learning through listening to songs. *SSLA*, 41, 745–768.

Pennington, M. C. (2019). "Top-down" pronunciation teaching revisited. *RELC Journal*, 50(3), 371–385.

Pennington, M. C., & Richards, J. C. (1986). Pronunciation revisited. *TESOL Quarterly*, 20(2), 207–225.

Peters, E. (2018). The effect of out-of-class exposure to English language media on learners' vocabulary knowledge. *ITL—International Journal of Applied Linguistics*, 169, 142–168.

Peters, E., & Webb, S. (2018). Incidental vocabulary acquisition through viewing L2 television and factors that affect learning. *SSLA*, 40, 1–27.

Philp, J., & Duchesne, S. (2016). Exploring engagement in tasks in the language classroom. *Annual Review of Applied Linguistics*, 36, 50–72.

Pica, T., Holliday, L., Lewis, N., & Morgenthaler, L. (1989). Comprehensible output as an outcome of linguistics demands on the learner. *SSLA*, 11, 63–90.

Picken, J. (1988). Let the students judge. *Modern English Teacher*, 15(4), 39–41.

Pienemann, M. (2003). Language processing capacity. In C. Doughty & M. H. Long (Eds.), *The handbook of second language acquisition* (pp. 679–714). Blackwell, Malden, MA.

Pike, K. L. (1947). *Phonemics*. University of Michigan Press, Ann Arbor, MI.

Pinter, A. (2017). *Teaching young language learners*. Oxford University Press, Oxford.

Politzer, R., & McGroarty, M. (1983). A discrete point test of communicative competence. *IRAL*, 21(3), 180–191.

Prince, P. (2013). Listening, remembering, writing: Exploring the dictogloss task. *Language Teaching Research*, 17(4), 486–500.

Purcell, E. T., & Suter, R. W. (1980). Predictors of pronunciation accuracy: A re-examination. *Language Learning*, 30(2), 271–287.

Purvis, K. (1983). The teacher as moderator: A technique for interactional learning. *ELT Journal*, 37(3), 221–228.

Ranta, L., & Meckelborg, A. (2013). How much exposure to English do international graduate students really get? Measuring language use in a naturalistic setting. *Canadian Modern Language Review*, 69(1), 1–33.

Renandya, W. A., & Farrell, T. S. C. (2011). "'Teacher, the tape is too fast!" Extensive listening in ELT. *ELT Journal*, 65(1), 52–59.

Reves, T. (1982). The group-oral examination: A field experiment. *World Language English*, 1(4), 259–262.

Richards, J. C. (1969). Songs in language learning. *TESOL Quarterly*, 3(2), 161–174.

Richards, J. C. (1974). *Error analysis: Perspectives on second language acquisition*. Longman, London.

Richards, J. C. (1990). *The language teaching matrix*. Cambridge University Press, Cambridge.

Riddiford, N., & Newton, J. (2010). *Workplace talk in action*. LALS, Victoria University of Wellington, Wellington.

Ridgway, T. (2000a). Listening strategies—I beg your pardon? *ELT Journal*, 54(2), 179–185.

Ridgway, T. (2000b). Hang on a minute! *ELT Journal*, 54(2), 196–197.

Riley, P. M. (1972). The dicto-comp. *English Teaching Forum*, 10(1), 21–23.

Robb, K. (2018). An integrated skills approach to speaking and listening. *Modern English Teacher*, 27(1), 31–32.

Robinett, B. W. (1965). Simple classroom techniques for teaching pronunciation. In *On teaching English to speakers of other languages* (pp. 135–138). NCTE Delaware.

Rodgers, M. P. H. (2018). The images in television programs and the potential for learning unknown words: The relationship between on-screen imagery and vocabulary. *ITL International Journal of Applied Linguistics*, 169, 191–211.

Rodgers, M. P. H., & Webb, S. (2011). Narrow viewing: The vocabulary in related television programs. *TESOL Quarterly*, 45(4), 689–717.

Rodgers, M. P. H., & Webb, S. (2017). The effects of captions on EFL learners' comprehension of English-language television programs. *CALICO Journal*, 34(1), 20–38.

Roever, C., & McNamara, T. (2006). Language testing: The social dimension. *International Journal of Applied Linguistics*, 16(2), 242–258.

Romanko, R. (2017). *The vocabulary demands of popular English songs*. Unpublished PhD thesis,, Temple University Japan, Tokyo.

Rossiter, M. J., Derwing, T. M., Manimtim, L. G., & Thomson, R. I. (2010). Oral fluency: The neglected component in the communicative language classroom. *Canadian Modern Language Review*, 66(4), 583–606.

Rost, M. (2016). *Teaching and researching listening* (3rd ed.). Routledge, New York.

Saito, K. (2013). Reexamining effects of form-focused instruction on L2 pronunciation development: The role of explicit phonetic information. *Studies in Second Language Acquisition*, 35(1), 1–29.

Sato, M., & McDonough, K. (2019). Practice is important but how about its quality? Contextualized practice in the classroom. *Studies in Second Language Acquisition*, 41, 999–1026.

Sawyer, J., & Silver, S. (1961). Dictation in language learning. *Language Learning*, 11(1 & 2), 33–42.

Sayer, P. (2005). An intensive approach to building conversation skills. *ELT Journal*, 59(1), 14–22.

Schlecty, P. (1994). *Increasing student engagement*. Missouri Leadership Academy, Jefferson City, MO.

Schmidt, R. W. (1992). Psychological mechanisms underlying second language fluency. *SSLA*, 14, 357–385.

Schmitt, N., & Meara, P. (1997). Researching vocabulary through a word knowledge framework: Word associations and verbal suffixes. *SSLA*, 19, 17–36.

Service, E. (1992). Phonology, working memory, and foreign language learning. *The Quarterly Journal of Experimental Psychology*, 45A(1), 21–50.

Service, E., & Kohonen, V. (1995). Is the relation between phonological memory and foreign language learning accounted for by vocabulary acquisition? *Applied Psycholinguistics*, 16, 155–172.

Sheen, R. (1992). Problem solving brought to task. *RELC Journal*, 23(2), 44–59.

Sheen, Y. (2004). Corrective feedback and learner uptake in communicative classrooms across instructional settings. *Language Teaching Research*, 8(3), 263–300.

Shin, D., & Nation, I. S. P. (2008). Beyond single words: The most frequent collocations in spoken English. *ELT Journal*, 62(4), 339–348.

Siegel, J. (2016). A pedagogic cycle for EFL notetaking. *ELT Journal*, 70(3), 275–286.

Siegel, J. (2019). Teaching lecture notetaking with authentic materials. *ELT Journal*, 73(2), 124–133.

Simcock, M. (1993). Developing productive vocabulary using the "Ask and answer" technique. *Guidelines*, 15, 1–7.

Singleton, D. (1999). *Exploring the second language mental lexicon*. Cambridge University Press, Cambridge.

Skehan, P. (1998). *A cognitive approach to language learning*. Oxford University Press, Oxford.

Skehan, P. (2014). Before and after the task: Potential research-based contributions. *OnTask*, 4(1), 4–10.

Skehan, P. (2015). Limited attention capacity and cognition: Two hypotheses regarding second language performance on tasks. In M. Bygate (Ed.), *Domains and directions in the development of TBLT: A decade of plenaries from the international conference* (pp. 123–156). John Benjamins, Amsterdam.

Skehan, P., Xiaoyue, B., Qian, L., & Wang, Z. (2012). The task is not enough: Processing approaches to task-based performance. *Language Teaching Research*, 16(2), 170–187.

Spada, N. (1997). Form-focussed instruction and second language acquisition: A review of classroom and laboratory research. *Language Teaching*, 30, 73–87.

Stahl, S. A., & Vancil, S. J. (1986). Discussion is what makes semantic maps work in vocabulary instruction. *The Reading Teacher*, *40*(1), 62–67.

Stenstrom, A. (1990). Lexical items peculiar to spoken discourse. In J. Svartik (Ed.), *The London–Lund corpus of spoken English: Description and research, Lund Studies in English 82* (pp. 137–175). Lund University Press, Lund.

Stevick, E. W. (1978). Toward a practical philosophy of pronunciation: Another view. *TESOL Quarterly*, *12*(2), 145–150.

Storch, N., & Aldosari, A. (2012). Pairing learners in pair work activity. *Language Teaching Research*, *17*(1), 31–48.

Strong, B., & Boers, F. (2018). The error in trial and error: Exercises on phrasal verbs. *TESOL Quarterly*, *53*(2), 289–319.

Swain, M. (1985). Communicative competence: Some roles of comprehensible input and comprehensible output in its development. In S. Gass & C. Madden (Eds.), *Input in second language acquisition* (pp. 235–253). Newbury House, Rowley, MA.

Swain, M. (1995). Three functions of output in second language learning. In G. Cook & B. Seidelhofer (Eds.), *Principle and practice in applied linguistics: Studies in honour of H.G. Widdowson* (pp. 125–144). Oxford University Press, Oxford.

Swain, M. (2000). The output hypothesis and beyond: Mediating acquisition through collaborative dialogue. In J. Lantolf (Ed.), *Sociocultural theory and second language learning* (pp. 97–119). Oxford University Press, Oxford.

Swain, M. (2005). The output hypothesis: Theory and research. In E. Hinkel (Ed.), *Handbook of research in second language teaching and learning* (pp. 471–483). Lawrence Erlbaum, Mahwah, NJ.

Swain, M. (2013). The inseparability of cognition and emotion in second language learning. *Language Teaching*, *46*(2), 195–207.

Swain, M., & Lapkin, S. (1998). Interaction and second language learning: Two adolescent French immersion students working together. *Modern Language Journal*, *82*, 320–337.

Swan, M. (2017). EFL, ELF, and the question of accuracy. *ELT Journal*, *71*(4), 511–515.

Swan, M., & Smith, B. (2001). *Learner English: A teacher's guide to interference and other problems* (2nd ed.). Cambridge University Press, Cambridge.

Swan, M., & Walter, C. (2017a). Misunderstanding comprehension. *ELT Journal*, *71*(2), 228–236.

Swan, M., & Walter, C. (2017b). A response to Jonathan Newton. *ELT Journal*, *71*(2), 245–246.

Sydorenko, T. (2010). Modality of input and vocabulary acquisition. *Language Learning & Technology*, *14*(2), 50–73.

Tahta, S., Wood, M., & Lowenthal, K. (1981a). Age changes in the ability to replicate foreign pronunciation and intonation. *Language and Speech*, *24*(4), 363–372.

Tahta, S., Wood, M., & Lowenthal, K. (1981b). Foreign accents: Factors relating to transfer of accent from the first language to the second language. *Language and Speech*, *24*(3), 265272.

Tauroza, S., & Allison, D. (1990). Speech rates in British English. *Applied Linguistics*, *11*(1), 90–105.

Taylor, B. P. (1982). In search of real reality. *TESOL Quarterly*, *16*(1), 28–42.

Tegge, F. (2017). The lexical coverage of popular songs in English language teaching. *System*, *67*, 87–98.
Tegge, F. (2018). Pop songs in the classroom: Time-filler or teaching tool? *ELT Journal*, *72*, 274–284.
Templeton, H. (1977). A new technique for measuring listening comprehension. *ELT Journal*, *31*(4), 292–299.
Terrell, T. D. (1982). The natural approach to language teaching: An update. *Modern Language Journal*, *66*(2), 121–132.
Thai, C., & Boers, F. (2016). Repeating a monologue under increasing time pressure: Effects on fluency, complexity, and accuracy. *TESOL Quarterly*, *50*(2), 369–393.
Thaine, C. (2018). EAP learners and pronunciation: Dealing with comprehensibility. *Modern English Teacher*, *27*(1), 19–22.
Thomas, G. I., & Nation, I. S. P. (1979). Communicating through the ordering exercise. *Guidelines*, *1*, 68–75.
Thornbury, S. (2001). *Uncovering grammar*. Macmillan Heinemann, Oxford.
Thorndike, E. L. (1908). Memory for paired associates. *Psychological Review*, *15*, 122–138.
Tinkham, T. (1993). The effect of semantic clustering on the learning of second language vocabulary. *System*, *21*(3), 371–380.
Tinkham, T. (1997). The effects of semantic and thematic clustering on the learning of second language vocabulary. *Second Language Research*, *13*(2), 138–163.
Todd, S. C. (1996). Why we should stop teaching our students to take notes: Evidence that the "encoding hypothesis" isn't right. In C. Reves, C. Steele, & C. S. P. Wong (Eds.), *Linguistics and language teaching: Proceedings of the Sixth Joint LSH-HATESL Conference* (pp. 201–222). University of Hawai'i, Second Language Teaching and Curriculum Center (Technical Report #10), Honolulu, HI.
Tomasello, M., & Herron, C. (1989). Feedback for language transfer errors: The garden path technique. *SSLA*, *11*, 385–396.
Trofimovich, P., & Gatbonton, E. (2006). Repetition and focus on form in processing L2 Spanish words: Implications for pronunciation instruction. *Modern Language Journal*, *90*(4), 519–535.
Tsui, A., & Fullilove, J. (1998). Bottom-up or top-down processing as a discriminator of L2 listening performance. *Applied Linguistics*, *19*(4), 432–451.
Tsui, A. B. M. (2012). The dialectics of theory and practice in teacher knowledge development. In J. M.-L. B. R. S. Hütter & S. Schiftner (Eds.), *Theory and practice in EFL teacher education: Bridging the gap* (pp. 16–37). Multilingual Matters, Bristol.
Tucker, C. A. (1972). Programmed dictation: An example of the P.I. process in the classroom. *TESOL Quarterly*, *6*(1), 61–70.
van Ek, J. A., & Alexander, L. G. (1980). *Threshold level English*. Pergamon Press, Oxford.
van Moere, A. (2006). Validity evidence in a university group oral test. *Language Testing*, *23*(4), 411–440.
van Zeeland, H., & Schmitt, N. (2013). Lexical coverage and L1 and L2 listening comprehension: The same or different from reading comprehension? *Applied Linguistics*, *34*(4), 457–479.

Vandergrift, L. (2007). Recent developments in second and foreign language listening comprehension research. *Language Teaching*, 40(3), 191–210.

Vandergrift, L., & Goh, C. (2012). *Teaching and learning second language listening: Metacognition in action.* Routledge, New York.

Vandergrift, L., & Goh, C. M. (2018). How listening comprehension works. In J. Newton, D. R. Ferris, C. M. Goh, W. Grabe, F. L. Stoller, & L. Vandergrift (Eds.), *Teaching English to second language learners in academic contexts: Reading, writing, listening, speaking* (pp. 161–181). Routledge, New York.

Vandergrift, L., & Tafaghodtari, M. H. (2010). Teaching L2 learners how to listen does make a difference: An empirical study. *Language Learning*, 60(2), 470–497.

Vanderplank, R. (2016). *Captioned media in foreign language learning and teaching.* Palgrave Macmillan, London.

Vasiljevic, Z. (2010). Dictogloss as an interactive method of teaching listening comprehension. *English Language Teaching*, 3, 41–52.

Vásquez, C., & Harvey, J. (2010). Raising teachers' awareness about corrective feedback through research replication. *Language Teaching Research*, 14(4), 421–443.

Wajnryb, R. (1988). The Dicto-gloss method of language teaching: A text-based communicative approach to grammar. *English Teaching Forum*, 26(3), 35–38.

Wajnryb, R. (1989). Dicto-gloss: A text-based communicative approach to teaching and learning grammar. *English Teaching Forum*, 27(4), 16–19.

Wajnryb, R. (1990). *Grammar dictations.* Oxford University Press, Oxford.

Walker, C. (1990). Large-scale oral testing. *Applied Linguistics*, 11(2), 200–219.

Walker, J. (2010). *Teaching the pronunciation of English as a lingua franca.* Oxford University Press, Oxford.

Wang, Y. (2019). Effects of L1/L2 captioned TV programs on students' vocabulary learning and comprehension. *CALICO Journal*, 36(3), 204–224.

Waring, R. (1997). The negative effects of learning words in semantic sets: A replication. *System*, 25(2), 261–274.

Waring, R., & Takaki, M. (2003). At what rate do learners learn and retain new vocabulary from reading a graded reader? *Reading in a Foreign Language*, 15(2), 130–163.

Watts, N. R. (1986). Developing aural anticipation and prediction strategies. *English Teaching Forum*, 24(1), 21–23, 29.

Webb, S. (2002). *Investigating the effects of learning tasks on vocabulary knowledge.* PhD thesis, Victoria University of Wellington.

Webb, S. (2005). Receptive and productive vocabulary learning: The effects of reading and writing on word knowledge. *SSLA*, 27, 33–52.

Webb, S. (2010a). Pre-learning low frequency vocabulary in second language television programs. *Language Teaching Research*, 14(4), 501–515.

Webb, S. (2010b). Using glossaries to increase the lexical coverage of television programs. *Reading in a Foreign Language*, 22(1), 201–221.

Webb, S., & Nation, I. S. P. (2017). *How vocabulary is learned.* Oxford University Press, Oxford.

Webb, S., Newton, J., & Chang, A. (2013). Incidental learning of collocation. *Language Learning*, 63(1), 91–120.

Webb, S., & Rodgers, M. P. H. (2009a). The vocabulary demands of television programs. *Language Learning*, 59(2), 335–366.

Webb, S., & Rodgers, M. P. H. (2009b). The lexical coverage of movies. *Applied Linguistics*, *30*(3), 407–427.

Webb, S., Sasao, Y., & Ballance, O. (2017). The updated Vocabulary Levels Test. *ITL International Journal of Applied Linguistics*, *168*(1), 33–69.

Webb, W. B. (1962). The effects of prolonged learning on learning. *Journal of Verbal Learning and Verbal Behavior*, *1*, 173–182.

West, M. P. (1941). *Learning to read a foreign language and other essays*. Longman, London.

West, M. P. (1960). *Teaching English in difficult circumstances*. Longman, London.

White, R. V. (1978). Teaching the passive. *ELT Journal*, *32*(3), 188–193.

Whiteson, V. (1978). Testing pronunciation in the language laboratory. *ELT Journal*, *33*(1), 30–31.

Williams, J. (2005). Form-focused instruction. In E. Hinkel (Ed.), *Handbook of research in second language teaching and learning* (pp. 671–691). Lawrence Erlbaum, Mahwah, NJ.

Willis, D., & Willis, J. (2009). Task-based language learning: Some questions and answers. *The Language Teacher*, *33*(3), 3–8.

Willis, J. (1996). *Exposure to spontaneous speech using recordings. A framework for task-based learning*. Longman, London.

Wilson, M. (2003). Discovery listening: Improving perceptual processing. *ELT Journal*, *57*(4), 335–343.

Winitz, H. (Ed.). (1981). *The comprehension approach to foreign language instruction*. Newbury House, Rowley, MA.

Winke, P., Gass, S., & Sydorenko, T. (2013). Factors influencing the use of captions by foreign language learners: An eye-tracking study. *The Modern Language Journal*, *97*(1), 254–275.

Wintz, H., & Bellerose, B. (1965). Phoneme-cluster learning as a function of instructional method and age. *Journal of Verbal Learning and Verbal Behavior*, *4*, 98–102.

Wolf, J. P. (2013). Exploring and contrasting EFL learners' perceptions of textbook-assigned and self-selected discussion topics. *Language Teaching Research*, *17*(1), 49–66.

Wood, D. (2006). Uses and functions of formulaic sequences in second language speech. *Canadian Modern Language Review*, *63*(1), 13–33.

Wood, D. (2009). Effects of focused instruction of formulaic sequences on fluent expression in second language narratives: A case study. *The Canadian Journal of Applied Linguistics*, *12*(1), 39–57.

Wu, Y. (1998). What do tests of listening comprehension test? A retrospection study of EFL test-takers performing a multiple-choice task. *Language Testing*, *15*, 21–44.

Yashima, T. (2002). Willingness to communicate in a second language: The Japanese EFL context. *The Modern Language Journal*, *86*(1), 54–66.

Yasui, M. (no date). *Consonant patterning in English*. Kenkyushu, Tokyo.

Yeldham, M. (2018). Viewing L2 captioned videos: What's in it for the listener? *Computer Assisted Language Learning*, *31*(4), 367–389.

Yeldham, M., & Gruba, P. (2014). Toward an instructional approach to developing interactive second language listening. *Language Teaching Research*, *18*(1), 33–53.

Yeldham, M., & Gruba, P. (2016). The development of individual learners in an L2 listening strategies course. *Language Teaching Research*, 20(1), 9–34.

Yuan, F., & Ellis, R. (2003). The effects of pre-task planning and on-line planning on fluency, complexity and accuracy in L2 monologic oral production. *Applied Linguistics*, 24(1), 1–27.

Index

4/3/2 8–9, 13, 16, 61, 71, 87, 114, 137–138, 157, 159, 177–178, 180, 210–211, 213, 219, 221–222, 260

Academic Word List 123, 185, 189, 262
age 17, 94–95, 99, 252, 273, 276, 279
agony column 138, 266
Aladdin 64–66
ask and answer 145, 178, 220, 275
ask and move 32

best recording 178, 219
bingo 21, 30, 35
bottom-up 40–42, 52, 62, 64, 90, 216, 277
brainstorming 158, 212
buzz groups 56

captions 66–70, 263, 265, 274, 279
challenge 29, 62–65, 78, 90, 144, 210, 226
children's movies 64–66
class judgement 145
collocation 4, 175, 184, 189–190, 193, 278
collocations 4, 75, 86, 175–176, 207–208, 275
complete the map 129
completion dictation 79
comprehensible input, vii 4, 12, 19, 21, 43, 60, 121, 276
comprehension approach 38–40, 139, 272, 279
consciousness raising 74, 190
controlling the teacher 71, 133, 138, 271
conversational cloze 237, 260, 267
correcting pronunciation mistakes 110

correction 81, 85, 102, 108, 114, 121, 192–200, 204, 267–268
could you repeat that? 134, 265
course book 20, 22–23, 164–182, 261
curriculum design, ii 240, 244, 269

deep processing 48, 56
delayed copying 82–83, 267
delayed repetition 82, 178–180
describe and draw 234
descriptions 14, 29–31, 35, 44–45, 48, 55, 102, 108, 181, 231
dictation 8, 13, 61, 74–91, 107, 114, 123, 164, 168–169, 177–178, 204, 224–225, 228–229, 231, 242, 260, 273, 275, 277
dictation for a mixed class 79
dictation of long phrases 78
dicto-comp 86–87, 267, 274
dicto-gloss 278
disappearing text 26, 89
discover the answer 134
distinguishing sounds 113
don't be tricked 106
dycoms 234

error analysis 193–194, 266, 274
expert groups 87
extensive listening 3–4, 9, 12, 16, 34, 60–73, 142, 164–165, 167–169, 176–177, 181, 261–262, 274
extensive reading 3–4, 13, 16, 60–61, 68, 142, 164–165, 171–172, 176–177, 181, 208, 218, 272
extensive viewing 64, 68

find the differences 136
fossilised pronunciation 93

four strands 1–3, 9–14, 16, 71, 93, 110, 118, 176, 181, 204, 214, 244, 272
fusion of the four skills 87, 264

goals 1–2, 13–15, 49, 52, 58, 74, 90, 92, 94, 113, 118, 124, 135–136, 154, 156–157, 161, 176, 202–204, 206, 213, 216, 220, 223, 225–226, 244, 260
group oral exam 234, 267
guided dictation 78

headlines 71, 177–178
hints 35, 263

identifying sounds 104–105, 113
imitation 109, 238, 263, 267
immediate repetition 177–178, 180
incidental learning 4, 10, 187, 278
information transfer 21, 30, 34, 36, 47–51, 53, 56, 88, 157, 159, 213, 219–220, 232, 271, 273
input hypothesis 5, 268
input theory 4
intensive listening 12, 60–61, 164, 168–169
interactional listening 39
interactive reading 70–71
interviews 28, 71, 163, 201, 219–220, 228, 233, 237, 246, 267, 271
interviews and scales 233
intonation 41, 93, 99–100, 110–111, 113, 169, 257, 276
it's my word! 189

jigsaw 125, 208, 212, 259

keep up 47, 106, 159

linked skills 177–179, 182, 215, 218–219, 222
LIST 220
listen again 208, 213, 218
listen and choose 45
listen and do 21, 29, 34, 114, 133, 138, 157
listen and draw 34, 45, 59, 213
listen and enjoy 34
listening grids 28
listening to pictures 30, 34, 217, 270
listening to questions 216

listening while reading 51, 168–169, 218
long turns 61, 141, 154

memory span 84, 266, 268
MINUS 19, 59
moderation 155
modify the statements 129
multi-word units 8, 12
multiple-choice sounds 106
multiple-choice speaking tests 237
multiword phrases 174–175

name it! 216
narrow listening 4, 60, 69, 178, 263
negotiated syllabus 19–20, 262
negotiation 47, 51, 115, 120–125, 128–135, 162, 265, 269–270
New Vocabulary Levels Test 173, 225, 270
notetaking 266, 275

odd one out 33
one chance dictation 78
oral cloze 44
oral reproduction 88–89
outcomes 147, 178, 211, 215
output hypothesis 5, 276

padded questions 46
partial dictation 231
pass and talk 151
peer dictation 79
peer input 71
peer interaction 60
peer talks 71, 114, 219
perfect dictation 80
phonological awareness 17
phrase by phrase 79, 89–90, 123, 231
picture ordering 21, 34, 44–45
planning 1, 14, 33–34, 111, 139–145, 148, 152, 154–156, 195, 206, 210–212, 220, 227, 241, 261–262, 264, 272–273, 280
playback speed 65
pop songs 70
positioning 30, 267
practicality 214, 227, 229–231, 239, 242
pre-dictation exercises 76
predicting 52, 219
prepared talks 16, 145, 153, 180
problem solving 275
pronouncing to hear 107

pronunciation 7, 13–16, 33–35, 61, 84, 92–119, 167, 169, 176, 196, 228, 259–270, 273–279
pronunciation instruction 93, 270, 277
pushed output 121, 139–163
pyramid procedure 128, 155, 159, 178, 220

quicklistens 61, 63, 205, 218, 221–222, 270
quizzes 28

ranking 50, 124, 128–129, 135, 138, 211, 220
rating scales and lists 232
read-and-look-up 83
reading while listening 62–63
recorded cloze 232
rehearsed talks 220
reliability 227–231, 239–240, 242
remedial work 195–196
repeated listening 8–9, 16, 42, 51–53, 61, 63, 167–169, 213
repeating sounds 108
repetition 164, 166–167, 170–171, 176–182
reproduction exercise 88, 114
responding to statements 231
retelling 86–87, 144, 151, 178–179
role plays 35, 162, 212, 228, 234, 238
running dictation 74, 78

same or different 32, 35, 44–45, 114, 138, 211–212, 234, 277
self-assessment 223, 232, 239, 242
sentence dictation 81
shadowing 109, 208, 266
short turns 61, 141
Shrek 65–66
slurring and bracketing 108
sound dictation 107
speed control 62–63, 81, 222
speed reading 8, 13, 53, 55, 211, 262
speeded listening 61, 177–178
split information 35, 73, 110, 114–115, 124–126, 128, 132, 134, 136, 138, 140, 150, 198, 211–212, 220, 234–236
stress 41, 48, 89, 93–94, 96, 99–100, 110–112, 169, 196, 257
strip story 6, 129–130, 138, 266
substitution tables 7, 16, 24, 26, 35–36, 89, 137
subtitles 64–66, 68–69, 168, 266
surveys 28, 193
survival vocabulary 9, 18, 71, 166, 175

testing the teacher 109
text with questions 231
time-on-task 2, 67, 140
top-down 40, 52, 64, 86, 90, 93, 216, 273, 277
topic types 55–56, 88, 158, 250
Toy Story 65–66
transactional listening 39
transformation exercises 190
triads 158
triplets 106
twenty questions 32, 138

unexploded dictation 81, 177–178
Updated Vocabulary Levels Test 173, 225, 279
using the written forms 103

validity 227–231, 237, 239, 242, 277
varied repetition 11, 176–177, 179–180
verbatim repetition 12, 176–179
visit and listen 218
vocabulary cards 187, 204

walk and talk 32
washback 230, 237
what is it? 26–27, 31, 34–35, 44, 266, 271
whiteboard reproduction 114
word detectives 189
word part analysis 181, 187

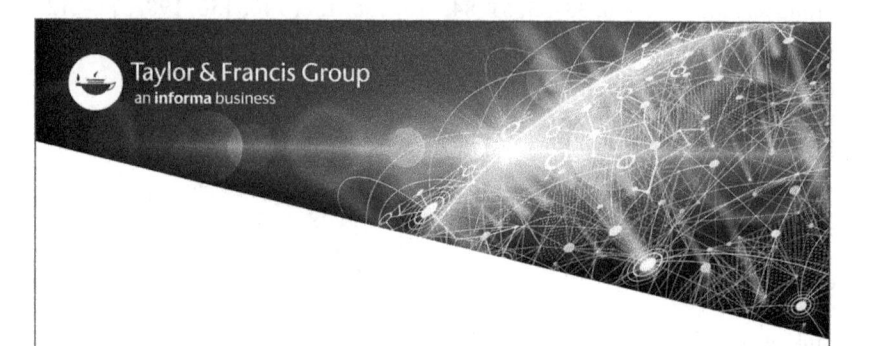

Taylor & Francis eBooks

www.taylorfrancis.com

A single destination for eBooks from Taylor & Francis with increased functionality and an improved user experience to meet the needs of our customers.

90,000+ eBooks of award-winning academic content in Humanities, Social Science, Science, Technology, Engineering, and Medical written by a global network of editors and authors.

TAYLOR & FRANCIS EBOOKS OFFERS:

- A streamlined experience for our library customers
- A single point of discovery for all of our eBook content
- Improved search and discovery of content at both book and chapter level

REQUEST A FREE TRIAL
support@taylorfrancis.com

Routledge — Taylor & Francis Group
CRC Press — Taylor & Francis Group

Milton Keynes UK
Ingram Content Group UK Ltd.
UKHW021455091124
450960UK00006B/24

9 780367 195533